Praise for *The Tao of Democracy*

FIVE STARS: Utterly Sensational — Basic Book for Humanity - I cannot say enough good things about this book. Tom Atlee gets credit for defining a "bottom up" approach that is sensible and implementable. This book is about collective intelligence for the common good, and it is a very fine book. — Robert D. Steele, Amazon Top 100 Reviewer

FIVE STARS: *The Tao Of Democracy* **offers the reader a positive viewpoint** on and for creating a democracy founded upon wisdom, citizen participation, and a culture of dialogue. A thoughtful and philosophical work written specifically to stave off the impending self-destructive side of current civilization. — *Midwest Book Review*

Co-intelligence — the ability to generate or evoke creative responses and initiatives that integrate the diverse gifts of all for the benefit of all — is the path to building a world that will work. Intelligence of this sort operates on many different levels, and in this easy to understand and very important book Atlee shows us how to apply it to building a holistic politics. **A useful guidebook for world-transformers.** — *Tikkun*

The Tao of Democracy suggests "co-intelligent" democratic decision-making can and will result in far simpler and s⁀⁀ able solutions. Atlee has assembled many examples ⁀⁀ ce/ citizen deliberation which have made ⁀⁀ es throughout the world. This is as m⁀⁀ ⁀e as it as a philosophical treatis ⁀ **the essential wisdom to mak⁀** Seavey in *HopeDance*

***The Tao of Democracy* is a dee⁀** ⁀gn study of what **wise self governance can really** ⁀ke. It describes many tools and techniques to harness our collective wisdom to solve social and environmental problems so we can move from power politics to cooperative and holistic politics. Readable and accessible, it is full of stories and anecdotes demonstrating the magic of this newer approach. — Barbara L. Valocore in *The Bridging Tree*

The Tao of Democracy is **a concise and well-written guide to a new form of participatory democracy at its finest,** where concrete results emerge hand-in-hand with increased human intimacy and solidarity. — Elisa Mishory in *What Is Enlightenment?*

In *The Tao of Democracy* you will find:

- **New forms of activism, citizenship and politics** that are not only non-adversarial but are potent enough to create a world that works for all.

- **Ways to bring wisdom to politics and governance** so that our future gets shaped by common sense, insight and creativity arising from We the People.

- **A hopeful vision** of healthy democratic societies that can heal and consciously transform themselves when they need to.

- **True stories of ordinary people** who became smarter and wiser together than they were separately.

- **Powerful approaches to collaboration, dialogue and deliberation**—from citizens' juries to permaculture to the choice-creating process, and much more...

The Tao of Democracy gives you ideas, information, tools, books, websites, people, organizations and a vision that can make all the difference in the world.

*The emerging integral culture ...
has got to be
a co-intelligent culture.*

Paul H. Ray, Ph.D.

co-author of *The Cultural Creatives*

The Tao of Democracy

Using Co-Intelligence
to Create
a World That Works for All

by

Tom Atlee

with

Rosa Zubizarreta

THE WRITERS'COLLECTIVE Cranston, Rhode Island
Independent Books for Independent Readers

The Tao of Democracy:
Using Co-Intelligence to Create a World that Works for All
By Tom Atlee, with Rosa Zubizarreta

Library of Congress Cataloging-in-Publication Data

Atlee, Tom, 1947-
   The tao of democracy : using co-intelligence to create a world that
works for all / by Tom Atlee with Rosa Zubizarreta.— Rev. ed.
        p. cm.
Includes bibliographical references and index.
   ISBN 1-932133-47-X (TP : alk. paper)
   1. Democracy. 2. Social change. 3. Intellect. I. Zubizarreta-Ada,
Rosalma. II. Title.
   JC423 .A83 2003
   321.8—dc21
                                        2002156128

Printed in the United States of America

10 9 8 7 6 5 4 3 2 1

Published by The Writers Collective
Cranston, Rhode Island

To my daughter,
Jennifer Atlee,
and to the designers and agents of transformation
whose worldwork
even today
is building stronger bridges
of survival, meaning and joy
between her generation
and the seventh generation after her.

And to
that seventh generation,
who are watching us,
waiting for us,
and praying.

And to that prayer.

*We have it in our power
to begin the world again.*

Thomas Paine

Common Sense (1776)

CONTENTS

Prologue | i

Co-intelligence wakes up in a fertilizer factory

Introduction | vii

Exploring this book

Section I
An Overview of Co-Intelligence

Section II
Making a Whole Difference Together

Section III
Creating a Wise Democracy

Section IV
Citizenship Toward a Wiser Civilization

CO-INTELLIGENCE
WAKES UP IN A
FERTILIZER FACTORY

Ever since I was a child, I wanted to make the world a better place. I was raised in a progressive family and participated actively in the political and cultural intensity of the 1960s. For two decades, I worked with numerous organizations bent on saving the world through political action, personal transformation or both. But I became increasingly frustrated with their dysfunction and combativeness. My efforts to change them and to build bridges between them were largely fruitless. Still, I carried on in my activist efforts, not knowing where else to turn to help remedy the tragedies of civilization.

Then came the cross-country Great Peace March for Global Nuclear Disarmament, a true watershed event in my life. The peace march – a mobile tent city of 400 people walking across the U.S. – was an exercise in daily interdependence and direct democracy. I suddenly found myself living lessons I had learned from ancient spiritual traditions and the leading edge of science – that we are all connected; we are all co-creators of the seamless fabric of life.

The more I reflected on this, the more it seemed to me that our social and environmental problems arise from our behaving *as if* we are separate from each other and nature. The march also opened my eyes to the fact that adversarial activism fails to take interconnected–ness seriously – and that social change work grounded in interconnectedness looks *very* different from what many activists are used to.

And then I saw something that transformed my world. I began to sense larger, deeper forms of intelligence that we are all part of, that we are all co-creating, and that flow through us.

I remember the day I had my first inklings that intelligence might be more than how smart each of us is individually. It was in early June 1986, three months into the Great Peace March. We had embarked from Los Angeles in March 1986 as a dramatic mobile public relations event with a cast of 1200 marchers and staff. Two weeks later our parent organization, ProPeace, went bankrupt, abandoning us in the Mojave Desert. 800 marchers went home. 400 of us stayed. Somehow, we managed to reorganize ourselves and walk across the country, united only by our compelling vision of global nuclear disarmament and our determination to reach our country's capital.

Our leadership could not have been more tenuous, conflicted and diffuse. Our governing councils had virtually no power to enforce their decisions. By all traditional logic, the whole operation should have just fallen apart and blown away. There was no way it should have been able to work or survive. But it did. And in the process, it became an extraordinary crucible for personal and collective learning and transformation.

The fertilizer factory

Among the scores of life-changing incidents on that peace march, one day in particular stands out in my mind:

> After three months on the road, our mobile community had become deeply divided. Some marchers were adamant that we should all march together to make a good impression and attract positive publicity. Others wanted to walk at their own pace, strung out along the road, attuned to the beauty of nature and stopping to chat with farmers and schoolchildren. Advocates of each approach saw the other approach as a threat to the march's peacemaking mission. The situation started to get nasty. People threatened to leave the march unless they got their way. Then a simple miracle occurred.
>
> Somewhere in Colorado, a heavy late-afternoon storm drenched us as we tried to pitch our multicolored tents in a soggy field near a fertilizer factory. The storm became a deluge. Hundreds of us retreated into the smelly, cavernous confines of the factory. As we stood there dripping and jostling, joking and complaining about our lives, we noticed a couple of marchers setting up a microphone and portable speakers. When the makeshift sound system was ready, they suggested we use this time to speak from our hearts about the issue that divided us. So we did that.
>
> Taking two minutes each, we shared passion and perspective with one another for more than two hours — weeping, cajoling, steaming and sweating in the muggy fetid air. Quite unexpectedly, as we talked and listened with great intensity, the answer to our problem began to emerge. We knew we had fully heard one another when the answer became as obvious as the rain on the sheet-metal roof.

All of us realized what we would do for the next few months: we would walk together through the cities (where there were rushing crowds, traffic, and media) and strung out in the countryside (where farmers and children had time to talk and nature had time to be beautiful). It was so simple, and it handled all our concerns.

On cue, the storm subsided. We dispersed into the glistening dusk, a healed community ready to continue on our path together.

As I headed across the flooded campsite to my tent, my mind was racing. I realized that something amazing had just happened, something so subtle I had almost missed it: In spite of all our talking, we had not made a decision. We had just stopped talking when we *knew*.

"The March Mind"

In the months that followed, we were orchestrated by our newly shared understanding. We called it "city mode/country mode." Like iron filings arrayed by a magnetic field, each of us manifested the orientation of the whole with nobody policing it. We even understood why a few marchers marched to a different drummer, and we did not hassle them about it.

I had never before been in a meeting like the one that generated this alignment. Nobody had been in charge. It was as if we had become a single sentient being, "The March," and our diverse thoughts and feelings had become the thoughts and feelings of this single but ambivalent March-mind wrestling with its problem. Increasingly, as the meeting unfolded, I had heard other marchers voice the thoughts in my head and the feelings in my heart. I had begun to sense us all sailing on a river of meaning that we had called up from our collective depths. It carried us to exactly the place we needed to go.

"Let us put our minds together..."

Five months later the march was over. November leaves twittered in chilly gusts as we said tearful good-byes and our last Maryland campground slowly emptied. Only a few dozen tents remained when I headed home, with my life and my awareness profoundly changed. I was haunted by an inchoate vision, an inkling of possibility I could not quite put my finger on.

I wrote:

> *I can't shake the feeling that I'm witnessing a metaphorical dawn, that the darkness is giving way, that in the next few years I will see the edge of the sun and know that we, as a planet, have made it.*

In the decade since then, I searched intently for the path I knew was there. In 1992, I was browsing through Jerry Mander's *In the Absence of the Sacred,* when a quote leapt off the page. It was from Oren Lyons, Faithkeeper of the Turtle Clan of the Onandaga Iroquois, describing traditional tribal councils. He said, "We meet and just keep talking until there's nothing left but the obvious truth." That was it! That was what had happened to us on the march.

I wondered: What is it that the Iroquois have known about for centuries, that I only "discovered" on the Great Peace March in 1986? Why don't we do it more often? As smart as we are individually, we are so seldom intelligent *together.* Brilliant, angry activists get in one another's way. Powerful nations squabble themselves into oblivion. Once-successful organizations shrink and vanish, unable to respond to change.

Further investigation led me to see that these tragedies have something to do with our using intelligence
in isolated ways, for our own ends, engaging only a
piece of ourselves. I realized that "truths" we find with
our individual smarts are *inevitably* partial. But I also
saw that we can transcend that limitation. The answers
we need lie in our own wholeness, and in our intercon-
nections with each other and the world. Maybe if we
were to take our wholeness and interconnectedness
seriously, engaging our full selves, together with each
other and the world around us, we would discover wiser,
greater truths and saner, more joyous ways of living.
And we could co-create a better future together.

In the beginning, my search turned up a variety of
ways that we can use to work together better in our
groups, organizations, and communities. As I continued the process, I began to discover that there are ways
that we can begin to apply these principles to our larger
political processes as well, in order to begin to create a
truly better world for everyone.

The more I learned, the more I discovered that thousands of people are holding pieces of this emerging
puzzle. I was determined to understand how their many
approaches and insights fit together. That exploration
has produced this book. It has also changed me, profoundly. Now I do believe I see the edge of the sun. We
have not made it yet, as a species. But, finally, I know
that we can.

EXPLORING THIS BOOK

*Let us put our minds together and see what kind of life
we can make for our children.*

— SITTING BULL

This book was written for all the people who want a
better world than we have now. It is especially written
for social change agents, community organizers, spiritually motivated activists, and the millions of people
sociologist Paul Ray calls "cultural creatives" – the co-
creators of a new culture. If you happen to be someone
who has left activism because it was too adversarial –
or if you feel called to be more active in response to the
suffering, danger or tremendous possibilities you see
in the world – this book is for you, too. I wrote it as an
invitation to everyone who is seeking to transform our
human culture in conscious, collaborative, life-affirming ways.

Its purpose is two-fold. First, I want to introduce
you to the co-intelligence perspective – a vision of what
intelligence might look like if we deeply understood
wholeness, interconnectedness and co-creativity.

Next, and most importantly, I want to explore how
we might use the perspective of co-intelligence to transform our troubled democracy into a living system ca-

pable of creating a world that works for all, by generating the collective wisdom we need to creatively address our twenty-first century problems, opportunities and dreams.

The political vision of this book

I called this book *The Tao of Democracy* because Lao-Tzu, the founder of Taoism, is famous for his insistence that when leaders lead well, people feel that they did it themselves, and that it happened naturally. Democracy is, in the end, about creating processes that allow people to empower themselves, not about Great Leaders saving the people. This book is about increasing the capacity of We the People, as a whole, to govern ourselves wisely, thereby realizing the dreams of all democratic visionaries from Lao-Tzu to Thomas Jefferson.

At the core of the political vision in this book is a straightforward, simple, and yet revolutionary thesis that flings open the doors to positive democratic change:

> *Given a supportive structure and resources, diverse ordinary people can work together to reach common ground, creating wise and deliberate policy that reflects the highest public interest.*

Around the world thousands of people have experimented with democratic innovations based on this premise. In this book, I explore the evidence that these "citizen deliberative councils," in their many forms, can be used to help us resolve social problems much more wisely than we do now. I also explore the possibility that these innovative institutions, combined with other aspects of co-intelligence, could produce *a new culture capable of consciously evolving itself.*

Our collective predicament as a species

Such democratic innovations are critical at this moment in history to deal with the crisis-generating capacity of twenty-first century civilization:

> *Collectively, we are creating effects in our world beyond our collective ability to comprehend what we are doing, at a speed that surpasses our collective ability to reflect and respond.*

It does not take a rocket scientist to see where this is headed. Our civilization is racing headlong into massive breakdown or breakthrough – or both. This book is about consciously choosing breakthrough. It is about breaking through to conscious evolution and conscious co-creation of our collective future.

Most of you are undoubtedly all too aware of our considerable social and environmental problems. I will not burden you with the usual litany, although Chapter 15 takes a deeper look at these challenges. But in this introduction, I would like to further develop the point I make above, about the imbalance between our capacity to create and our capacity to respond to the consequences of our creations, as communities and nations.

It is clear to many of us that, in the very near future, our lives will be changing even more dramatically than we have already experienced. Our vast collective power – our technological and economic power – is so great that we are creating impacts far beyond what is called "the human scale" – that scale of everyday life where we evolved with a certain balance between our powers of creation and our powers of response.

Gone are the days when the worst we could do was conquer a neighboring tribe or overgraze a local hill-

side. We are reaching a point where individuals and
small groups will be able to create, or destroy, almost
anything. We have moved beyond the scale of centime-
ters and miles down into the microscopic, even sub-
atomic realms, and up into the planetary and inter-
stellar realms, from angstroms to light years, from
nanoseconds to gigabytes. We break up atoms and
chromosomes. And collectively we change forests to
deserts. We litter the upper atmosphere with layers of
space junk zooming around earth at hundreds of miles
an hour. Our inventions are transforming the lives of
our grandchildren's grandchildren – and we do not have
the foggiest notion how. And we are doing all of this
faster and faster, more and more, bigger and bigger.

Meanwhile, individually, we can directly comprehend only a tiny fraction of what we are collectively
doing. Our individual senses, nervous systems and
brains are not capable of taking in the gigantic effects,
both current and potential, that our civilization's creativity is capable of generating. Our nervous systems
are set to respond to what is here and now and obvious: we can not *feel* radiation, the population explosion, the vital information missing from our newspaper, the disappearing ozone layer. And when we are
faced with any significant piece of the full information,
we get overwhelmed.

Stop and think about this for a minute.

*We cannot individually comprehend the range,
depth and detail of the consequences we are
collectively generating for ourselves.*

Well, if we cannot appreciate our circumstances individually, perhaps we can do it collectively. Unfortunately, our democracy is not designed for that. Even in
those rare instances when it is not being manipulated
by special interests, it operates on elections and polls,

on the numerical adding up of our individual opinions. Logically speaking, this cannot do the job that is required; if we can not individually comprehend our circumstances, adding all our individual incomprehensions together will not improve our understanding.

The need for collective intelligence and wisdom

It is clear we need far better ways to perceive our world, to reflect on it, to act and to learn from what is going on around us. Of course, we need these things as individuals. But most of all, and urgently, we need these capacities as whole societies – indeed, as a civilization.

The language I use to talk about this is that *we need greater collective intelligence than our democracy is able to deliver in its current form.* It is not that we need a better collection of intelligences, a mere sum of all our individual smarts. We need something that is significantly larger and more synergistic than that, an intelligence that is bigger than the sum of its parts.

In other words, we do not need *collected* intelligence. We need *collective* intelligence, a coherent integration of our diversity that is greater than any or all of us could generate separately, just as an orchestra is greater than the sum of its instruments. We need a new kind of collectivity that does not repress individuality, diversity and creativity but that, instead, allows us to arrive at creative consensus without compromise. We need a shared power that calls forth the best in all of us and cherishes our diversity for the riches it contains.

Furthermore, we need to apply an unprecedented level of collective wisdom to all the challenges we face. Right now, there is much wisdom on earth, scattered here and there. But our collective actions as societies are clearly not wise. It is far too easy to imagine that the problem is "out there," with all of the various powerholders and interests groups that keep the wise solutions that already exist from being implemented. But if we find ways to work with one another across a wide range of differences, we could then create the broad-based coalitions we need in order to implement the wisdom that we have.

We need ways to focus our full capabilities – heart, mind, soul, and gut – on our collective situation. We need to be informed by big-picture sensibilities, aware of our potential for both catastrophe and evolution, for both co-stupidity and collective wisdom. We need methods that can help us deepen and expand our thinking, feeling and dreaming, and we need ways to weave it all together, collaboratively, into a shared future. Co-intelligence is the capacity to do that, individually and collectively.

Co-intelligence

Co-intelligence is a capacity. It is also the field that explores theories and practices dealing with the dynamics of that capacity and how to use and enhance it. There are many tools available for this task, as you will find in this book. As a culture, we have abundant insight and know-how that just need to be pulled together and aligned so our whole society can see and think and feel and dream more effectively together.

When we succeed at that, we will not merely be saving ourselves from disaster. When we become fully capable of wisely co-creating a better future, we will be taking a giant step forward into conscious cultural evolution.

It is time for us to take that step.

Exploring the landscape of this book

This book is arranged so that later chapters build on earlier ones. But it is also possible to explore areas you are interested in by dipping into relevant chapters.

- In particular, if you are interested in **democracy**, take a look at Sections III and IV – looking over chapters whose titles appeal to you.
- If you are interested in what all this has to do with **Taoism** or **spirituality**, check out Chapters 4 and 20.
- A very condensed summary of **co-intelligence** is available in Chapter 1.
- If you learn best through **stories** and **examples**, Chapters 2, 12 and 13 will be your cup of tea.
- If you collect **methodologies** and **processes** (as I do), you will likely find Chapters 7, 8, 13, 14, 16 and 17 of special interest.
- For better understanding of the democratic design innovation most central to this book – **citizen deliberative councils** – read Chapters 12-14.
- **Activists** will find Chapters 5 and 19 thought provoking.

The purpose of this book, as noted above, is two-fold: to introduce you to co-intelligence, and to show how co-intelligent processes and systems can help us solve our collective problems wisely.

Sections One and Two introduce you to the basic ideas and conceptual models of co-intelligence, illustrated with a variety of stories, examples and descriptions of co-intelligent methods and processes.

You will discover a key **definition of co-intelligence** – "what intelligence would look like if we took wholeness, interconnectedness, and co-creativity seriously." Co-intelligence moves beyond IQ-based theories to offer a view of intelligence that is fully alive and far more comprehensive than individual reason.

In Section One you will also learn about **six manifestations of co-intelligence**: multi-modal intelligence, collaborative intelligence, resonant intelligence, collective intelligence, wisdom, and universal intelligence. Focusing on the fourth and fifth of these, collective intelligence and wisdom, we proceed to Section Three, the heart of the book: an exploration of how co-intelligence can transform our public affairs, the area of life that we usually think of in terms of politics, governance, citizenship and activism.

Section Three tackles that realm head on and in detail, describing how we can create a conversation-rich **deliberative democracy** that naturally and dependably produces **community wisdom**. It offers an overview of co-operative and holistic politics, as well as the role that **citizen deliberative councils** can play within this larger picture. Citizen deliberative councils are the key innovation featured in this section. Hundreds of these councils have already been held around the world, in a wide variety of forms and contexts. When you get a glimpse of this compelling story, currently invisible to most Americans, I expect you will see how great a difference these councils could make if popular demand led to their widespread use as a regular part of our democratic system.

Section Four explores how we might proceed with this and why we must. After delving into the dynamics that have made current forms of **citizenship** almost meaningless, this section describes the emergent "culture of dialogue" and many ways people are tackling public issues together. It explores the co-creative, non-adversarial conversation, participation and action that can transform twenty-first century cultures. And finally, it takes a look at the kinship between **co-intelligence and the Tao.**

After reading reflections on people who are involved in this emerging movement for a co-intelligent culture, you can explore some ideas for becoming a part of this movement, yourself.

At the end of the book you will find an **annotated bibliography** of books that have contributed to the development of co-intelligence.

What is now possible

Remember the thesis I said was fundamental to this book:

> *Given a supportive structure and resources, diverse ordinary people can work together to reach common ground, creating wise and deliberate policy that reflects the highest public interest.*

This book explores the many ways in which this statement is true, and how we can use this truth to transform our world. While some amount of supportive structure and resources are essential to this process, it is by no means a prohibitive amount, especially considering the resources that we spend in other areas and the mounting cost of our thorny social and environmental problems.

Fostering collective intelligence on a society-wide level is a project that requires complementary top-down and bottom-up strategies integrated so that they feed back into each other. A broad movement in support of citizen deliberative councils can lead to the use of this highly-effective means of harvesting the "people's wisdom" on behalf of the common good.

If we created such a movement (see page 276) – and as it succeeded – those periodic citizen deliberative councils would provide high quality, dependable public judgments about public issues that concern us all. Although they would be "only" temporary small groups of ordinary citizens, they would do their work and make their statements from the "top" of our political culture. Instead of highly placed public officials deciding everything with one eye on fickle "public opinion," we'd have groups that reflected the evolving, thoughtful, informed wisdom of our whole community or society, speaking clearly into official deliberations and into the widespread conversations going on naturally all the time at the grassroots.

This new feedback loop between the top and the bottom would continue as the conclusions of these councils, and the stories of their participants, catalyzed more such conversations, generating a broad base of support at the community level to make the wise course-corrections our society needs.

You may consider this book an introduction – and invitation – to **the Co-Intelligence Institute's websites**: *co-intelligence.org* and *democracyinnovations.org*. They contain extensive additional information on all these subjects.

With your support and whatever energy and insight Life sends through us, further books and projects will be forthcoming.

May it prove to be a great and fruitful journey for us all.

Coheartedly,

Tom Atlee
Eugene, Oregon
July, 2002

Section I

An Overview of

Co-Intelligence

CHAPTER 1

WHAT IS CO-INTELLIGENCE?

For the last ten years, I have been exploring the following question:

> *What would intelligence look like if we took wholeness, interconnectedness and co-creativity seriously?*

As it turns out, this question has many interesting answers. I decided I needed a name for the larger category that could hold all of the various answers I was discovering. After considering the names "holistic intelligence" and "connected intelligence," I decided upon "co-intelligence."

My favorite definition of co-intelligence is

> *the ability to generate or evoke
> creative responses and initiatives
> that integrate the diverse gifts of all
> for the benefit of all.*

So what is co-intelligence, in practice? Co-intelligence manifests in very diverse ways, not unlike life, itself. After all, when we ask What is Life?, we don't get a simple answer. We know that life manifests in such wildly different phenomena as birds, grass, reproduction, human consciousness, natural selection, suffering, love and vitality, among many other things. The word "life" allows us to usefully consider these diverse phenomena as expressions of one larger category – *life*.

Similarly, I have found that co-intelligence manifests in many ways that are as distinct and yet as intertwined as the manifestations of life. If we see these manifestations as expressions of a single capacity, it helps us explore how they relate to one another, and how we might use them and enhance them.

Six basic manifestations of co-intelligence

As part of my inquiry, I realized that if we are indeed going to take wholeness, interconnectedness and co-creativity seriously, we are going to have to face some very challenging implications:

- **First**: Intelligence must involve more than logical reason, since rationality constitutes only a tiny piece of our full capacity to learn from and relate to life.
- **Second**: Intelligence must involve more than learning how to control and predict things, since that does not engage the powerful co-creativity of life.
- **Third**: Intelligence must be far more than personal, since even ants can together generate an intelligence that's greater than they have individually.
- **Fourth**: Intelligence needs to reach far beyond the obvious, since whatever is obvious is connected to things that aren't so obvious, and intelligence should engage with the wholeness and relatedness of things, as much as possible.

- **Fifth**: Intelligence should be able to arise among us and through us, as a result of our kinship in the interconnected family of life.
- **Sixth**: It would seem likely that some form of intelligence would exist beyond us – in and beyond the living world – built into the very wholeness of life.

Starting with these challenges, I developed the concept of co-intelligence on the basis of six revolutionary premises:

1. **There is more to intelligence than brains and logic.** Many varieties of intelligence are available to us. So co-intelligence can manifest as multi-modal intelligence.

> **MULTI-MODAL INTELLIGENCE** means there are many ways to learn, know and engage with the world. Our bodies, minds, hearts and spirits contain a full palette of intelligences – emotional, analytic, intuitive, kinesthetic, narrative, moral, and so forth. We can use more of these and integrate them better, especially in synergy with other people, since we are all capable in such different ways.

> It is of the utmost importance that we recognize and nurture all of the varied human intelligences ... If we can mobilize the spectrum of human abilities, not only will people feel better about themselves and more competent; it is even possible that they will also feel more engaged and better able to join the rest of the world community in working for the broader good.
>
> Howard Gardner
> *Multiple Intelligences: The Theory in Practice*
> (HarperCollins, 1993)

2. There is more to intelligence than successfully predicting and controlling things. We can creatively respond to life and join with its energies. So co-intelligence often manifests as collaborative intelligence.

> **COLLABORATIVE INTELLIGENCE** means finding and working with all the available allies and cooperative forces around us – and there are many. There are always energies, both existing and potential, with which we can fruitfully align – even within the heart of adversaries and within the problems we face. Working with one another, with nature, and with the natural tendencies in us and the world, we can accomplish more with less, and enjoy it more.
>
> > Rather than asking, 'What can I get from this land, or person?' we can ask, 'What does this person, or land, have to give if I cooperate with them?'... Everything is a positive resource; it is up to us to work out how we may use it as such.
> >
> > Bill Mollison
> > *Permaculture: A Practical Guide for a Sustainable Future* (Island Press, 1990)

3. There is more to intelligence than individual intelligence. Co-intelligence often manifests as collective intelligence, the intelligence we generate together through our interactions and our social structures and cultures. Inclusiveness (finding effective ways to include all of the parts of the larger whole) and the creative use of diversity are two key elements for increasing collective intelligence.

> **COLLECTIVE INTELLIGENCE** means that families, groups, organizations, communities and entire

societies can act intelligently as whole, living systems. What we believe, what we do, and how we
organize our collective affairs can make or break
our collective intelligence. We could improve our
collective intelligence to a point where humanity
not only survives and flourishes into the foresee-
able future, but also consciously evolves.

> Now more than ever we need to be in active conver-
> sation with others. No one can do it alone. We need
> access to our collective intelligence to address the
> questions that are critical to our common future [and
> to] make our collective intelligence visible to ourselves
> and each other on a larger and larger scale.
>
>   The Cafe Collaborative
>   *theworldcafe.com/ComConversation.html*

**4. There is more to intelligence than solving the
problems in front of our faces.** Co-intelligence often manifests as wisdom – seeing the big picture,
the long term – an integral intelligence that puts it
all together even as it focuses on the essence of the
matter.

WISDOM means seeing beyond immediate appear-
ances and acting with greater understanding to
affirm the life and development of all involved. It
involves balance, mystery and tolerance of ambi-
guity and change. The expanded perspective that
accompanies wisdom fosters wonder, humility,
compassion and humor.

> Our greatest need at the present time is perhaps for
> a global ethic – transcending all other systems of al-
> legiance and belief – rooted in a consciousness of the
> interrelatedness and sanctity of all life. Such an ethic
> would temper humanity's acquired knowledge and

power with wisdom of the kind found at the heart of
the most ancient human traditions and cultures – in
Taoism and Zen, in the understandings of the Hopi
and the Maya Indians, in the Vedas and the Psalms,
in the very origins of human culture itself.

Federico Mayor, Director-General of UNESCO
"Crucible for a common ethic"
in *Our Planet* 8:2, Aug 1996

**5. There is more to intelligence than a solitary ca-
pacity exercised within the life of one entity.** Attuned to life, intelligence evokes a fuller, deeper intelligence in and around it. So co-intelligence often
manifests as resonant intelligence.

RESONANT INTELLIGENCE is intelligence that
grows stronger or fuller as it resonates with other
sources or forms of intelligence, or which deepens
in empathic response to life.

Our availability to each other, our ability to dream
each other's dreams and experience each other's bi-
ographies is part of the interpenetrating wave of the
current time...We are being rescaled to planetary
proportions, as we become resonant and intimate
with our own depths.

Jean Houston's online *News,*
March 19th, 2001

**6. There is more to intelligence than human intelli-
gence.** Intelligence is a property of the universe and
of all that is in it – and perhaps beyond it. I call this
manifestation of co-intelligence universal intelligence.

UNIVERSAL INTELLIGENCE is, in my understanding, the intrinsic tendency for things to self-orga-

nize and co-evolve into ever more complex, intricately interwoven and mutually compatible forms. Our human intelligence is but one manifestation of that universal dynamic. The more we are conscious of universal intelligence and connect ourselves to it, the more intelligence (and wisdom) we will have to work with.

Others might describe Universal Intelligence as the mind or will of God or Spirit. Both perspectives derive from observing a certain intelligent pattern in the way the world is organized and/or sensing an intelligent Presence in and around us, and finding that there is guidance there.

> The harmony of natural law...reveals an intelligence of such superiority that, compared with it, all the systematic thinking and acting of human beings is an utterly insignificant reflection.
>
> Albert Einstein
> *The World As I See It*

I've found that co-intelligence at its best consists of these very special phenomena – multi-modal intelligence, collaborative intelligence, collective intelligence, wisdom, resonant intelligence, and universal intelligence – all mixing and matching in a thousand different ways. Of course, each of these six manifestations of co-intelligence is itself co-intelligence. At the same time, our understanding of co-intelligence deepens and grows richer the more dimensions it has.

Co-intelligence, then, is a new paradigm for understanding intelligence. When we think of intelligence in the conventional manner, as a way in which an individual gains dominion over his or her world, we have lost something vast and important. I propose, instead, that intelligence is fundamentally about creating and re-creating wholeness, coherence, and fittedness. We apply our intelligence to make things right, good, or beautiful, to discover truth and reality, to make sense of things, to support our health and well-being. All of these are forms of wholeness, coherence, and harmony.

Sometimes this harmony is broken by doubt, challenge, or change. At such times, our intelligence seeks a higher-level coherence that will make new sense out of our experience. Healthy, intelligent individuals do this all the time. In society, as well, old ideas and realities are challenged and changed. Science, art, academics, politics, and social change movements are just a few of the ways we have of institutionalizing our societal learning process.

In our culture, it is customary to think of intelligence as something we either have or do not have, and to link intelligence with economic success. The reality is that all of us as humans are intelligent, and use our intelligence throughout our lives to address the challenges we face. At the same time, we can always learn better ways to apply our intelligence.

Similarly, co-intelligence is always present as an intrinsic aspect of life. At the same time, we can always enhance the co-intelligence available in a given situation.

We can do this by learning better ways to collaborate with others and by learning to create more effective and sane organizational structures. We can enhance co-intelligence by learning to cultivate our various ways of knowing and by considering "the big picture" and the long-term consequences of our choices. And we can enhance co-intelligence by connecting more deeply with the promptings of universal intelligence in and around us.

At its core, co-intelligence is simply intelligence that takes the wholeness of life fully into account. As we reexamine our understanding of intelligence, we realize that there is more to intelligence than we previously thought available to us. It is up to us to develop it and put it to good use. And we do not need to do it alone!

CHAPTER **2**

TALES AND COMMENTARIES

The more we notice and use co-intelligence, the more attuned we will be to the wholeness, interconnectedness, and co-creativity of life in and around us. It is not too much to say that the whole world is alive with potential co-intelligence. We can join, evoke and work with it, but first we have to notice it and recognize the situations that cry out for it to be used. Sharing stories about our experiences with co-intelligence can help sensitize us to its presence and possibilities.

The following stories offer some examples of co-intelligence in action. In the commentaries that follow each story, I explore some of the lessons we might draw from each example.

STORY 1

A GIFT FROM A SHEPHERD

Having trouble with your neighbors? A farmer in Indiana was bothered by his neighbor's dogs who were killing his sheep. The traditional way that sheepraisers counter this problem is with lawsuits, or barbed wire fences, or even with shotguns as a last resort. This man had a better idea. He gave his neighbor's children lambs as pets. The neighbors

*then tied their dogs up voluntarily. In the process,
the families became friends.*

The Oswego Valley Peace & Justice Council,
cited in *Peace Network News*, May 1994.

When there is a problem or a conflict, we often create
distance or walls between ourselves and the trouble so
it will not disturb us. We shut our doors, we turn our
heads, we call the cops. Co-intelligence, on the other
hand, seeks to build relationship, support cooperation
and enhance life. The farmer may well have asked
himself, "How can I get these folks to join me in protecting my sheep?" Notice how different that is from:
"How can I stop these folks from killing my sheep?"
This difference — a spirit of cooperation rather than of
resisting or dominating — is an important feature of
co-intelligence. It usually requires a good deal more
creativity and courage to put into practice. But it builds
bonds that will make future problems much easier to
solve, and makes life more deeply enjoyable, as well.

STORY 2

"THE WORLD'S MOST UNUSUAL WORKPLACE"

*When I took over Semco from my father twelve years
ago* [writes Ricardo Semler, CEO of a Brazilian company that manufactures large industrial equipment],
*it was a traditional company in every respect, with a
pyramidal structure and a rule for every contingency.*

*One of my first acts was to throw out the rules.
We whittled the bureaucracy from twelve layers of
management to three and devised a new structure
based on fluid concentric circles to replace the traditional rigidly hierarchical corporate pyramid.*

*[Although in many societies] almost everyone be-
lieves people have a right to vote for those who lead*

them, democracy has yet to penetrate the workplace. [But at Semco,] before people are hired or promoted to leadership positions, they are interviewed and approved by all who will be working for them. And every six months managers are evaluated by those who work under them. The results are posted for all to see. This employee review builds on one of Semco's great strengths, our transparency. At our company people can always say what's on their minds, even to their bosses — even when it's about their bosses. It is instilled in our corporate culture that everyone should be willing to listen, and admit it when they are wrong.

Our people are free to speak their minds, without fear. Two or three times a year we distribute a questionnaire called "What Does the Company Think?" The results are published for all to see.

We have people who agree with very little of what we think and are still here, unapologetic and unfettered. A touch of civil disobedience is necessary to alert the organization that all is not right. We do our best to let [such people] speak their minds even though they often become thorns in our sides.

We don't believe in cluttering the payroll with ungratifying, dead-end jobs. Everyone at Semco, even top managers, fetches guests, stands over photocopiers, sends faxes, types letters, and dials the phone. We don't have executive dining rooms, and parking is strictly first-come, first-served.

And we encourage everyone to mix with everyone else, regardless of job. The idea is that we all can learn from one another.

Profit sharing is democratic. We negotiated with our workers over the basic percentage to be distributed — about a quarter of our corporate profits, as it turned out — and they hold assemblies to decide how to split it. It's up to them.

We believe it is essential that all company communications, especially those intended for the work-

ers or the public, be absolutely honest. All financial information at Semco is openly discussed. Indeed, our workers have unlimited access to our books (and we only keep one set). To show we are serious about this, Semco, with the labor unions that represent our workers, developed a course to teach everyone to read balance sheets and cash flow statements.

In restructuring Semco, we've picked the best from many systems. From capitalism we take the ideals of personal freedom, individualism, and competition. From socialism we have learned to control greed and share information and power. The Japanese have taught us the value of flexibility.

Semco has grown sixfold despite withering recessions, staggering inflation, and chaotic national economic policy. Productivity has increased nearly sevenfold. Profits have risen fivefold.

> edited excerpts from Ricardo Semler
> *Maverick: The Success Story Behind
> the World's Most Unusual Workplace*

Ricardo Semler used his leadership position to help the system he is leading (Semco) self-organize for the benefit of all stakeholders. His step-by-step transformation of power relationships, expectations, corporate structures, cultural assumptions, responsibility, opportunity, conflict, learning and the quality and openness of communication all suggest he has a rare natural understanding of co-intelligence. His work arose from his respect for people and his belief that their intelligence and motivation would be expressed at the organizational level if they were just set free in an intelligently designed system. He understands the co-intelligent foundation of democracy: that the people who can most effectively shape decisions are those who are affected by those decisions.

STORY 3

A CHIMPANZEE AT STANFORD

[Change agent Fran Peavey writes:] *One day I was walking through the Stanford University campus with a friend when I saw a crowd of people with cameras and video equipment on a little hillside. They were clustered around a pair of chimpanzees — a male running loose and a female on a chain about twenty-five feet long. It turned out the male was from Marine World and the female was being studied for something or other at Stanford. The spectators were scientists and publicity people trying to get them to mate.*

The male was eager. He grunted and grabbed the female's chain and tugged. She whimpered and backed away. He pulled again. She pulled back. Watching the chimps' faces, I [a woman] began to feel sympathy for the female.

Suddenly the female chimp yanked her chain out of the male's grasp. To my amazement, she walked through the crowd, straight over to me, and took my hand. Then she led me across the circle to the only other two women in the crowd, and she joined hands with one of them. The three of us stood together in a circle. I remember the feeling of that rough palm against mine. The little chimp had recognized us and reached out across all the years of evolution to form her own support group.

Quoted from Fran Peavey
Heart Politics

Co-intelligence arises from our interconnectedness, our relatedness to each other and everything. And then it turns around and builds upon that relatedness to make something good happen. In this story, the female chimp was able to use her collaborative intelligence to reach

across the barrier of species (and most likely, past negative experiences with humans as well) in order to find
supportive allies.

STORY 4

MEASURING COMMUNITY HEALTH

*In 1992 one hundred citizens — ranging from a cor-
porate executive to an activist, from a priest to a
teacher — formed the Sustainable Seattle Civic Panel.
They wanted to build their city's "long-term cultural,
economic and environmental health and vitality, with
emphasis on long-term." But how?*

*They wondered: How does anyone know whether
a community is getting more or less sustainable?
How do you measure sustainable progress?*

*They broke up into 10 topic groups — economy,
education, health, environment and so on. Each group
brainstormed a long, lively list of possible measurements. But then they had trouble winnowing down
their burgeoning lists! After investing over 2500 volunteer hours in the project, they finally settled on 99
indicators of Seattle's sustainability. Their list —
which they presented to the public in a dramatic reading interspersed with stories, quotes and poems —
included:*

- *Hours of work at the median wage required to
  support basic needs.*
- *Percentage of employment concentrated in the
  top 10 employers.*
- *Wild salmon runs in local streams.*
- *County population and growth rate.*
- *Average travel time from selected starting points
  to selected destinations.*
- *Percentage of the population that gardens, and
  that votes in primary elections.*

- *Tons of solid waste generated, and recycled, per person.*

Sustainable Seattle is now unearthing and publicizing actual numbers for as many of these indicators as possible — and getting city institutions to measure and report them on a regular basis. Then they will initiate programs to get those indicators moving in the directions people want them to go. With sustainability consultants, awards, checklists and publicity, their efforts will start to make a real difference in the quality of life in their city.

This powerful program, run on a shoestring, could be done by any community.

Donella H. Meadows — Dartmouth College professor, systems analyst, and co-author of The Limits to Growth *and* Beyond the Limits to Growth *— commented: "The indicators a society chooses to report to itself about itself...reflect collective values and inform collective decisions. A nation that keeps a watchful eye on its salmon runs or the safety of its streets makes different choices than does a nation that is only paying attention to its GNP [Gross National Product — the sum of its economic transactions]. The idea of citizens choosing their own indicators is something new under the sun — something intensely democratic."*

Based on "Using Salmon Runs and Gardens
to Measure Our Well-Being,"
a syndicated column by Donella H. Meadows,
seen in *Timeline*, Sept./Oct. 1993

"Growth" has been a buzzword in our society. More is better. But are more people, more highways, more factories, and more consumption intrinsically better? Cancer, too, is growth — growth out of step with the larger system it depends on, the body. A co-intelligent community, conscious of its internal and external interconnectedness, would not tend to seek endless growth of its material "standard of living" at the expense of the long-term health of itself and its environment. Rather, it would seek sustainable development of its "quality of life," as manifested in the welfare of its members, the vitality of its culture and the health of the natural environment in which it was embedded.

So let us suppose a community wants to promote its quality of life and not just "growth." How can it think, feel and respond as a coherent, conscious entity? This is a question of societal intelligence – society-wide collective intelligence. Societal intelligence depends (among other things) on feedback. Just as our senses give us feedback — information, pleasure, pain — so also a community needs feedback to sense what it needs to do and how successful it is being. Having indicators — and which indicators it has — makes a tremendous difference in how intelligent a community or a society can be.

What makes Sustainable Seattle's story even more co-intelligent is the fact that their indicators were derived from, and brought together, diverse perspectives: many people's views, human/eco–logical needs, long-term/short-term perspective, and so on. An important part of co-intelligence is the wisdom to expand our perspective to embrace a wider view.

For more information on quality of life indicators, see *co-intelligence.org/P-qualtylifeindicators.html.*

STORY 5

WHY FIGHT WHEN YOU CAN ALL WIN?

After years of traditional adversarial community organizing, Mike Eichler realized he was winning battles but losing wars. He created a new community organizing style called consensus organizing.

He was hired by an organization of Pittsburgh, Pennsylvania's top corporate leadership, to help create a strategy for economic development in the nearby Mon Valley – an economically and socially devastated steel-mill region. He got corporate support by being broadly inclusive in his projects – reaching beyond the adversarial activists who had targeted local corporations in the past – and by instituting recognizably high standards in the organizations formed to work with him, including strict answerability for any funds. He got support from community activists by ensuring that all projects would be fully controlled by the community. He helped create eighteen new community coalitions of businesses, social services, unions, religious organizations and resident leaders in Mon Valley cities and towns.

These coalitions of ordinary low-income citizens and institutional partners successfully completed a number of real estate projects needed by their communities. Then they banded together as the Mon Valley Initiative to increase their clout with the county and the state. New leaders rapidly emerged and developed who could deal in these political and policy-making realms. They began cultivating relationships with policy makers and opinion leaders from across the state. Their sophisticated regional agenda impressed the corporate leaders who first funded the effort, and emerged as a major force in regional economic development.

Edited from reports at
cpn.org/COI and *consensusorganizing.com*

In consensus organizing, community organizers learn all they can about the "downtown interests" (the local powerholders) and about the community and its grassroots leaders. The downtown interests and grassroots community leaders often oppose each other and tell stereotypical stories in which their opponent plays an ineffective or malevolent role. Consensus organizers try to identify a project, such as a job training program, that is of interest to both the community leaders and downtown interests. Then they engage the parties in real dialogue about that program only, leading to productive collaborations and new relationships. Later, those relationships can be used to make real progress on other community issues, since the stereotyped us-vs-them stories have been replaced with a belief in the possibility of shared exploration and shared benefits.

This community organizing strategy takes wholeness, interconnectedness and co-creativity very seriously: Organizers pick a small project the whole community can get behind (wholeness) and then build relationships (interconnectedness) as they work on it together (co-creativity). Those relationships then have healed the community just enough to pick a larger project with which to start the whole cycle over again.

STORY 6

YOU NEVER KNOW WHO WILL BRING IN YOUR NEXT $20 MILLION

On Thursday, October 21, 1993, The Rockport Company closed down for two days to explore new directions. They held an "open space" meeting – a form of conferencing in which attendees self-organize into workshops and task groups with little direction. The bean counters objected to the costs of suspending operations, but company president John Thorbeck was adamant. Almost the entire workforce attended.

The conference was held in a cavernous warehouse. People from all levels of the corporate hierar-

*chy mixed together in dozens of groups discussing
company issues and possibilities. Managers, line
workers, supervisors, clerical staff and dock workers had unprecedented access to each other.*

*As the warehouse hummed with excited energy,
a security guard (who was not a Rockport employee)
wandered among the shelves, crates and circles of
people. He lingered over a discussion of new products, finally pulling up a chair. "He mentioned that
he spent a lot of time on his feet and would love to
wear the kind of comfortable shoes that Rockport
made," writes Srikumar S. Rao in* Training *magazine. "But his company would never buy them because they didn't 'look right' as part of a guard's
uniform. Why couldn't the company redesign the
uppers so that they met the security company's uniform specifications?"*

*Suddenly the guard found himself barraged with
questions. Someone pulled some shoes off the shelves
and started cutting them up and fitting parts together.
Within a few hours, they had sketched out the new
product idea. "Rockport is proceeding to develop such
a line of shoes," writes Rao. "If it is an average per-
former in the market, [CFO Anthony] Tiberii expects
sales of about $20 million per year."*

Compiled from a talk by Harrison Owen,
founder of Open Space Technology
and from Srikumar S. Rao,
"Welcome to Open Space,"
Training, April 1994

Inclusiveness and collaboration are two trademarks of
co-intelligence. Many other ideas emerged from this
particular Open Space gathering, but I find it significant that the most profitable idea came from someone
who was not an employee. The willingness of the group
to embrace an outsider made the company millions of

dollars. That willingness was no accident: the spirit and structure of the Open Space approach treats everyone as creative, responsible peers and helps them welcome unexpected developments. The processes, structures and cultures we operate with can make all the difference in how co-intelligent we end up being.

STORY 7

AWAKENING THE POWER AND WISDOM OF A COMMUNITY

Four hundred years ago the village of Maliwada, India, was a thriving agricultural center, producing fruits, vegetables, and wines. In 1975, it had little water, no sanitation, and few crops. Over 2,000 villagers barely eked out a subsistence living. Muslims and Hindus of many different castes lived with centuries of mutual distrust. The villagers knew about their prosperous past, but it seemed long gone and hopeless to recreate.

Discussions began based on two questions: "What would it take to have prosperity exist again in this village? What can you do to make that happen?" Gradually, as ideas began to pour forth, perspectives changed. Hindus and Muslims talked together excitedly about how to clean out the ancient well. Brahmins and Untouchables discovered in a joint meeting that all despaired at the lack of medical care for their sick children. They all wanted to create a health clinic in the village. Hope began to creep into their voices and eyes. What had seemed totally impossible suddenly became doable. People organized and tapped resources they had forgotten they had.

They acquired loans from a bank and received government grants. They built a dam, a brick fac-

tory, and the clinic. The shared vision of what they wanted for themselves and their community allowed them to go beyond their personal and cultural differences and continued to motivate them. Each success made them stronger, more confident, more self-assured. Today, Maliwada is a prospering village.

When transformation like this takes place, the news travels. Nearby villagers wanted to know how they could do this...

Quoted from Patricia R. Tuecke
"Rural International Development,"
in *Discovering Common Ground*
by Marvin R. Weisbord, et al.
(Berrett-Koehler, 1992)

The process used above in rural India was developed by the Institute of Cultural Affairs (ICA) in the 1960s in a collaborative effort with citizens of an urban ghetto on Chicago's Westside. It has now been used in over 30 countries to help communities self-organize for "self-sustenance, self-reliance, and self-confidence." A notable feature of ICA's approach is its transcultural applicability. ICA demonstrates that simple, co-intelligent techniques for evoking the previously untapped knowledge, vision and collaborative capacities in a community can have universal application. ICA's respectful, catalytic approach helped each community design programs "that met local needs and reflected authentic cultural style" (a positive use of diversity) and that give them an opportunity to "shape their own destiny instead of being victims of their situation" (co-intelligent co-creativity). I'm particularly struck by the way their process distributes leadership: Who is leading—the facilitators who catalyze the question-asking sessions and offer support, or the people of the community who together create and operate the programs? This shared, multi-dimensional form of leadership, in sharp contrast to hierarchical control-based leadership, is one hallmark of co-intelligence.

STORY 8

CO-INTELLIGENT PRISON WORK

The prison population in the U.S. doubled from 1981-1991, and has doubled again in the past five years [writes Manitonquat (Medicine Story), a Native American elder who runs a program in New England prisons. He is spiritual leader and Keeper of the Lore for the Assonet band of the Wampanoag Nation in what we now call New Hampshire.] *Yet there seems to be no alternative but to clamor for more of the same approach that is not working. A little like saying if your present medicine is not effective, then you should keep taking more of it until it works.*

[The prison program I work with is based on an indigenous understanding of] how to live a life that is harmonious and in balance. We notice that things tend to want to heal, to come to balance, to become better, and that human beings want in fact to learn, to become more aware, more conscious, and to make things better.

[In our prison program] we encourage spiritual growth and seeking, because a whole human being must be aware of more than himself, that there is a vast mystery beyond our consciousness to which we must have some relation.

[At the start of each meeting] we greet our common mother, the Earth. And then we greet her other children – those that put down roots into her, those that crawl under her skin, those that run about on her as we do, those that swim in her waters and those that fly on her winds. Each one has a different gift that they bring to the web of life, and that web depends on all these gifts.

Our people noticed long ago that the circle is the basic form of Creation [so we sit in a circle].   In the circle, all are equal: there is no top or bottom, first or last, better or worse. The talking stick will be passed, and each one who holds it may speak for as long as he needs and chooses. Everyone else will listen and give the speaker his attention and respect. It is not necessary that you agree with a speaker in order to respect him. You respect him by listening and keeping your mind open to hear his words, as well as to feel his heart and what lies between the words. Each man holding the talking stick is asked only to be honest.

This teaching of respect is spiritual wisdom to our people, because we have found over the ages that it functions and makes our lives work, makes them better, and when we depart from this wisdom at any time we make mistakes and regret it. Therefore we are taught to respect the Earth, as our own mother, to respect all things in Creation, all forms of life, and all other human beings regardless of their age, sex, color, nationality, or belief.

Most of these prisoners have never in their lives been listened to with respect. Very few have any persons in their experience who have shown them respect in any manner at all. So for them to hold the talking stick and feel all that attention, respectful, supportive attention, it becomes a really powerful and liberating experience.

[We tell prisoners] "No one was ever like you in all the universe, and there will never be another one like you again. Therefore only you have your special gift, and you are the only one who can give it away. You will not feel right, will not fulfill your purpose until you give it away. The rest of us need to receive your gift and hear your story."

[Every] human being [starts out] loving, joyful, intelligent and creative. That's how every one of these prisoners began, these criminals, these men with

shattered lives who may have shattered others' lives. [But] every prisoner I have listened to has suffered some level of abuse in those tender, vulnerable early years of childhood – physical abuse very often, sexual abuse, or just terrifying emotional abuse by one or more adult care-givers, coupled with some level of isolation and abandonment.

After some years in a prison circle, men find themselves so changed that it is hard for them to believe that they once were the people who committed their crimes...Having been rescued by a circle, having seen that the most human society is one that lives by the ideals of respect and honesty, equality, closeness and caring, these men want never to be isolated again, never to be without the support and the love of a circle of real human beings.

[We also use] the sweat lodge – an almost universal purification ceremony among native cultures of North America. The well-known Northern European version of a sweat lodge is the sauna. In a Native American sweat lodge, people sit together in total darkness in a low domed structure made of saplings set in the ground in a circle and bent over and tied to each other in pairs and then covered with blankets and canvas. Pouring water over red-hot stones in a central pit creates the steam.

In my way of leading a sweat purification ceremony, I use four rounds, or sections, one for each direction, in which I focus on healing the body, the mind, the heart, and the spirit. The ceremony is very intense and may last over two hours, and the experience cannot be translated adequately into words. [It seems to] burn out their past, their troubling thoughts and feelings, the tension of life in prison, and their worries about the outside world.

[And sometimes I have used Re-evaluation Co-Counseling, a peer counseling practice through which these prisoners] learned that they can allow them-

*selves to feel feelings which are terrifying and pain-
ful and enraging, and that they will not go crazy or
get bummed out forever, but will actually relieve themselves of old burdens, gain more power, and think
more clearly.*

*Out of [this] circle of men hidden behind their [dys-
functional psychological] patterns comes a family of
brothers with common grief, common despair, common desire, common fear, and common hope. Old
timers take the new ones under their wings and set
them straight. They begin to look at everyone – parents, siblings, wives, children, friends, enemies – as
human beings that once were innocent children but
got loaded with distress with no support to deal with
it, and developed the patterns that now make them
so difficult to relate to. As their attitude changes, they
feel better ... [and even] see other inmates and especially some of the difficult guards in this way, too.
They become less confrontational, sometimes down-
right sympathetic, and report great changes in those
encounters as well.*

*[When these prisoners leave prison they should
have their] own half-way houses, staffed by the ex-
prisoners themselves, where newly-released prisoners can have the ongoing support of a circle. Going
from a circle in the prison to a circle on the outside
would be an easy transition for them, within a way
that is familiar and empowering. Here the men would
find counseling, to understand their way into the new
social world, to relate to their families and friends,
and to find employment and housing.*

edited from *Ending Violent Crime* by Manitonquat

Manitonquat's program, which has run for more than
a dozen years, is attractive to mainstream folks for two
reasons: it works and it is cheap. Only five to ten percent of the convicts who complete Manitonquat's pro-

gram revert to criminal activities which land them in prison again (compared to a general recidivism rate of 65-85% in the overall prison population). As a volunteer, he serves 120-150 inmates in seven state prisons with only about $100/month in travel expenses. He estimates that if he worked full-time on a small salary he could provide bi-weekly programs for up to 1000 inmates and train people to do what he does with a two-week training program.

He also notes that the convicts he works with are eager to use the same practices to heal the young men on the streets, in the gangs and in the juvenile correctional system. They want to build job programs and start ex-con businesses, especially environmental ones. He infects these men with his desire "to replace the pyramid of domination with the circle of equality and respect."

****

As you can see, co-intelligence is a basket which we can use to gather examples of intelligence used in the service of healing and wholeness. On the Co-Intelligence Institute website at *co-intelligence.org*, you can find many other stories and examples that exemplify co-intelligence in action.

Co-intelligence is also a lens we can use to look more closely at these examples and stories, so that we can better understand their underlying operating principles. Familiarity with the framework of co-intelligence can help us apply these principles more systematically throughout our society, in order to create a world that truly works for all.

CHAPTER 3

WHOLENESS, INTERCONNECTEDNESS AND CO-CREATIVITY

We have been exploring "co-intelligence" as a new way to understand and relate to intelligence, from the perspective of wholeness, interconnectedness and co-creativity.

To get a better grasp on what this means, let us take a closer look at some of the implications of taking wholeness, interconnectedness and co-creativity seriously.

When we take wholeness seriously...

We include more of what is involved – and more of who is involved – in any situation with which we are dealing. Even as we weigh what is relevant and appreciate our limits, we continually stretch our ability to embrace a more comprehensive view of reality: more viewpoints, approaches, diversity, nuances and complexity. We want to get a sense of the whole picture – or as close to it as we can get.

We recognize there is more to whatever we are dealing with than we can articulate and analyze. We sense into it, looking for hints of the bigger story, the underlying feelings, the growing edges of the situation, the mystery. We make sure our intelligence involves more than our own logic and individual smarts – that it involves things like emotion and intuition and each other – so we can embrace life more deeply.

When we take wholeness to heart, we realize there is much more to us – as whole individuals and groups – than any particular label, role or aspect of who we are. Everyone is bigger than their name or function, or our estimation of them, and therefore worthy of respect – even when we do not like them. This is true of every thing, as well. Practitioners of permaculture (a system of "permanent agriculture") apply this insight by designing productive ecosystems in which each element – each animal and plant, each piece of land or water – performs multiple functions which utilize its unique qualities.

When we take wholeness seriously, we are committed to moving beyond "either/or" and "win/lose" to the more inclusive posture of "both/and" and "win/win." We also are committed to thinking long-term, as do the Iroquois – considering the consequences of our actions for the next seven generations.

We explore the role of circumstances, environment, culture and other contexts as factors influencing outcomes. We recognize that taking things out of context is one of the best ways to miss the whole point.

We see the effects of not taking wholeness seriously in our criminal justice system. For the most part, our communities take little or no responsibility for the misdeeds of their members. Instead of helping to heal the damage done to the community – by facilitating reparations and mutual efforts to learn from the damage in order to prevent its recurrence (as is done in many tribal communities) – we remove offenders to isolated cells at great expense, often making them even more criminal.

When we take wholeness seriously, we ground our ideals in wholeness. For example, since the words health, healing, wholesome, integrity and holy all refer to wholeness, we give these values high priority in our personal, economic and community lives. The work of people like Gandhi and Rudolph Steiner embody this effort to nurture wholeness at every level of life. These inspiring leaders showed ways to develop whole people who can sustain healthy communities together, with a sense of sacredness, working in harmony with nature.

When we take interconnectedness seriously...

We recognize that we are not alone in the world, but are embedded in human and natural communities. We share our fate with these communities: Global weather and global economics are teaching us this, catastrophe by catastrophe.

When we take interconnectedness seriously, we seek to understand the relationship between people, things, life forms, fields of study, approaches, etc. – considering the relationships between them as equally important or more important than their individual characteristics. We use that understanding to establish peer synergistic relationships wherever we can. More often than not, we find that healthy relationships are the solution – or at least a powerful resource for finding the solution. Individual solutions for addiction, for example, do not succeed as well as collective solutions that utilize the peer support of recovering addicts.

When we take interconnectedness to heart, we realize the power of shared realities, shared vision, shared stories, shared experience and the sort of communication systems that support such sharing. One of the most powerful techniques for creating bridges between ideological enemies is to have each person share the story of how he or she came to hold his or her beliefs. This is one way in which we can allow our common humanity to shine through our differences.

When we really understand interconnectedness, we do not focus on trying to control or blame individual people, situations, and problems. Instead, we take a relational and systemic perspective to help heal the whole. We may follow the example of family systems therapists who attend to a family's patterns of interaction, not allowing a scapegoat to take the blame for an entire family's dysfunction.

When we take co-creativity seriously...

We examine our own role in whatever circumstance we find ourselves. We seek out all actual and potential allies instead of focusing on opponents.

When we take co-creativity to heart, we avoid nailing down blame or isolating single linear causes for any condition or event. To the best of our ability, we try to understand and address the many causes and fields of influence at work co-creating any situation.

Furthermore, we acknowledge the dance of order and chaos which is inherent in a co-created reality (since no one is actually in charge) and learn to let go of attachment, certainty and our need for control. In fact, when we are really proficient at co-creativity, we let go of control *in order to enhance* productive self-organizing systems; our lack of attachment *enhances* serenity and responsiveness; our lack of certainty *enhances* openness and ability to learn. All of this enhances our ability to co-create as partners with the life around us.

In sum, co-intelligence involves stretching our sense of what is needed, what is relevant, and who is involved in any given situation. It involves stretching in the direction of wholeness, interconnectedness and co-creativity.

CHAPTER 4

RESONANT INTELLIGENCE

In the next section of this book, we will explore a variety of co-intelligent practices we can use to help our groups, organizations and communities become more co-intelligent. In preparation for doing so, it may help to take a closer look at resonant intelligence as the foundation for a different kind of leadership.

In Chapter 1, I wrote:

> There is more to intelligence than a solitary capacity exercised within the life of one entity. As it attunes to life, intelligence evokes a fuller, deeper intelligence in and around it. Resonant intelligence is intelligence that grows stronger or fuller as it resonates with other sources or forms of intelligence, or which deepens in empathic response to life.

Resonance is an energetic response among similar things, which arises from their similarity, especially in the absence of barriers to that response.

A vibration in one tuning fork sets off the same vibration in a similar tuning fork – the nearer it is, the stronger the response. A memory shared by one Vietnam vet sets off a flurry of memories in another Vietnam vet – especially in a supportive group setting where participants have come to know themselves and one another well, and thus have lowered the psychological and interpersonal barriers that could block resonance.

The core commons

As human beings, our experience of resonance arises from what we share or what we have in common with one another or with the world around us. Several realms of kinship with life support this phenomenon:

- **Group**: We feel special connection with people with whom we share significant ties, characteristics or experiences. Family members, war buddies, single mothers or cancer survivors – "we can relate." Even when the "vibes" are not pleasant, they tend to be more intense because of the resonance. Tribal and national resonances are also found at this level of kinship.
- **Humanity**: Deeper down, we feel kinship with all other people. We share a tremendous amount in common simply by being human. We often call this "our common humanity."
- **Animals**: Then there is our kinship with animals – especially our intelligent, infant-nursing, often furry relatives, the other mammals – such as dogs, cats, horses, dolphins, and monkeys. Most pets are mammals, but most people can empathize with any animal that is like us in any way.
- **Life**: We also can have feelings for plants and other life forms. We can respond to all forms of life, since we are living creatures, too.
- **Earth**: Most of us feel deeply at home with sunsets, mountains, oceans, and the rain – and the way the moon and stars look. We are part of the earth, and kin with everything on it. Every atom in our bodies has been part of this planet for eons, flowing through life in all its forms, including its winds, seas and lands.
- **Universe**: Some people even identify with the entire universe, saying (with considerable scientific

evidence) that humans are "star dust" and that "we are the universe becoming conscious of itself."

- **Spirit:** Finally, at perhaps the deepest level, as spiritual beings, we recognize other spirits and other creatures as part of our larger spiritual family. Many people experience spiritual kinship in all of the realms described above.

Combined, I call these kinship realities – these facts of our relatedness – our *core commons* – the biological, human and spiritual kinship deep within all of us. This "core commons" is the rich soil that nurtures our most basic values, such as compassion, respect, and integrity. And it is also the basis for the energetic responsiveness of resonance. The fact that the common core exists in all of us means that you can evoke its resonance within me – and the resonance between us can cause it to come alive in our larger group – and a group, in the right conditions, can cause it to resonate in the wider population.

So somewhere deep inside us, our sense of goodness, our connection to spirit, and our natural earth consciousness are all blended together into a seamless sense of right relationship and healthy, wholesome behavior. Sometimes this common core is buried, and sometimes it is very much alive and vivid in our consciousness. The more we are in touch with the kinship realities that make it up – in ourselves and each other – the more resonance becomes possible, allowing these deep forms of intelligence to resonate from one person to another.

This is "co-resonant wisdom" – the wisdom that is evoked in one person or group by someone else's powerful love, integrity, inquiry, empathy or other pure invitation to common humanity or life. Resonant intelligence, or the ability to evoke co-resonant wisdom in others, is what made Gandhi and King so effective. Our core commons – our shared patterns of human, biological, and spiritual kinship – can, if we attend to them, point us towards connection, towards healing, towards life, towards making our actions and our solutions wiser. The fact that we can evoke these things in one another is remarkably empowering.

"ALL MY RELATIONS"

Resonant intelligence arises from, and supports, a sense of kinship, a lived reality of relatedness. We treat one another like sisters and brothers when we ground ourselves in our common humanity or life. Those who see their God or essential goodness in themselves and in everyone else have a powerful capacity to resonate with people around them. Those who see sacredness *everywhere* resonate and commune with the whole world and everything in it. Everything becomes an expression of the sacred Beloved or the spirit of Nature – and, as such, an opportunity for offering love, respect, and consideration.

Other forms of resonance are grounded in nature. Deep ecologists recognize that we have much in common with other life forms and even with rocks, rivers and landscapes. We share common ancestors, chemical patterns (DNA, water, salt), a common atmosphere and our planetary home. And we share that undefinable dynamic energy we call life. Upon this shared aliveness rests our ability to commune with nature and with one another as living beings. Many Native Americans see the living world as "all my relations." We all can realize this relatedness and act on it. Resonant intelligence thrives on this level of conscious interconnectedness.

Of course, we may feel resonance with a more limited set of humans, with whom we share certain beliefs, identities and narratives about life. Most people identify with a particular religion, lifestyle, nation, or culture. Sometimes, these more limited kinds of resonance are built around a "common enemy" and do not include a sense of connection to the larger whole.

Yet the existence of a "core commons" means that there is always a way that we can attempt to bridge the differences that tend to keep us separate at a more limited level of resonance. As many religions point out, direct offerings of love appeal to the fundamental truth of our deeper shared humanity. For example, Kathryn Watterson's *Not By the Sword* tells the story of a wheelchair-bound diabetic neo-Nazi Klansman who was terrorizing a local Jewish cantor. The cantor and his family responded by offering sincere friendship. The heartful communications and actions from these people he despised generated profound resonance in the Klansman's heart and mind. Finally, they broke through his shell. When the now former Klansman died of his disease soon thereafter, it was in the home of the cantor, as a member of his family.

Resonant leadership

The potential for resonance among all beings suggests that there are forms of leadership that call forth deeper patterns of resonance among people. We could call this resonant leadership.

At the surface level of this phenomenon we find resonant appeals to patriotism and team spirit. On the dark side of this important but shallow resonant leadership are demagogues who evoke an exclusive, alienated tribal resonance that lifts their followers out of self-concern into deep feelings about their group or country – and about its enemies. Hitler, for example, was a profoundly resonant leader. The problem was that he concentrated on a very shallow level of the core commons, the level of the tribe, and grounded it in exclusion rather than inclusion.

Today's world urgently needs forms of resonant leadership that are strong enough to accept, include and honor all the differences we find among us. We need leadership that calls forth our resonance at the deepest levels of our core commons – our natural and spiritual kinship. This can, of course, include deep feelings for our group or our country, but only as they are embedded in a strong sense of connection to other groups and countries, and to the larger world.

From a co-intelligence perspective, the highest form of resonant leadership would give people awareness, tools and institutions to support their deep resonance with one another, with all members of the human family, and with the natural world, all at the same time. This book is intended to support that emerging leadership.

USING OUR LEADERSHIP TO NURTURE RESONANT INTELLIGENCE

One of the ways that all of us, regardless of where we are, can use our leadership to support resonant intelligence is simply to share. All kinds of sharing support the process of resonance: sharing of ideas and stories; of possessions and wealth; of interests and fears; of hearts and meals; of activities and conversations; of singing and dancing; of the past, the present and the future.

We can nurture resonant intelligence by sharing, by appreciating that which we already share, and by creating cultures, institutions and practices that increase or sustain sharing. Sharing creates and sustains relationship, expanding our ability to perceive our common ground while lowering the barriers to resonance.

Yet it is important to be able to share not just what we have in common, but our differences as well. Paradoxically, when we create a safe space where each of us can share our diversity – that which makes us unique and individual and different – we are often able to experience our shared humanity on a much deeper level. In this way we are often able to arrive at creative consensus without compromise, as in the opening story about the fertilizer factory. In Chapter 7, we will be exploring a variety of different tools that we can use to help create safe environments for speaking our truths in the various groups to which we belong.

When we speak our own truth, even when we fear it may alienate others, it can encourage others to also look within and find what is true for them. Likewise, when we take an action that is motivated by principle, or even when we propose something new, we may find ourselves at first standing alone, or encountering some initial resistance. Yet if we maintain a spirit of inclusivity and connection with others, we often find that others are inspired or moved by our actions, and ripples of resonance begin to form.

Resonant intelligence is often intertwined with our experience of collective intelligence, especially at a group level. Experiences of high collective intelligence in groups are almost always accompanied by unforgettable experiences of resonance, where we may feel "as though we are one larger organism," accompanied by a strong sense of "flow." Therefore, many people identify collective intelligence – the capacity to be effective together – with a group experience of resonance or "collective consciousness." Among the many aspects of collective intelligence at the group level, this is certainly one of the most compelling.

Resonant intelligence and the core commons are fundamental to understanding how collective intelligence can bring forth the wisdom we need to address the challenges of the twenty-first century. In the rest of this book we will explore how to generate collective intelligence at different levels of human life, building a foundation for a co-intelligent vision of holistic politics and conscious cultural evolution.

As we bring the spiritual principles of
interconnection and interdependence
into the material world,
we can make them the basis
for political action
and ... quicken the spirit
of world transformation.

U.S. Representative
Dennis Kucinich

Section II

Making a

Whole Difference

Together

CHAPTER **5**

REACHING BEYOND
ADVERSARIAL ACTIVISM

All things are possible once enough human beings realize that everything is at stake.

— NORMAN COUSINS

Things undreamt of are daily being seen, the impossible is ever becoming possible. We are constantly being astonished these days at the amazing discoveries in the field of violence. But I maintain that far more undreamt of and seemingly impossible discoveries will be made in the field of nonviolence.

— M. K. GANDHI

My dictionary defines activism as "assertive, often militant action" to oppose or support a controversial position. That conventional definition bristles with battle.

This chapter offers a different definition of activism – one that can include everyone concerned about making a better world. It explores a novel vision of activism that embraces the gifts of engagement while offering alternatives to oppositional approaches. Yet the paradox is that some-

> *times principled oppostion is still required in or-*
> *der to advocate for non-adversarial approaches*
> *to conflict.*
>   *This new activist vision recognizes human dif-*
> *ferences and conflicts as natural, essential aspects*
> *of life. But it seeks to use them creatively to ex-*
> *pand our awareness, develop our capacities and*
> *further the common good. I invite you to join me*
> *in nurturing this emerging energy to heal and*
> *transform the world.*

I should begin by saying that I consider myself an activist. To me, activism is simply the focused exercise of citizenship – intentional, active participation in public life toward some desired end. Some activists advocate, some question, some listen, some invite and inspire. Some focus on a problem, some on a cause, some on a solution or a vision, some on a process or a way of being. But we all want something to change. We want a better world. And we think that better world is so important that we put a significant part of our lives into working for it.

Activism, of course, is not passive. Activists *act,* hoping to have a real effect on the policies and activities of institutions, on the views and behaviors of the public, and on the well-being of a particular community or interest group. In short, activism reaches beyond the familiar basics of citizenship, such as voting and voicing opinions, to have a greater impact on the affairs of society.

In this book the term "activist" is intended to include social change agents, community organizers, cultural catalysts, people involved in "engaged spirituality," facilitators of social transformation and anyone else working for a better world.

If you are reading this book, I suspect that includes you. I invite you to explore some new approaches to our work for the world, and how we might go about it.

Activism informed by co-intelligence

The perspective of co-intelligence can inform our activist work in different ways. For example:

- we can seek to operate on the assumptions of wholeness, interconnectedness and co-creativity;
- we can advocate co-intelligent solutions to problems (such as the prison program in Chapter 2);
- we can use co-intelligent methods, such as dialogue, to pursue our goals;
- our goal, itself, can become the creation of ways in which people can collaboratively arrive at solutions to their (and our) collective problems.

Given the kinds of problems that our society is facing, one of the most urgent needs I see is this last option – to advocate for the use of co-intelligent methods to increase the capacity of society as a whole to act in a co-intelligent manner. As a society, we need tools to help us address diversity in a positive and productive way, to more creatively meet the challenges that we face. One particularly useful method for doing this involves *citizen deliberative councils,* which I will be describing in more detail in Section Three. As activists, we can advocate for the use of citizen deliberative councils and other co-intelligent methodologies in their own right. Alternatively, some hot current issue (such as a technology-related crisis) can become an opportunity for promoting the idea that we need more collective intelligence and for offering practical approaches to address the situation at hand.

Thoughts on the evolution of activism

For years, most of the people I knew, including myself, thought of our work as *social change activism.* But then I started meeting people who saw themselves as *facilitators of cultural transformation*, a term which suggests deep shifts in fundamental cultural assumptions. I liked that. It seemed a more accurate description of what I did.

More recently, I have been thinking about another category of activism that may be even more appropriate to describe what I am suggesting here: *social process activism*.

> *Co-intelligent social process activism acts on behalf of better ways for the society as a whole to change and transform ITSELF.*

Accomplishing this, of course, requires certain other changes and transformations, but they all relate to that shift in *social process and capacity.*

Since so much traditional activism is adversarial, some people might wonder if such social process work should even be called "activism." I would like to suggest that activism is bigger than its adversarial forms. Although I believe adversarial activism has an important role to play in making the world a better place, I think it also has its limits. And those limits have left many people who sincerely want change disenchanted with current approaches to activism.

Many of us are already familiar with the limits of adversarial activism. Being against something does not build that which is needed, nor does it tap into the resources hidden in people and institutions we may be fighting. Neither does it illuminate how our own approaches may be reinforcing the very problem we may be trying to change. Although critical analysis of what is wrong can hone our awareness, concentrating on adversarial struggle can contract our thinking and limit the possibilities we see.

Of course, some kinds of nonviolent direct action can be necessary in existing political systems in order to bring distracted citizens and resistant power-holders into dialogue on important issues. Yet if direct action is not held within the larger context of a call for creative dialogue, it can become simply another way in which we are attempting to impose our views, however noble, on others.

THE URGE TO MOVE BEYOND PROTEST

As I developed as an activist, I found myself chafing against the limits of protest and contention. I began to search for other approaches and for a larger picture that would show me how diverse forms of activism fit together into making a better world. As I did so, I realized that I was not alone. My own evolution as an activist was part of a larger shift. Other activists were also having trouble with the adversarial energy of most progressive political work. The antagonism that was at the heart of anti-war, anti-pollution, anti-corporate globalization, anti-oppression work was not only projected against what we were trying to change, but often pitted activists against one another, making good group experience difficult. The emphasis on values, which is the strength of so much activism, was often used by us to attack each other for lack of this or that principled belief or behavior. In too many progressive and green groups, many of us experienced a lack of compassion and patience with one another, and a narrowness of sensibility that made some of us feel claustrophobic. It was out of this raw material that the enemies of progressive activism conjured up the idea of "political correctness."

I was only one of many activists and would-be activists who dropped out of traditional political protest in frustration, searching for more life-affirming approaches to building a better world. Some of us went into community work, helping stakeholders to come together or communities to develop shared visions, or we joined the intentional community movement. Some of us took up spiritual paths or explored various aspects of the human potential movement, feeling that individual transformation was a necessary foundation for social change. Some of us moved into the arts or became performers, sometimes taking our creations into the streets. Others found ways to make a difference through computer networking and programming, or in the organic and natural foods movements, or through various "green technologies," environmental law, eco-philosophy, and green architecture and city planning. Some of us went into organizational development or facilitation work, seeking ways to shift corporate activity or organization in more positive directions or to improve nonprofit effectiveness. Many became teachers, at all levels of education, or presented remarkable new ways and worldviews in workshops attended by the rest of us.

Many of these one-time activists evolved into core members of an important and rapidly growing subculture identified by Paul Ray and Sherry Ruth Anderson as "cultural creatives" *(culturalcreatives.org),* who now make up about a quarter of the adult U.S. population. The ecological, social, spiritual and personal development concerns that inform this sector of the population cause them to be in the forefront of cultural transformation.

Many of these aptly named cultural creatives developed the very ideas, methods and organizations that I have written about in this book. I have learned a tremendous amount from them. These leaders and innovators have sought to make a better world, and have been creating ways to do so for decades. My own view is that those cultural creatives who were activists, myself among them, have never actually left the world of activism. Rather, we have changed it. Although there are thousands of adversarial activists still actively protesting and fighting, I do not believe activism is primarily adversarial any longer. More and more creative folks have found ways to make a significant difference in collaborative and holistic ways. Their work has inspired me to come up with this new framework and language that I have called "co-intelligence," and I hope that my work offers useful coherence to the many visionaries it embraces. At the same time, most co-intelligent activity has unfolded within the social and cultural spheres, and many of us have felt powerless to bring this new sensibility to bear on the realm of politics. Therefore, the third section of this book focuses on applying a co-intelligent perspective to our political system.

There are many facets to co-intelligent activism, and I will be exploring this subject in greater depth in Chapter 19. Here I would like to offer an overview and address some of the basic assumptions of this emergent approach.

A DESIRABLE UNFOLDING

At a very deep level, I believe that those of us who are beginning to build a more co-intelligent society – a global wisdom culture – are stepping into a totally different game. One of the biggest differences about this new activism is that everything in the old world – the old structures, all the experiments and methodologies, even the problems and catastrophes, *everything,* is a resource for what we are beginning to do. *And what we are beginning to do is different in kind from anything that we have tried to do before.* We are shifting from thinking of social change as an effort to solve problems and achieve an ideal society, to realizing that social change is an ongoing process that we can enhance and make wiser. Our goal is no longer *a desired state* for society, but rather *a desirable unfolding* of society. In other words, we are not trying to engineer a new society to our specifications so much as trying to jumpstart certain innovations which will (we hope) elicit society's conscious and continuous re-creation of itself to its own changing specifications, as needed, to meet the challenges, changes and opportunities it faces.

So we are not actually talking about utopia any more. Perhaps we are talking about *utopiation* – an ongoing journey towards ever-better societies.

A vision of a co-intelligent wisdom culture

I first ran across the term "wisdom culture" in conversations about indigenous cultures where wisdom has been highly honored, cultivated and articulated for millennia. Members of these tribes see life as a great learning and growing experience, not just a matter of pleasure, pain, survival and death.

But these tribal wisdom cultures tend to be coherent, with single dominant worldviews, lifestyles and socio-spiritual practices. For very long stretches, they experienced little dissent with regard to their basic assumptions. Although many of these indigenous cultures have included a tradition of real respect for diversity among individuals, they have often tended to be quite intolerant of "other ways," as part of the cultural mechanism that allowed tribal cultures to live side-by-side yet maintain their own distinctiveness. This sense of cultural coherence has been an important factor in the struggle for survival that indigenous cultures have waged in the face of encroachment by other, mostly European, cultures.

In contrast, today's global culture is highly pluralistic. Paradoxically it is becoming both more so and less so. Individuals, groups and sub-cultures demand recognition and assert their pride, even as they rub elbows, eat each other's cuisine, and kill each other.

Stimulating, mediating and eroding all this cultural variety is the dominant post-modern market-oriented mega-culture that commodifies and exploits diversity, but does not honor deep traditions, real uniqueness, or wisdom. So, while indigenous wisdom cultures may serve as an inspiration in many ways, there is much that we need to invent and create anew in order to address our current circumstances.

So what kind of wisdom culture might be possible for us? What does it mean to speak of a global culture that is not reductionist and homogenized? At the very least, a global wisdom culture would need to know how to use diversity to generate or access deeper, broader, higher forms of wisdom than any person or culture could alone. Instead of a utopia, it would be a culture consciously engaged in a continuous process of growth and transformation. It would be characterized by a high capacity for collective reflection, as well as the ability to nurture wise and diverse forms of self-organization in organizations, communities, and societies worldwide. This is the vision that sustains my work in co-intelligence.

If we lived in such a culture, we would see:

- many forms of high quality dialogue, at all levels of society;
- widespread respect for diversity within the context of a well-understood common ground;
- institutionalized feedback loops and synergies which enhance community health, vitality, insight and sustainability;
- participatory processes for self-governance at all levels, including collaborative visioning, policy-generation, problem-solving, administration and oversight;
- widespread understanding of the advanced social technologies (many of them part of our indigenous heritage) that allow us to reach creative consensus without compromise;

- a spirit of partnership with one another and the world around us – a sense of co-creating a vibrantly good shared life together;
- leadership that persistently nurtures the capacities of individuals, groups, communities and whole societies so they can better function in independent and interdependent ways, without top-down dependencies.

This vision is grounded in the co-creative philosophy noted in previous chapters. It is based on a shift in perspective that begins with recognition of a simple fact:

> *Together we create our communities, our societies, and our world. We are always doing this, together. We can do it more consciously, intentionally and responsibly.*

Given any condition we want to change, we can ask:

- What are we doing to co-create and sustain this problem – through our beliefs, attitudes, behaviors and systems?
- What do we want to co-create together?
- What beliefs, attitudes, behaviors, agreements and systems would help us co-create what we want instead of what we do not want?
- What beliefs, attitudes, behaviors, agreements and systems would help us ask and answer these questions together – and act on what we learn – most effectively?

CHAPTER **6**

COLLECTIVE INTELLIGENCE

As we explore ways to generate more effective groups, organizations, institutions, and other human systems, it may help to begin by taking a closer look at collective intelligence.

In my own experience, when I investigate the problems that we face in the world today, I seldom find individual evil. I usually find basically good, intelligent people *collectively* generating discord and disaster – in families, groups, organizations, nations and the world. Meanwhile, in their own lives, from their own perspective (and usually that of their loved ones), most of them are doing perfectly good, decent things. How can this be?

As you may have gathered already, I believe that *individual* intelligence is not enough. If we wish to successfully deal with the various social and environmental challenges we face today, we need to develop far more *collective* intelligence as a society and as a global civilization.

To date, much has been learned about how to develop collective intelligence within organizations – usually to help corporations become more competitive in the global market. Good work has also been done to increase collective intelligence in civil society at the community level, especially to deal with local environmental conflicts.

Yet comparatively little effort has been applied toward building collective intelligence in the public sector, for governance and social system design. In order to ensure our success as a species, we will need to apply what we have learned about collective intelligence to improve our capacity to create sustainable social, political, and economic systems that work well for everyone involved.

This much is clear: *Given the right conditions* – conditions which have been created in numerous environments around the world on many occasions – communities and societies can collectively reflect on their problems and possibilities, and collectively choose and implement effective, even brilliant solutions and initiatives. Understanding collective intelligence can help us fulfill the original dream of democracy: the participatory determination of our collective fate.

Collective intelligence at different levels of society

Given the central importance of collective intelligence, let us take a closer look at this phenomenon. The following examples show how collective intelligence might be applied at a variety of levels: in groups, organizations, communities, states, and whole societies.

GROUPS

An individual IQ test compares individuals' problem-solving skills with the problem-solving capabilities of others their age. In a similar manner, we could demonstrate the existence of group intelligence by comparing how well various groups solve problems.

In a classic experiment, group intelligence was measured by presenting small groups of executives with a hypothetical wilderness survival problem.* All-female teams arrived at better solutions (as judged by wilderness experts) than all-male teams. The women's collective problem-solving capabilities were enhanced by their collaborative style, while the men's efforts to assert their own solutions led them to get in each other's way. Significantly, the resulting difference in collective intelligence did not occur because the individual women were smarter than the individual men, but rather because of a difference in gender-related group dynamics.

This example also shows how collaborative intelligence can enhance a group's collective intelligence. When people align their individual intelligences in shared inquiries or undertakings, instead of using their intelligence to undermine each other in the pursuit of individual status, they are much more able to generate collective intelligence.

In the pursuit of collective intelligence, organizations often invest in many kinds of "team-building" approaches in order to generate greater collaboration within groups. In Chapter 7, we will be describing a number of simple, low-cost approaches that can be used to help neighborhood, community, and activist groups develop greater collaborative and collective intelligence.

ORGANIZATIONS

Can a whole organization exhibit intelligence? In November 1997, 750 forest service employees used a technique called Open Space Technology to create, in just three days, a shared vision of change, including action plans. The vision that this group generated covered all

---

* Lafferty and Pond, *The Desert Survival Situation*, cited in Marilyn Loden, *Feminine Leadership*.

facets of forest service activity, and the employees were genuinely excited about implementing the action plans they themselves had developed. This one-time exercise had a lasting effect upon the larger system.

Several organizations and networks, such as the Society for Organizational Learning *(solonline.org),* research and promote the capacity for organizational intelligence by helping corporations build a culture of ongoing, high-quality dialogue that examines the whole-system dynamics in and around the organization. Just as group intelligence depends on things such as group process, organizational intelligence depends on organizational factors. These factors range from an organizational culture that promotes dialogue to organizational memory systems (files, records, databases, minutes, etc.). They include systems that collect and utilize feedback (learning inputs) from inside and outside the organization, as well as efforts to understand the feedback dynamics (cycles and interdependencies) that govern the organization as a living system. When such things are in place, an organization can create, accumulate and use understandings and solutions which become part of the organization itself – knowledge that outlasts the tenure of individual employees and executives. In other words, the *organization* is learning, exercising its intelligence and applying it in life the same way an individual does.

One particularly interesting innovation is chaordic organization. The term "chaordic" was coined by Visa co-founder Dee Hock to describe complex, self-organizing systems that manifest both chaotic and orderly qualities. In *The Birth of the Chaordic Age,* he describes how a chaordic organization, such as the Internet, is not so much a thing as a pattern of agreements about interactions which help voluntary participants achieve certain shared goals or visions, guided by certain agreed-on principles. Such organizations provide workable alternatives to conventional command-and-control structures. **The Chaordic Commons** *(chaordic.org)* is a non-profit organization dedicated to making this work available in the world.

As mentioned earlier, much of the research on how to generate collective intelligence has taken place within the private sector. Unfortunately, all too many corporations are still playing a destructive role within our larger system, and are using their enhanced collective intelligence to consolidate power and consume resources faster. This is in part because society has yet to change the fundamental "rules of the game," including how corporations are chartered and monitored.

Nonetheless, if we are to survive as a species, we need to apply our knowledge of collective intelligence to larger and nobler ends than profit. Our non-profit, community, and social change organizations can improve their capacity for creating effective change by applying the knowledge that has been gained about collaborative leadership, whole-system planning, self-directed work teams, and a host of other innovations.

COMMUNITIES

What would community intelligence look like? Perhaps we see a budding example of it in Chattanooga, Tennessee, which in the early 1980s was reeling from local recession, deteriorating schools, and rising racial tensions. Several dozen citizens formed Chattanooga Venture, an on-going, cross-class, multi-racial organization that involved hundreds of people in an inclusive effort to set and achieve community goals. Of 34 specific city-wide goals set in 1984, 29 were completed by 1992, at which point **Chattanooga Venture** again convened hundreds of citizens to create new community goals. Among the goals realized through this process was the creation of Chattanooga's Neighborhood Network, which organized and linked up dozens of neighborhood associations to help people co-create a shared future right where they lived, enhancing their community intelligence even further. Chattanooga Venture provides a glimpse of the sort of ongoing collective intelligence we could build to solve problems, to learn together, and to generate a better life right at home.

There are many other inspiring examples of the effort to develop community intelligence. Many of these have been carried out using the approach of **Asset Based Community Development** (ABCD). This community organizing approach does not directly address a community's problems or treat citizens as clients in need of services from government and nonprofit agencies. Rather, it sees citizens as assets and as co-creators of their community. ABCD organizers help citizens discover, map and mobilize the assets that are hidden away in all the people who live in their community, as well as in the community's informal associations and formal institutions. Those resources, brought out of their isolation and into creative synergy with each other, are then used to realize the community's visions. See John P. Kretzmann and John L. McKnight's *Building Communities from the Inside Out* or *nwu.edu/ IPR/abcd.html*.

STATES AND PROVINCES

A statewide example of collective intelligence can be found in the efforts of the non-profit **Oregon Health Decisions** (OHD), which involved thousands of diverse, ordinary Oregonians in in-depth conversations about how to best use limited health care funds. Hundreds of such meetings in the 1980s resulted in the legislature mandating in 1990 the use of community meetings to identify the values that should guide state health care decisions. With experts "on tap" to provide specialized health care knowledge, citizens weighed the trade-offs involved in over seven hundred approaches to deal with specific medical conditions, and decided which should be given preference.

In general, approaches that were inexpensive, highly effective, and needed by many people (which included many preventative measures) were given priority over approaches that were expensive, less effective and needed by very few people. Although clearly some people would not get needed care under this system, it was pointed out that some people did not get needed care under the existing system. The difference was that in the old system, it was poor people who fell through the cracks by default. In the new system, Oregonians were trying to make these difficult decisions more consciously, openly and justly. So they tapped into the collective intelligence of their entire state, weaving together citizen and expert contributions into a wisdom greater than any person or group could have generated separately.

NATIONS AND WHOLE SOCIETIES

Admittedly, increasing the level of collective intelligence on a national or societal level can be a daunting proposition. How can we begin to involve everyone in a dialogue about the issues we face, when working at such a large scale? I offer the following paragraphs as a "preview" of a longer story that we will be exploring in Chapter 12. I believe that it offers some ideas about avenues to explore if we wish to invite a deeper national dialogue.

One weekend in June 1991, a dozen Canadians met at a resort north of Toronto, under the auspices of *Maclean's*, Canada's leading newsweekly. They had been scientifically chosen so that, together, they reflected all the major sectors of public opinion in their deeply divided country. Each of these people had accepted the invitation to attend this weekend event, where they would be engaging in dialogue with people whose views differed from their own strongly-held beliefs. The dialogue was facilitated by Harvard University law professor Roger Fisher, co-author of the classic *Getting to Yes*, and two colleagues. These ordinary citizens had never engaged in a process like this before. They started with widely divergent positions, and little trust among them. The process took place under tremendous time pressure, as well as under the eye of a camera crew from CTV television who was recording the event for a special public-affairs program. Nonetheless, these folks succeeded in their assignment of developing a consensus vision for the entire country of Canada. Their vision was published in four pages of fine print, part of the thirty-nine pages that *Maclean's* devoted to describing their efforts in their July 1, 1991 issue.

This experience was a very moving event for all who participated in it or witnessed it. *Maclean's* editors suggested that "the process that led to the writing of the draft could be extended to address other issues." Assistant Managing Editor Robert Marshall noted that earlier efforts, including a parliamentary committee, a governmental consultative initiative, and a $27 million Citizens' Forum on Canada's Future, all failed to create real dialogue among citizens about constructive solutions, even though those efforts had involved 400,000 Canadians in focus groups, phone calls and mail-in reporting. "The experience of the *Maclean's* forum indicates that if a national dialogue ever does take place, it would be an extremely productive process."

The *Maclean's* experiment is a type of gathering that I call a **citizen deliberative council**. These councils are diverse groups, somewhat like a jury, who are called together as a microcosm of "We the People" in order to learn, dream, and explore problems and possibilities together while the rest of society observes their deliberations. This approach can dramatically change the political environment, as subsequent government decisions are made in a context of greater public wisdom, sophistication and consensus. In Chapters 13 and 14 we will be taking an in-depth look at citizen deliberative councils as a promising approach for generating collective intelligence on a societal level. Many types of these citizen councils have been used in at least sixteen countries.

As we have seen, collective intelligence is a phenomenon that can occur at various levels. Yet, what do all of these examples of collective intelligence have in common? What makes all these forms of collective intelligence similar?

Inclusion and the intelligence of democracy

At all levels, from groups to whole societies, the degree to which various perspectives are included increases the collective intelligence of the whole. Collective intelligence increases as it creatively and constructively includes diverse relevant viewpoints, people, information, etc., into collective deliberations.

Historically, practical considerations have allowed everyone's voice to be heard only in small groups, such as town meetings. In its ideal form representative democracy was imagined to provide legitimate, manageable small groups (legislative, administrative and judicial bodies) through which (at least theoretically) the voices of whole populations could be channeled. However, over time, our legislatures, executives and judges have become both less representative and less responsive – a situation that has led many of us to reconsider our political and governmental arrangements.

But there is good news: Simultaneous with this development, humanity has been developing powerful tools which could solve these problems. For example, the citizen deliberation councils described earlier could be combined with sophisticated use of media, especially telecommunications and powerful group processes that foster the creative use of diversity. Furthermore, the national councils could be used to spark more and better dialogue at the local level.

This idea combines only a few of the hundreds of approaches that are currently available. I hope to show in this book that there are many social innovations that we could weave together in a variety of ways to create remarkable enhancements to our present system. If we take this challenge, I believe we will find ourselves poised on the edge of our next evolutionary leap in democracy – not just as an alternative to tyranny, but as an inclusive path to society-wide collective intelligence and wisdom.

In the next chapter, we will look at a number of social innovations that allow us to generate deeper democracy and greater collective intelligence in our personal relationships, community groups, nonprofit organizations and social change movements. This, in turn, can lay the groundwork for creating deeper democracy in our social system.

CHAPTER 7

WAYS TO HAVE
REAL DIALOGUE

Dialogue is a central aspect of co-intelligence. In my co-intelligence work, I usually define dialogue as

shared exploration towards greater understanding, connection and positive possibility.

To the extent any method or conversation serves this purpose, I consider it dialogue.

In essence, co-intelligence is dialogic, co-creative, co-evocative, exploratory, synergistic, responsive. That is what the "co-" is all about.

Dialogue plays an obvious role in collaborative and collective intelligence. We can only generate higher levels of intelligence among us if we are doing some high-quality talking with one another, exploring together, working together. When we are in dialogue, whatever we are thinking and feeling joins the thoughts and feelings of others in a shared flow of evolving meaning, carrying us to new, deeper understandings none of us foresaw. Through dialogue we can also more fully encounter one another, and discover who each of us really is beneath our assertions and defenses. In many forms of dialogue we find ourselves sharing feelings, intuitions and stories that reveal our common humanity and strengthen our relationships with one another. As connection and common ground grow, all sorts of things become possible that were not possible before.

As we change the quality of the conversations between us, we create greater synergy among us. We find ways to honor the differences between us and engage with them as a source of creativity and growth. In this way we become smarter together than each of us is individually. And that is the essence of collective intelligence.

Through dialogue "a new kind of mind begins to come into being," observed quantum physicist and dialogue innovator David Bohm, "based on the development of common meaning ... People are no longer primarily in opposition, nor can they be said to be interacting, rather they are participating in this pool of common meaning, which is capable of constant development and change" (quoted in Peter Senge, *The Fifth Discipline*). Believing that our mental constructs are primary barriers to direct participation in this flow of shared meaning, Bohm created a conversational approach – Bohm Dialogue – which helps people suspend their assumptions and move towards more direct encounters with their own experience and with each other.

There are a variety of different approaches to dialogue, and while Bohm's method is valuable, it is by no means the only one. As consultant Harrison Owen suggests, "Dialogue is people truly listening to people truly speaking."

At the same time, not every form of communication is dialogue. For example, one-way communication is not dialogue, especially when it involves powerful people or institutions lecturing to a relatively powerless audience, or mass media pushing manipulated information.

However, since I have an inclusive sense of dialogue, I often think in terms of a *spectrum of dialogue* that reflects different levels of quality in conversation. A highly controlled conversation in which participants are restricted to a fixed agenda might be near the low end, while exploratory dialogue to which people bring their whole selves to engender lively co-creativity might be at the high end. But it is all dialogue.

That approach makes it unnecessary to engage in arguments (unfortunately all too common) over whose restrictive definition of dialogue is better. Under the heading *dialogue* I think we can safely include all forms of *talking things out* and *coming up with shared insights and solutions.* After all, even mediocre dialogue is preferable to people fighting and killing each other.

And as to what makes one form of dialogue better than another form, I suggest that the more creative and transformational it is, the better. That is why I have chosen the following tools.

A handful of tools

Let us look at some methods we can use to generate high-quality dialogue and greater co-intelligence in our personal relationships, as well as in small and large group interactions. It is my hope that the more experience we have in our own lives with a different quality of conversation and relationship, the more we will want to create and support new forms of self-governance that also reflect these qualities.

LISTENING CIRCLES

You may already be familiar with listening circles (also known as talking stick circles and Council) as a simple way for a small group of people to deepen the quality of their conversation, hold divergent views, and equalize the power dynamics in a situation. If not, it can be a good place to start.

Listening circles are inspired by the kind of councils practiced by indigenous tribal peoples all over the world. They may well be part of our shared human legacy: our hunter-gatherer ancestors sat around campfires for hundreds of thousands of years before settling down as farmers.

In essence, a listening circle is:

People sitting in a circle
listening deeply
and speaking from the heart.

Sitting in a circle helps us to fully see each other as peers sharing meaning, creativity, and a common center. "Speaking from the heart" means being grounded in our experience, our feelings and in things that are truly important to us. It means being honest, taking risks, being real, allowing the vitality and emotion we feel to find its way into our voice when we speak.

Many of us discover that we are naturally moved toward a more heartfelt form of expression once we find ourselves in the safe "container" created by the circle. The circle is designed to create a group where each of us can be heard without judgment or negative consequences. Together, we create a "safe space" for the truth.

Instead of interrupting one another, people practice patience by speaking in turn, going around the circle. Often a breakthrough happens when someone takes a risk and speaks particularly poignantly. This courageous act can open the door for others to speak from their hearts, and the intimacy of the circle deepens.

A well-functioning circle should help those who usually speak a lot to say less and those who are usually reticent to say more.

A "talking stick" (or other object) is often used to designate whose turn it is to speak. The ritual act of passing the talking stick around the circle shapes the structure and quality of our dialogue.

Often, the more times we go around the circle, the deeper it goes. When our scheduled circle time is up, or when we pass the stick around the whole circle with none of us speaking, the stick returns to the center and our circle is done.

If the group is new or large, the person who has convened the circle will often set the tone and get things started, as well as signal the end of the meeting. A smaller group or a more experienced group may proceed more informally.

There are, of course, some situations in which circles do not work as well. If there are more than a dozen people, a basic circle format can prove unwieldy, unless participants are highly committed to the practice of patience! Twenty people is probably an upper limit for most listening circles – although some circles have been done with hundreds of people.

The use of circles has been growing widely in the last several decades. From women's consciousness raising groups and other peer support groups, to Stephen Covey's family meetings and the circles now used for team-building within corporations, the circle is a powerful container for creatively engaging the diversity present in any group.

For more information, you may want to refer to Christina Baldwin's *Calling the Circle: The First and Future Culture* and Jack Zimmerman and Virginia Coyle's *The Way of Council.*

CIRCLE VARIATIONS

Several variations of circle process can be helpful in conversations that are more loosely structured than the listening circle process described above. For example, "popcorn" is a variation in which each speaker returns the talking-stick to the center, instead of passing it to his or her left. It can then be picked up by anyone. In some popcorn circles, people are asked not to speak twice until everyone has spoken once.

Sometimes a group may wish to open with a formal go-round, and then shift into more free-flowing dialogue. In such cases, the talking-stick can sit in the center while everyone talks informally, until someone (usually a quieter or less assertive person) feels the need to pick it up. At that point, the current speaker can finish, but the person with the talking-stick goes next. When he or she is finished, the stick is returned to the center, and the conversation continues freely. Alternatively, if the person who just spoke wishes to invoke more circle energy, he or she might pass the stick around, inviting everyone to shift into a more measured mode of conversation.

Yet another variation is to place a chime, bell, or tuning fork in the center of an open dialogue circle, that anyone can ring when he or she feels the conversation becoming too heady, speedy or contentious. Before the conversation begins, people are invited to pause whenever the bell is rung, and then resume their conversation with a more thoughtful energy.

GESTURES OF CONVERSATIONAL PRESENCE

Like listening circles, this simple yet powerful conversational innovation allows for a deeper dialogue to emerge in a small group without the need for a facilitator. The use of hand gestures to communicate one's state of mind and heart in a conversation helps participants self-regulate the pace and flow of their conversation. With practice, the hand gestures can flow into conversation effortlessly and creatively as needed, making a significant difference in how the conversation feels and progresses.

Michael Bridge invented this series of gestures to help equalize power between those who are more verbal and those who are less so. The gestures expand our attention in the conversation beyond an exclusive focus on what individuals are saying, to include the quality of what is taking place between us. They serve as a simple feedback system for the person who is speaking and can help move a group towards a more synergistic flow where individual creativity and collective process support each other.

Here are some of the gestures, to get you started in your own explorations. Once you get the hang of them you will likely want to create new ones of your own. And, as with any living language, there can be multiple shades of meaning depending upon the context.

OFFERING PRESENCE

Placing palms together in the traditional gesture of prayer is used as a non-verbal greeting in many cultures. It can also be used to convey the message "I have full attention to offer," especially in response to the next gesture, *The Stirring*.

THE STIRRING

Placing hands clasped (as in prayer) with two index fingers pointing upward can be used to signal that "there is something stirring within me." It is not so much a request to speak as an honoring and sharing of what is taking place inside one's self. Nevertheless, a speaker who observes someone making this sign might respond by offering their attention, either immediately or at the next opportune moment.

REQUESTING ANOTHER'S VOICE

Placing palms together, pointing towards another person can be used as a simple substitute for: "John, you haven't said anything in a while. I'm wondering what you are thinking." Or, if we see someone making the *Retreat* sign (or the *Stirring* sign), we might use the *Requesting* gesture to inquire about what is happening with that person.

RETREAT

Placing hands fully clasped is used to convey that one's attention is withdrawing or becoming unavailable. The speaker may continue to speak if he or she so wishes, but the *Retreat* gesture makes it clear that the listener cannot be held accountable for any words that are being directed at him or her.

If one feels overwhelmed by another's words, the *Retreat* sign, followed by a *Requesting* sign pointing towards the speaker, invites him or her to move to a deeper level of communication. This might be equivalent to, "I am having a hard time listening to what you are saying, and I am wondering what you are feeling or what it is you are really wanting." This combination of *Retreat* followed by *Request* is called ASKING FOR A DEEPER VOICE.

ASKING FOR ATTENTION

Placing hands clasped, two index fingers and two middle fingers pointing up tells others that whatever is stirring within me has become more urgent. I may be in distress, or overwhelmed with excitement.

PAUSE

Placing hands clasped, pinkies pointing upwards is used to request or signal a brief interruption. For example, it can be used by a listener as a substitute for: "I'm really interested in what you are saying right now, and I need to take a break to use the bathroom" – or it could be used to request reflection time to process what's been said, and/or to invite the speaker to take a breath.

Alternatively, the *Pause* gesture might be used by a speaker to signal, "I see that something is stirring within you, and I am just about to reach the end of my train of thought."

These six basic gestures comprise the core of this simple, elegant, and highly flexible tool for increasing the quality of small-group communication. Enjoy!

(Much of this essay was edited from "Gestures of Conversational Presence" by Michael Bridge and Rosa Zubizarreta in *Communities* magazine, Issue 109. Reprinted with permission from *Communities* magazine, *fic.ic.org/cmag* or 800-462-8240. For more information on the gestures, you may contact Michael Bridge directly at *bmichael@neteze.com*.)

STRATEGIC QUESTIONING

When a person or group has a problem, strategic questioning can help bring forth new understandings and energy for change.

Strategic questioning assumes that those involved in a situation are the best sources of useful insight and do-able solutions about that situation. The innovator of strategic questioning, change agent Fran Peavey, puts it this way: "Strategic questioning assumes that the direction and energy for change is contained in the people involved in the situation, but that it must be brought to the surface and helped to ripen, individually and collectively. Strategic questions are designed to do that."

Strategic questions do not have one answer, and certainly not one the asker knows. Strategic questions need to be asked in a real spirit of inquiry and curiosity, because they could generate any number of unexpected answers. Not only that, they often generate changes in the person trying to answer them, because strategic questions help people put their attention in particularly fruitful areas, and sometimes a shift takes place. In fact, the shift may be more important than the answer.

When Fran Peavey was starting a project in India to save the Ganges from pollution, only men came to the meetings. So she asked (genuinely curious) "Where are the women?" She asked it a few times and, sure enough, women started to show up at the meetings.

"Often a very powerful question will not have an answer at the moment it is asked, but will sit rattling in the mind for days or weeks as the person works on an answer," says Peavey. "So don't be disappointed if a great question does not have an answer right away. The seed is planted, the answer will grow."

So the unfolding of good answers is in many ways more important than the answers themselves. During that unfolding, peoples' relationship to the situation comes into focus and evolves, and the *will* to create change emerges. The power of an answer derives only from the truth and passion that lie buried in the heart of the answerer, suggests Peavey. The power of the question itself is merely its leverage in releasing that truth and passion into the world to generate change.

Strategic questions succeed to the extent they move people from old ways of thinking and acting to new ways that work better. Peavey notes that some questions have more leverage than others. "A good strategic question opens the options up. A long lever question opens up more possibility for motion than a short lever question. 'Why don't you move to Sydney?' would be a short lever question. A longer lever question would be 'Where do you feel you'd like to move?' or 'What is the meaning of this move in your life?'"

Strategic questioning assumes that "the world is far more complex and exciting than two options would indicate; but having two options creates the idea that a decision, however limited, is being made." A strategic questioner tries to get beyond that. "A friend whose daughter had run away was trying to decide whether to let her get on the train in a few hours, or to go to the train and insist that she come home. We worked at that level for a while, and then a new option came up – why not run away with the daughter and take the twelve hours on the train to sort things out."

HOW TO DESIGN STRATEGIC QUESTIONS

Strategic questions can:
- find where attention is focused: e.g., "What are you most concerned about in your community?"
- clarify what is seen or known: "What effects of this situation have you noticed?" (Peavey notes: "I do not refer to the situation as a problem, for that may work against creative thinking.")
- clarify what is felt: "What sensations do you have in your body when you think or talk about this situation?"
- identify ideals, dreams and values: "What about this situation do you care so much about?"
- identify the change view: "What will it take to move the current situation towards the ideal?"
- evoke personal involvement: "What do you like to do that might be useful in bringing about these changes?"
- get something started: "With whom do you need to talk about this?"

Note: Questions later in the above list tend to be longer-levered than questions nearer the beginning.

THINGS TO AVOID:
- 'why' questions – which tend to rationalize the present rather than explore options
- disguised suggestions (i.e., "Have you considered...?") which are manipulative

- yes/no questions – which wrap up without generating real exploration
- closed questions – which limit our sense of possibility. For example, feel the increasing openness of the following questions: "Why don't you work on poverty?" "What keeps you from working on poverty?" "What would need to be different, for you to work on poverty?" "What kind of support would help you work on poverty?"

(The quotes and strategic question examples are excerpted from Fran's booklet "Strategic Questioning: An Experiment in Communication of the Second Kind," compiled from talks she gave in 1988-1992. I have dropped the ellipses to ease reading.)

For more information, see *geocities.com/Athens/ Parthenon/3722/strategic.html* or the lengthy chapter on strategic questioning in Peavey's *By Life's Grace* or write *fpeavey@igc.org*.

DYNAMIC FACILITATION AND THE CHOICE-CREATING PROCESS

To "facilitate" means to "help make easier." If the goal in a conversation is to have meaningful and powerful dialogue, then the role of a facilitator is to help make it easier for the group to do that.

Dynamic Facilitation, created by consultant Jim Rough, is a leading-edge process designed to help groups have meaningful conversations, access their creativity, and discover practical breakthroughs to challenging situations – even in the midst of divergent opinions, strong emotions, and conflicting beliefs. This style of facilitation produces a highly co-creative form of dialogue called the "Choice-Creating Process" in which people and ideas change as the conversation unfolds and new possibilities emerge that were not present before. As a result, it can serve us well in a situation where we want to increase the level of collective intelligence.

In Dynamic Facilitation, the facilitator does not try to hold the group to a pre-established agenda. In fact, the only agenda are the thoughts and feelings of participants as they emerge in the process. However, the facilitator works very actively to draw out each person's perspective, including the solutions that each person imagines might be the best course of action. The facilitator actively "protects" each person's contribution by listening deeply to it, reflecting it and recording it on chart paper where the whole group can see it.

Whenever a conflict emerges, the facilitator "expands the space" to make room for the full range of divergence present in the group. Instead of trying to reconcile differences, the facilitator simply acknowledges and makes room for the various perspectives, solutions, concerns, questions, etc., that are offered by participants.

The facilitator keeps an ongoing record of the group's conversation. Ideally, he or she will add each person's contribution to one of four charts:

- Challenges (also known as "Inquiries" or "Problem Statements"),
- Solutions (also known as "Possibilities" or "Options")
- Concerns, and
- Information (also known as "Perspectives" or "Data").

If space constraints are severe, the facilitator will record all contributions on a single numbered list. In any case, chart paper filled with participants' contributions soon covers the walls, and the group begins to get a clearer picture of the challenges, solutions, concerns, and information they all bring to the conversation. In the process, group members naturally begin to move toward greater creativity and more inclusive possibilities in response to the larger picture that is emerging.

To get the process rolling, we might begin by asking the group a simple question such as, "What would you like to work on today?" Usually someone is willing to offer an initial topic, such as "making our business more environmentally responsible." The facilitator will ask the participant if he or she can reframe the topic as a question (usually a "how" question like "How can we make a profit and still be environmentally responsible?") and will record it on the Challenges page. Next, the facilitator may invite that same group member to share any "solutions" to that problem that he or she may have. Instead of treating any solutions as proposals to be defended, they are simply written on the Solutions page.

Usually, those initial solutions will provoke concerns among other group members. Any person who has a pressing concern is invited to share it, and his or her thoughts are recorded on the Concerns page. The facilitator will often invite the same person to share any alternative solutions that might be underneath their concerns.

Sometimes, instead of proposing another solution, someone may say, "Wait a minute. We're barking up the wrong tree. There's actually another (or much deeper or broader) problem here..." The facilitator would write that new question or problem statement on the Challenges page, and invite the person to share any solutions to this new problem that he or she may have.

Just as when we are putting together a jigsaw puzzle, there is no need to worry about following any particular sequence. We do not need to work at holding the conversation to a linear train of thought. What we are doing instead is helping each piece to get "put out on the table," and spending enough time with each person so that he or she feels fully heard.

If Bill responds to a suggestion from Sarah by yelling "That's absurd! That would distract us from our basic mission here!" the facilitator's job would be to both protect Sarah and to create space for Bill to share his concern. The facilitator might say to Bill, "Please address your concerns to me. I want to make sure I am understanding your concern, so I can record it. But could you hold it a minute? I want to first make sure I've understood what Sarah was saying, and that I've heard her completely."

After making sure that Sarah's contribution has been accurately understood and recorded, the facilitator would turn back to Bill. "Okay, let me see if I understand. You see things very differently. You have a concern that we are deviating from the basic mission." After recording Bill's concern, the facilitator may ask some follow up questions: "What is your sense of the basic mission?" (Bill's response to this might be recorded on the Information chart.) "What question do you feel we should be addressing?" (Challenges chart) "What would be your answer to the question you just proposed?" (Solutions chart).

If, when someone's turn came to speak, that person said, "We're forgetting there are thousands of people involved here who are not part of this group," we would write that on the Information sheet. Again, we would follow-up with some open-ended questions to elicit any problem-statements and/or solutions that person may have.

In this way, the facilitator helps the group translate its conflicts into Concerns, Information, Challenges and Solutions. By honoring and protecting each member's contribution, the door is kept open to greater creativity and collaboration. In some ways the facilitator's job is very simple...to listen deeply to everyone, and to keep the creative momentum going by following the group's energy and trusting the group's own emerging process.

In addition to listening, recording, and trusting the group's emergent process, one of the main jobs of the facilitator is to ask for the group's help in taking turns so that everyone is not speaking at once. From time to time, the facilitator may also need to ask the group to wait while checking in with someone, so that the group does not move on too quickly and steamroll over someone in the process.

TRUSTING THE UNFOLDING PROCESS

In the early stages of dynamically facilitated meetings, people tend to share things they already knew when they walked in – their sense of the problem, their ideas about what should be done, their concerns and information. The facilitator's job is to draw out all of those pieces of the puzzle into view. As the process unfolds, people begin to engage with the evolving collective picture that is taking shape. At first they may feel overwhelmed by the complexity. But natural human ingenuity soon begins to emerge, and the group starts discovering new and creative ways to engage with the situation they are facing. Quite commonly, breakthrough solutions start cropping up. Of course, each breakthrough brings a whole new level of challenges and questions, and participants begin to become quite energized and involved in the creative process. At that point, the facilitator's job may be to remind the group of where they began, and how much they have accomplished, since the process of accomplishing goals and discovering new ones can be an endless one.

However, the meeting itself is not endless. Instead, it often feels like it went by much more quickly than conventional meetings. When it is time to end a session, it is the facilitator's responsibility to invite the group to create a brief summary or "bookmark" of the group's current situation that can serve as a starting point for the next time the group meets.

For more information and Dynamic Facilitation training, contact: Jim Rough & Associates, 1040 Taylor Street, Port Townsend, WA 98368 / 360-385-7118; fax 360-385-6216; *jim@ToBe.net; tobe.net; cointelligence.org/ P-dynamicfacilitation.html.* Email *seminars@tobe.net* to order *A Dynamic Facilitation Manual and Reader* by Rosa Zubizarreta and Jim Rough.

OPEN SPACE TECHNOLOGY

Open Space Technology is a large-group process designed to help any group self-organize a conference, without the time and expense involved in obtaining keynote speakers and scheduling workshops. Instead, the process is designed to elicit maximum participation and creativity from all participants, in order to generate a blossoming of collaboration, synergy, and collective wisdom.

The format of Open Space was formulated in the mid-1980s by organizational consultant Harrison Owen when he discovered that people attending his traditional conferences loved the coffee breaks better than the formal presentations and plenary sessions. Combining that insight with his experience of African village life, Owen created a revolutionary form of conferencing.

As unusual as it may seem at first, Open Space conferences have no keynote speakers, no pre-announced schedules of workshops, no panel discussions, no organizational booths. Instead, in the first hour, participants learn how they are going to create their own conference based totally on their passion about the topic and their responsibility for their own experience. Almost before they realize it, they become one another's teachers and leaders.

The main task of the facilitator is to explain the process to the group. Anyone who wants to initiate a conversation or activity is to write it down on a large sheet of paper in big letters and then stand up and announce it to the group. Ahead of time, the facilitator has prepared a simple grid containing self-stick notes with possible meeting times and locations. Each person who wants to initiate a conversation or activity selects one of those pre-established times and places, posts it on their big paper, tapes their proposal to the wall, and then sits down. When everyone who wants to has announced and posted their initial offerings, participants mill around the wall, checking out possible activities and putting together their personal schedules for the remainder of the conference. The first meetings begin immediately.

Harrison Owen suggests that, as apparently chaotic and fun as Open Space can be, in reality it is more highly organized and productive than the best conference planning committee could possibly manage. Unleashing people's real passions and heartfelt conversations generates a whirlwind of activity. Instead of being pre-planned by the organizers, the content emerges from the participants and is guided by a handful of simple Open Space principles.

SOME PRINCIPLES OF OPENNESS

Four key principles are:

1. Whoever comes are the right people.
2. Whatever happens is the only thing that could have.
3. Whenever it starts is the right time.
4. When it is over it is over.

And then there is The Law of Two Feet: "If you find yourself in a situation where you aren't learning or contributing, go somewhere else." This law releases participants to flit from session to session. Owen calls such folks bumblebees because they cross-pollinate all the workshops. Furthermore, participants who go off by themselves he calls "butterflies" because they create quiet centers of non-action for stillness, beauty, novelty or random conversations to be born.

Open Space conferences can be done in one day, but the most powerful go on for two or three days, or longer. Participants gather together briefly as a large group during the mornings and evenings to share experiences and propose new workshops. The rest of the day is spent in rich conversation. Even meals are come-when-you-can affairs that go on for hours, filled with bustling dialogue. After a few days of this, an intense spirit of community usually develops that is all the more remarkable considering that everyone is doing exactly what he or she wants to do.

Open Space conferences are particularly effective when a large, complex organization or activity needs to be thoroughly reconceptualized and reorganized. If a task is just too big and complicated to be sorted out "from the top," stunning results can often be obtained by tapping into the creativity of all participants. Open Space starts with the assumption that any system contains within it the seeds of everything that needs to happen, and offers an elegant combination of order and creative chaos to provide the whole system with an opportunity to self-organize into its best new configuration.

Conversely, Open Space is not recommended when the leaders of an organization have a great need for control, nor when there is no desire to generate creativity in an organization or network. While Open Space can certainly be used with small groups, other tools exist that can be more effective for team problem-solving, small-group facilitation, and/or conflict resolution.

For more information, see Harrison Owen's *Open Space Technology* or visit *openspaceworld.org*.

THE WORLD CAFÉ

The World Café refers to both a vision and a method of dialogue. Consultants Juanita Brown and David Isaacs stumbled on this approach early in 1995 when a rainstorm forced them to hold a large meeting indoors at their home. It has since grown into one of the leading forms of large-group dialogue.

The World Café process involves people gathering in small groups – often four or five to a table, as in a regular café – and talking about some "question worth asking" that they are all interested in. World Café organizers put the same kind of care into crafting a Café question that Fran Peavey puts into her strategic questions.

Ideally, the host creates a pleasant, warm, intimate environment – perhaps some music, flowers, and candles. Brown and Isaacs have found the café-style setting to have a profound effect on participants as soon as they enter the room. The tables usually have marking pens and paper tablecloths for doodling or making notes about emerging insights. The host welcomes participants and tells them (or reminds them of) the question they have come together to explore.

He or she then explains what will happen. "After [a set period of time, usually 30-45 minutes] I will ask you to bring your conversations to a close and move to new tables – except for one person you choose, who will remain at your current table throughout the session, as a table host, sharing with newcomers some of the ideas and questions that emerged from earlier conversations at the table." After that announcement, the conversation begins.

STIRRING THE POT

When the first round is up, the host rings a bell or chime or plays a flute or otherwise gently but persistently gets participants to wind down their conversations and listen up. She or he says, "If you haven't

done so, please decide who will be your table's host."
The group is reminded of the table host's function.
"When you've gone to other tables and gotten briefed
by that table's host, then all of you in the new group
can share what happened in your previous conversations and carry on the dialogue from there. Try to listen together for any patterns, insights or deeper questions that may be emerging."

At the sound of the bell or chime, everyone (except
table hosts) gets up and moves to another table, with
everyone mixing in with new conversational partners. At
the end of the second round, the Café host rings the bell
again, and says something like, "Let's wrap up the conversations now and move to different tables. Table hosts,
please remain at your tables and welcome your new ar-
rivals. Everyone share any high points that emerged from
the conversation at your last table and any connections
or new questions you're noticing, and then carry on your
dialogue." The conversation continues for a bit, and then
the bell is rung again and everyone mixes into still new
groups, and so on. Often participants return to their
original tables (and groups) to share "what they learned
when they were out in the world."

ENJOYING THE SOUP

Some time before the end of the Café, Brown and Isaacs
usually gather the whole group to share significant
insights and questions that have emerged. These are
posted up front where everyone can see them – often
using large self-stick notes or a large visual mapping
exercise facilitated by an interactive graphics special-
ist to "synthesize key insights and ideas." Sometimes
they take participants on tours of all the tables' tablecloths – and once even tried quickly compiling a Café
newspaper. Whichever approach they use, they think
of it as the whole group's "tablecloth," and stress the
importance of "making collective knowledge visible to
the group."

Although there is definitely an art to facilitating potent World Cafés, the basic conversation is very easy to facilitate – or, rather, host. It offers a large group a rare opportunity to explore important questions together, sharing what they come up with, all the while being in small groups where each person can have significant "air time."

MORE THAN A PROCESS

The World Café is more than a process. It is a vision or metaphor of the way life is. Juanita Brown notes that virtually every conversation, from the most prestigious and powerful to the most banal and seemingly insignificant, is part of vast interconnected self-organizing webs and networks of conversations. She sees these conversations as the way whole systems – organizations, communities and societies – "think together." "Reaching out in ever-widening circles," writes Brown, "members of small groups spread their insights to larger constituencies, carrying the seed ideas for new conversations, creative possibilities, and collective action." She emphasizes the point that all this happens naturally. Since the dawn of human society, such cross-pollinating networks of conversations have helped humanity "access collective intelligence, create new knowledge, and bring forth desired futures."

So the process of The World Café – the cross-pollinating flow of talk from table to table in a single room – mimics and enhances the vast global sea of criss-crossing self-organizing conversations of which it is a part.

For more information see *theworldcafe.com.*

OTHER APPROACHES

Other approaches to dialogue you may wish to explore include:

APPRECIATIVE INQUIRY

A process of generating new images of the future by asking questions about the best of the past and present. Practitioners of appreciative inquiry ask questions that "strengthen a system's capacity to apprehend, anticipate, and heighten positive potential." The assumptions underlying this approach are so radical that a new branch of organizational development practice has grown up around it. See David Cooperrider and Diana Whitney's *Appreciative Inquiry: The Handbook* or visit *appreciativeinquiry.cwru.edu.*

PARTICIPATORY DECISION-MAKING

The *Facilitator's Guide to Participatory Decision-Making* by Sam Kaner, et al., is a detailed guide to facilitating a traditional consensus process, organized so the clear, useful pages can be copied and used by the group. Kaner's work includes a map of how a group changes during its consideration of an issue, diverging into "the groan zone" and converging to a decision point. All stages in the process are well described, with options given for dealing with them.

PRINCIPLED NEGOTIATION

Principled negotiation is also known as *Interest-Based* or *Collaborative Negotiation.* To the extent a negotiation succeeds in meeting everyone's needs, it is a manifestation of group intelligence. The "principled" approach to accomplishing that was first codified and popularized in the best-selling 1981 classic *Getting To Yes: Negotiating Agreement Without Giving In* by Roger Fisher and William Ury of the Harvard Negotiation Project. Participants in principled negotiation are led to deconstruct their positions into "legitimate interests" that they are trying to meet, to formulate any apparent conflict as a shared problem, and to see each other as colleagues in solving that problem. Then they "invent options for mutual gain," evaluate those options, and make their final decisions based on co-created "objective standards" ("principles") of fairness and functionality. For a good overview see *colorado.edu/conflict/ peace/treatment/pricneg.htm.*

TRANSFORMATIONAL MEDIATION

Just as principled negotiation helps us shift our focus from "positions" to "legitimate interests," transformational mediation shifts our focus a step further, to the universal human need to balance one's self-concern with one's need to be connected to others. Seeking to restore that balance, transformational mediation does not focus on crafting an agreement between conflicted parties. Rather, it encourages participants' empowerment and perspective-taking as they explore what is going on in their conflict. Their emotions and stories about the past are welcomed as potential sources of valuable information and insight. The conflict process, itself, is tapped as a source of growth and learning. Any agreements that emerge tend to be very solid, since participants have not been "led" in any way towards them. For more information, see Robert A. Baruch Bush and Joseph P. Folger's *The Promise of Mediation: Responding to Conflict through Empowerment and Recognition* and explore *transformativemediation.org.*

Conclusion

All the tools introduced here – listening circles, gestures of conversational presence, strategic questioning, Dynamic Facilitation, Open Space Technology, World Café, Appreciative Inquiry, participatory decision-making, principled negotiation, and transformative mediation – were designed for the purpose of helping create a deeper dialogue, in the sense of "exploration towards greater understanding, connection, and positive possibility." Of course, there are many differences among them, and some are more structured and linear than others. In any particular situation, one of these tools may work better than others, just as a hammer might be more useful for some things than a wrench. Part of the work of co-intelligence is figuring out when a particular tool may be more useful than another. Yet all of these tools, as well as many others, constitute what organizational consultant Steve Wallis calls "Advanced Social Technologies" – methods that can play key roles as we work together to create a world that works for everyone.*

Some of the approaches mentioned in this chapter could play significant roles in the conversations that shape our national policies – and even our national political system. Closer to home, they can help us create healthy communities and sane and effective working relationships within our own community groups, non-profit organizations, and social change movements – and even in our relationships and families. With so many problems in our communities and the world, many of us do not invest sufficient time and attention on nurturing our own capacity to work co-creatively and to develop stronger relationships with one another. Supporting real dialogue within our own networks and organizations can be a significant step toward whole-system change, especially when coupled with the efforts to promote dialogue at a national level that we will be exploring in Section Three.

---

* Along these lines, I highly recommend getting involved with the new National Coalition for Dialogue and Deliberation (NCDD), which seeks to bring together the full range of practitioners, academics and activists working with all forms of dialogue, deliberation, conflict work, diversity work, community conversations, etc. *(thataway.org)*

CHAPTER **8**

OTHER APPROACHES TO CO-INTELLIGENCE

My own work with co-intelligence has been primarily focused on dialogue-based methods such as the ones described in the last chapter and the citizen deliberative councils that are the focus of the next section. However, as we move up to larger levels of system, other significant factors come into play. Often, these are more cultural or structural elements of the system – institutions, rules, assumptions, stories, and so on.

To illustrate how collective intelligence can be supported through approaches that are not primarily based on dialogue, we can look at two examples: the public library and the Web. These institutions are primarily forms of social memory. Libraries have for centuries contained the most honored records of civilizations. Public libraries made those memory records available to all parts of the social system. Today, the World Wide Web has emerged a way for society to keep its records in an updated form, has made those records instantly searchable, and allowed more members of the social system to add their records to the collective resource pool. While libraries still serve a useful function, and have their own set of benefits, the World Wide Web has dramatically enhanced our capacity for operational collective memory at a societal – even global – level.

Next, we shall look at another systemic approach for enhancing our collective intelligence.

REDEFINING SUCCESS

Assumptions around success – and the ways success is measured and rewarded – are among the most powerful shapers of thought, feeling and behavior, both individual and collective, in any social system. This is true of a family, an organization, a community or a society.

Currently, most countries measure their collective health and success by how much money they spend each year. This statistic, Gross Domestic Product (GDP),* does not include anything we do for ourselves, nor the production of homemakers, nor the production of nature, nor the volunteer work we do for our community or to improve our society. If it is not paid for, it is not recorded.

An articulate critic of this system, Marilyn Waring, has pointed out that by this measure the most successful oil tanker voyage in history was made by the Exxon *Valdez* in 1989. It ran aground, dumping 11,000,000 gallons of crude oil into pristine Alaskan coastal waters. Just think of the money that was spent as a result of that! There was the cost of the tanker and the oil, for starters. Then there were all the cleanup costs, the lawyers' bills, the insurance fees, and the compensations to all the fisherpeople whose livelihoods were devastated – to say nothing of all the donations to environmental groups that came pouring in. It was

---

* The earlier version of this statistic was Gross National Product (GNP).

monstrously expensive. And every dollar spent made the Gross Domestic Product rise, indicating a "growing, healthy economy."

Meanwhile, when you mow your lawn, diaper your baby, cook your dinner, and fix your bike or car, the Gross Domestic Product does not budge. And all those trees pumping out oxygen, and the rain watering the fields, and the ozone layer turning away deadly ultraviolet rays – none of that makes it to the accounting books. And the flowers? They are only good if you buy them. We will not say what that means about love.

Most remarkable of all, the Gross Domestic Product does not subtract any bad things that happen. If they cost money, however – like the Exxon Valdez – the GDP keeps on going up. Therefore, if you are healthy, it does not count. However, every visit to the doctor's office makes the GDP rise. And if your community is healthy – if there is no crime and the landscape is lovely and everyone lives simple, productive, meaningful, joyful lives, sharing lots of things so they do not have to work so many hours to buy their own – well, that is not nearly as significant as a community of harried city/ suburb commuters working 60 hours a week to maintain lives filled with stuff and spending lots of money on large police and security forces to keep the criminals away.

Statistics are a form of collective perception: We see the world through them. If the statistics are distorted, our perception is distorted. One way to increase the collective intelligence of our society as a whole is to create indicators and feedback loops that can give us useful information with regard to the real well-being of the whole society.

To increase our collective intelligence as a community, a state, a nation, and a society, we need to ask questions like: "What would 'quality of life' look like if it included all of us, even future generations?" and "How would we know we had it?" Many communities have already begun to explore alternative ways for measuring their quality of life, as in the Chapter 2 story entitled "Measuring Community Health." In addition, there are many proposals for national and international statistics of this type.

Although I do not believe it has yet been developed into a measurement system, perhaps the most radical reframing of national success that I have ever heard of is the one established by the King of Bhutan.

THE PURSUIT OF HAPPINESS

The isolated Kingdom of Bhutan, which is situated between China and India, gained some notice several years ago by declaring its official standard of success its "Gross National Happiness." In a speech before the United Nations in September 2002 *(un.org/webcast/ga/57/statements/020917bhutanE.htm),* Minister of Foreign Affairs Lyonpo Jigmi Y. Thinley explained:

> My country continues to be guided by our goal of promoting "Gross National Happiness" as opposed to simply targeting the enhancement of Gross National Product as the end of development. We believe that it is the responsibility of the government to create an enabling environment within which every citizen would have a reasonable opportunity to find happiness. Toward this, all our development strategies must subscribe to strengthening of the four pillars of "Gross National Happiness", which are namely i) ensuring of equitable and sustainable socio-economic development, ii) conservation of our fragile mountain ecology, iii) promotion of basic human values and culture, and iv) the strengthening of good governance.

According to a report from "60 Minutes," when approached by commercial interests wishing to purchase lumber from Bhutan's beloved forests, the government declined. To further protect forest ecosystems, they are developing solar power as an alternative to wood fuel. They forbid commercial mountain climbing to protect the spiritual integrity of their mountains, which have been made a national park. Drivers encounter signs to the effect of 'Please be gentle with our curves.' Only a few thousand tourists are allowed each year, mostly seekers of enlightenment and bird watchers.

Inspired by its Buddhist roots, Bhutan sees happiness as the Middle Way between tradition and modernization.

For more information about redefining success, see *co-intelligence.org/ P-qualtylifeindicators.html* or *rprogress.org*. An online book exploring these issues is Robert Theobald's *Reworking Success*. The Centre of Bhutan Studies' book *Gross National Happiness* is also available online. The *Calvert-Henderson Quality of Life Indicators* edited by Hazel Henderson, Jon Lickerman, and Patrice Flynn, is a proposed set of national quality of life statistics.

Of course, such proposals for new social institutions can be pursued more co-intelligently if their promotion involves widespread public dialogue. The differences in values that we encounter when we raise alternatives like this provide us with opportunities to engage a diversity of perspectives in ways that deepen into creative consensus without compromise.

While reframing success is a structural way of addressing collective intelligence, not all factors that influence collective intelligence are structural. Some, like the approach we will examine next, draw upon the power of creativity to help support collective understanding.

MULTIPLE-VIEWPOINT DRAMA

Among its many functions, art can support collective reflection in the culture as a whole. Sometimes it is a mirror showing us certain aspects of ourselves individually or collectively. Sometimes it explores important issues, looking at their moral dimensions, deeper meanings, and ramifications. Artists themselves do much of this reflection for us. When many of us have experienced a piece of art, its reflective gift becomes part of our shared awareness of life. When we actually discuss it, we make it come alive as *our* collective reflection.

The power of art is shown partly by the desire of dictators to control their country's artists. There is social power in art of all kinds.

In the paragraphs below, we will explore one form of art that can help a whole community – a whole country, even the whole of humanity – to see itself. This is whole-system reflection of the highest order. Art like this changes people's responses. Just as there is art that feeds political hatred and partisanship, so there is art that feeds political wholeness and understanding.

In fiction or documentary, video or performance, it is possible to present compelling vignettes of the many perspectives involved in any situation so that all viewpoints can be shared by a wide audience. I discovered the potential social power of this approach from the remarkable work of Anna Deavere Smith.

Smith has created a form of multiple-viewpoint docudrama through which she delves into the psychosocial dynamics that produce riots. "Fires in the Mirror," which I saw first in 1995, is a monologue about the conflict between African Americans and Hassidic Jews in Crown Heights, New York.

To prepare for her performance, Smith went to Crown Heights and interviewed a wide range of participants, from well-known figures to nearly anonymous bystanders and people hiding in their homes. Afterward, she carefully selected about twenty interviews and, from each one, chose several minutes of significant, passionate talk. She then thoroughly memorized not just the words, but the voice, mannerisms, and appearance of each person speaking.

Smith's performances consist of her presenting each
of these intent, diverse voices, one after the other. She
dresses for each character and performs that person's
words with full passion and reality. The light fades and
then, after a pause, a new character appears to tell us
another way of looking at what happened. By the fi-
nale, the audience has gained deep insights, not only
into the individual stories of these real-life characters,
but into the larger story that includes all of these diverse viewpoints. "There is no one answer, no one viewpoint or conclusion, that can hold all this complex reality," Smith seems to be saying. "Let go of your own
perspective for a while and let the full story sink in.
Enter into the larger whole that gave rise to this particular tragedy."

LAYERS OF MEANING

When I first saw a video of "Fires in the Mirror," what
seemed most compelling to me was not so much the
explicit tension between the diverse viewpoints, but the
solidity of the viewpoints themselves, the sense they
made within their own frames of reference, and their
mutual incompatibility. These remained, like an echo
or a scent, long after the performance drew to a close.
Later I also came to appreciate the message implicitly
communicated by the fact that Smith's face represents
every character she portrays: "We are all human. That
is the most important thing." She calls forth the heal-
ing-into-wholeness of our deep humanity.

One could easily argue that it is the solidity of viewpoints that leads to profound human tragedies. To the
extent we live out our stories in isolation and mutual
misunderstanding, we will create a larger story of mutual destruction, almost whether we want to or not.
To the extent we can step outside our insular stories
to realize the intrinsic logic of *everyone's* stories and of
our common humanity – Smith's very political message – we may become able to co-create collective sto-

ries more consciously, ones that are at least tolerable, perhaps mutually beneficial or even joyful.

Both "Fires in the Mirror" and "Twilight: Los Angeles" – a video of Smith's performance about the Los Angeles riots following the trial of Rodney King's assailants – are available from some libraries and video stores. The Public Broadcasting System, which produced both videos, sells "Twilight: Los Angeles" at *shop.pbs.org*.

The ability to hold diverse perspectives simultaneously is vital to co-intelligence. Art, as we have seen, offers one approach to help us. But this same work needs to be done with our other information sources. Here is an innovation to paint the big picture on any public issue.

POSSIBILITY/PROBLEM FOCUSERS

In his book, *Turning the Century*, futurist Robert Theobald suggests creating a new form of information for citizens. He calls this innovation the possibility/problem focuser – or p/p focuser. A p/p focuser is a body of accessible, engaging information that introduces people to the full range of opinions and options on a public issue. Theobald's idea reaches beyond the already excellent work of groups such as the **National Issues Forum** *(nifi.org)*, which create discussion booklets on diverse public issues.

Theobald suggests that teams be established to research and record diverse perspectives on various topics, to discover the extent to which the positions advanced are coherent and consistent, and to state the various credible views in understandable form. He felt that these documents should stress, in particular, the areas of agreement and disagreement as well as the causes and consequences of different positions to the extent these can be understood.

Research groups would not search for a single, objectively correct statement, but rather for a way to bring together divergent viewpoints. The results would be presented to decision-makers and the public so that the clash between various attitudes and proposals could be worked out in an intelligent and creative dialogue. Input from these dialogues would be used to update the p/p focusers on an ongoing basis.

P/P focusers could become available on many important topics at a number of levels of difficulty. To reach a wide audience, they could be customized to appeal to different perspectives – education issues would be presented differently for students and policy-makers, for example. They would also be presented in various media – through computers and in print, video, audio and interactive formats. These could be updated to reflect shifts in the landscape of opinion in light of changing realities.

To address the problem of potential bias, Theobald suggested that this not be a centralized process. Instead, diverse teams could produce competing p/p focusers on the most important topics. A central location would provide an index to the various p/p focusers available on a given theme, so that citizens would be free to choose the ones they found most useful. In this way, Theobald envisioned a co-intelligent "marketplace of ideas" – or rather, a marketplace of inclusive landscapes of opinion.

Moving from the landscape of opinion to the landscape of nature and human activities, we find one of the more remarkable co-intelligent practices in the world:

PERMACULTURE

The word permaculture is a contraction of permanent agriculture or, more broadly, permanent culture. Permaculture is an ecological design science – an approach to understanding and using the many ways in which parts of living systems interact or work together to generate harmony or dissonance among them. In his *Introduction to Permaculture,* founder Bill Mollison calls it

> a philosophy of working with rather than against nature; of protracted and thoughtful observation rather than protracted and thoughtless action; of looking at systems and people in all their functions, rather than asking only one yield of them; and of allowing systems to demonstrate their own evolutions.
>
> A basic question that can be asked in two ways is: "What can I get from this land, or person?" or "What does this person, or land, have to give if I cooperate with them?"
>
> Of these two approaches, the former leads to war and waste, the latter to peace and plenty.

Mollison advocates protecting wilderness areas from further encroachment, rehabilitating degraded or eroded land with forests and ground covers, and designing human living environments to sustainably satisfy people's real needs so they do not have to degrade their environment to survive. But his primary focus, one that applies to social systems as well, is on understanding and creating self-organizing living systems.

Permaculture principles that deal with this include (and here I quote or paraphrase from Mollison's *Introduction to Permaculture*):

- Order is found in things working beneficially together. The fact that neatness, tidiness, and straightness require extensive investments of energy yet produce little yield, tells us that these illusory forms of order are, in fact, nature in wild disarray. True order often lies hidden in apparent confusion, like a meadow, with its hundreds of hidden synergies.
- Design is a beneficial assembly of components in their proper relationships to serve a purpose.

- The role of beneficial authority is to return functions and responsibility to life and to people. If
  successful, no further authority is needed. The
  role of successful design is, therefore, to create a
  self-managed system. It is only by returning self-
  regulating function and responsibility to living
  things that a stable life system can evolve.
- Stupidity is an attempt to iron out all differences,
  and not to use them or value them creatively.

The permaculture movement is widespread. Thousands of people around the world practice it. There are
textbooks, classes and journals on the subject. See
permacultureactivist.net.

By arranging things so they assist each other,
permaculture home and landscape design reduces
work, walking distances and waste products. Here is
one of my favorite permaculture stories, showing such
collaborative intelligence, applied to the forces of nature right at home.

Jerome Osentowski's permaculture site in Basalt,
Colorado, has a greenhouse attached on the south side
of his house for quick access. His home and the greenhouse heat each other in the winter. Sunlight pen-
etrates the south-facing roof of the greenhouse and a
long compost pile rests against the wooden north wall,
consuming Jerome's garbage while generating useful
one hundred degree temperatures as the compost de-
cays. A large black metal tank filled with water soaks
up heat from the sun and radiates it out into the greenhouse. Carp and catfish in the tank not only provide
on occasional fish dinner; their wastes are carried
through a drip system to water and fertilize surrounding plants. Chicken and pigeon coops against the west
wall send bird body heat into the greenhouse instead
of the winter sky, and a small wood-fired sauna gets
fired up on extra-cold nights to heat people and all the
other denizens of the greenhouse. Jerome also uses a

"rabbit tractor" – a rollable wire mesh rabbit pen which he moves slowly (it takes months) over new garden beds. The rabbits eat the weeds and simultaneously fertilize the soil with their manure.

Permaculture is so powerful because it is an example of how we humans can learn to work "with" the rest of the natural world, instead of seeing ourselves as needing to struggle "against" Nature in order to survive. While most of the examples included in this book have to do with how humans can learn to work with one another, it is important to remember that *working "with"* is not necessarily limited to the human realm. Instead, our understandings of wholeness, interconnectedness, and co-creativity can be applied to our interactions with all beings, in all realms of existence.

One question that permaculture might leave us with is, "How might we extend permaculture's positive approach to diversity in the natural world, in order to create a positive approach to social diversity?"

CHAPTER **9**

THE LIST GOES ON...

In addition to the approaches to co-intelligence described in the last chapters, there are thousands of
others that exist, and more are being created every day.

Just to give you an idea of the range of approahes
available, here is a sampling of more than 120 of them.
For me, all of these approaches embody different ways
of applying our understandings of wholeness, interconnectedness, and co-creativity in order to generate
greater wholeness in ourselves, our communities, and
our world.

> Aikido ... anticipatory democracy ... The Big Pic-
> ture Puzzle ... biodynamic agriculture ... biologic
> ... bioregionalism ... brainstorming ... campaign
> finance reform ... Citizen Consensus Councils
> ... clearness sessions ... cob houses ... Co-coun-
> seling ... co-housing ... co-incarnational mani-
> festation ... co-operative education ... co-opera-
> tives ... the commons ... community ... commu-
> nity building ... complexity theory ... composting
> toilets ... consensus process ... contact improv
> ...creativity ... Curitiba ... dance ... Danish citi-
> zen technology panels ... deep diversity work ...
> Delphi process ... Despair and Empowerment
> work ... E-Prime ... eco-psychology ... ecovillages
> ... emotional intelligence ... Enneagram ... fam-

ily systems therapy ... feedback systems ... fishbowl ... flow ... focusing ... forgiveness ... fractal patterns ... full cost accounting ... Future Search ... fuzzy logic ... the Gaia hypothesis ... game theory ... Gaviotas ... global peace force ... graphic facilitation ... group awareness exercises ... group psychotherapy ... group silence ... groupware and other "electronic co-intelligence" ... healthy cities movement ... heart ... HeartMath ... Holistic Management ... holographics ... holon theory ... humor ... The I Ching ... imagineering ... improvisational theater ... indigenous science ... industrial ecology ... integraphs ... intentional community ... intuition ... jazz improvisation ... juries ... lateral thinking ... learning exercises and games ... learning organizations ... learning styles ... Less Work More Life ... Listening Projects ... Living Democracy ... mediation ... meditation ... Mondragon ... morphogenetic fields ... multi-cultural literacy and experience ... multiple intelligences ... mythology ... National Initiative for Democracy ... Natural Capitalism ... The Natural Step ... The New Story ... networking ... nonviolence ... Nonviolent Communication ... Noogenesis ... open focus ... open sentences practice ... The Option Process ... panarchism ... the partnership way ... personality typing ... planning cells ... popular education ... prayer ... precautionary principle ... Process Worldwork ... Project Vote Smart ... pyramid analysis ... Quaker meeting for worship for business ... retreats ... salons ... scenario and visioning work ... The Six Thinking Hats ... social dreaming ... storytelling ... study circles ... subsidiarity ... sustainability ... synchronicity ... synergic power ... systems thinking ... T-groups ... Tavistock ... team building ... transformational philanthropy ... transperspectivity ... values barometer ... Widening Circles exercise ... Wisdom Council ... the list goes on and on and on and on...

How do all these things fit together? What would happen if we used them all synergistically? Could they help us build a new culture, a wiser civilization?

These are central questions for those who are drawn to the field of co-intelligence. Many of the approaches above are described later in this book and on the co-intelligence website.

In the next section, I will describe a few additional approaches in more depth as we explore what I consider the most important application of co-intelligence – to politics, governance, citizenship and activism.

Section III

Creating a Wise

Democracy

CHAPTER **10**

DEMOCRACY
AND WHOLENESS

*Democracy is the rule of an interacting, interpermeating
whole ... We have an instinct for democracy because
we have an instinct for wholeness; we get wholeness
only through reciprocal relations, through infinitely expanding reciprocal relations. Democracy is really
[about] ... creating wholes.*

— MARY PARKER FOLLETT

In the twentieth century, science took many leaps forward. One of them was the realization that any whole
cannot be reduced simply to its parts. Even when we
fully understand all the parts, we may understand little
about the whole. We can miss the forest for the trees.
This insight is expressed in the oft-quoted phrase: "The
whole is greater than the sum of its parts."

Perhaps the most important factor that makes the
whole greater than the sum of its parts is *synergy* –
the energy of fruitful relationship. We can feel synergy
in groups that are exciting, compared to groups that
are dull. Synergy is present in our breathing: Every
time we breathe, we are engaging in synergistic ex-

change of oxygen and carbon dioxide with all the plants of the world. Synergy is everywhere in and around us: That humble oxygen we breathe, in synergy with the even more humble hydrogen, produces something *far* more than both of them together – the wet water that flows so powerfully through our bodies and our world. This is all synergy.

Understanding wholeness better

We need to understand wholeness better. Wholeness is vital. Wholeness has life in it. In wholeness, the parts are in fruitful relationship, which generates the energy of life. As noted earlier, words such as healthy, holy, wholesome, integrity, and community are all derived from roots related to wholeness.

While recent advancements in the science of wholeness have begun to permeate our culture in various ways, including certain leading-edge management books, we have yet to systematically apply these understandings to the public sphere. This book is based on the idea that we need more holistic democratic theories and practices to match our new holistic understanding of our world and the new challenges we have made for ourselves. Co-intelligence, or a holistic understanding of intelligence, can help us create the next evolutionary step of our democracy – a step that we need to take if we are to survive and flourish.

Without abandoning earlier forms of democracy, it is time to develop new political forms grounded in breakthrough understandings of what constitutes "the whole" of a community or society. The whole of a society is not embodied in a king – but neither is it embodied in a simple majority vote or opinion poll. It is embodied in the diversity of its parts and in their synergistic relationships and interactions.

New political theory and practice needs to under-stand and tap into the *system as a whole,* including all of the diverse viewpoints, capacities and relationships within it. To the extent we can facilitate fruitful rela-tionships among all its diverse parts, we will generate the creative energy and intelligence that any commu-nity or society needs to flourish. We need a politics grounded in this realization, designed to evoke this synergistic collective energy and intelligence, so that we can make decent, vibrant lives for ourselves, for our children, and for all the children of the future.

The political vision of co-intelligence was foreshad-owed by John Dewey in a 1937 speech entitled "De-mocracy as a Way of Life":

> The foundation of democracy is faith in...human in-telligence and in the power of pooled and cooperative experience...to generate progressively the knowledge and wisdom needed to guide collective action...[E]ach individual has something to contribute, whose value can be assessed only as [it] enters into the final pooled intelligence constituted by the contributions of all.

Forty-five years later Paul Hawken, James Ogilvy, and Peter Schwartz gave pooled intelligence a name in their book *Seven Tomorrows,* where they stated, "We need a collective intelligence of a kind that may not have characterized the human species in the past."

Such collective intelligence is, sadly, a rare phe-nomenon. Too often, even brilliant people behave in ways that add up to collective stupidity in the form of arguments and alienation, not to mention global warm-ing and Congressional deadlock. Often people are herded into dysfunctional behaviors by dysfunctional structures, processes, and cultural agreements they do not even recognize as problems. If those patterns (structures, processes, cultures) were made conscious, enhancing collective intelligence could become a project of the whole society: we could consciously redesign our society's systems for synergy, wisdom and conscious self-organization, rather than just drifting into dysfunctional messes.

That is the vision of the co-intelligent, holistic politics I want to share with you. That is what I mean by "wise democracy" – a democracy that can bring forth collective wisdom to save us from the rising tide of our collective folly and, using that wisdom, create a world that works for all.

What might "collective wisdom" look like?

In Chapter 6, we looked at what collective intelligence might look like at different levels of a system – groups, organizations, communities, and societies. Yet what might collective *wisdom* look like?

One way to understand collective wisdom is by analogy to individual wisdom. A wise person has perspective. If we are wise, we can see the big picture without losing sight of the small. We can see the part without losing sight of the whole. We can understand the partnerships of day and night, good and bad, the known and the unknown. We have observed how it all fits together, including our own limitations and immense ignorance – and that realization makes us humble, insightful and flexible. We are free to creatively see and respond to what is actually around us.

Interestingly, a community of people (whether a group, a company, a town or a nation) is better equipped to be wise than an individual. As individuals, we are inherently more limited than a community. Although we can consult books, friends, and critics, in the end we are limited to our own single perspective. We are, alas, only one person, looking at the world from one place, one history, and one pattern of knowing. A community, on the other hand, can see things through many eyes, many histories, and many ways of knowing. The question is whether it dismisses or creatively utilizes and integrates that diversity.

Communities are wise to the extent they use diversity well, in a cooperative, creative interplay of viewpoints that allows the wisest, most comprehensive and powerful truths to emerge. The more we know how to nurture and use the rich diversity of individual views and capabilities within our society, the more wise and democratic our society will be. We will resist small-minded leadership and even the dictatorship of the majority. We will cherish dissent as a wise individual cherishes doubt, as a door to deeper understanding.

However, as we all know, it is not easy to do something creative with diverse opinions and experiences. It is much easier to settle for lowest-common-denominator agreements, press for (or give in to) one-sided decisions, or enforce thoughtless compliance. However, a wise, democratic society would realize that such approaches inevitably overlook important factors and result in poor decisions. A public rush to judgment is comparable to an individual jumping to conclusions. In the long run, it only makes things worse.

Therefore, a major activity of a democratic community is developing the attitudes, skills, supporting processes, and institutions needed for people to engage creatively with their diversity, and discover creative consensus without compromise. In this process, communities leave domination and fragmentation (alienated individualism) behind. Those dysfunctional approaches arise from a false dichotomy between the individual and the group. In fact, individuality and community are two facets of the same thing – our alive humanity. Individuals and communities can only be whole and healthy when they nurture one another.

A different perspective on power and politics

To our normal awareness, a uranium rock is just a rock. But arrange its parts in a particular way, with the right processes, and it can blow up a city. To our normal awareness, a room filled with people is just a crowd. But arrange those people in the right way, with the right processes, and they can generate wisdom.

Both these forms of power derive from intelligent design and process. If we don't have the second power, the first power will likely destroy us.

And so we find evolution's experiment with human consciousness has reached a crisis: Will we design cultures with the power to generate wisdom before our awesome physical powers destroy the "experimental laboratory" – our world?

I invite you to consider co-intelligence as an antidote to blind human power. As a capacity that adds collective sight to our collective technical brilliance, it constitutes a vital next step in the evolution of both our consciousness and our power.

Many of you may already be familiar with the distinction between "power-over" (the power to dominate or control) and "power-with" (the power to generate effects through cooperation). Although these terms can be applied to our relations with nature (see the discussion of permaculture in Chapter 9), they were first created to describe social relations.

The distinction between power-over and power-with was first proposed nearly a century ago by the same person that I quoted at the beginning of this chapter. Early in the twentieth century, Mary Parker Follett wrote (in papers presented to the London School of Economics in 1933, excerpted at *onepine.demon.co.uk/ pfollett.htm*):

> It seems to me that whereas power usually means power-over, the power of some person or group over some other person or group, it is possible to develop the conception of power-with, a jointly developed power, a co-active, not a coercive power.

Politics is basically about social power in all its manifestations. Power is the ability to influence or shape reality. *Political* power is the ability to shape or influence *social* reality: our relationships and everything that happens in our collective, public life.

The most basic form of power is simply the power to do things. I make this seemingly obvious point to stress that power is not necessarily about controlling or dominating. This basic form of power is intimately connected with freedom and capacity. In order to do things, we need to be free from certain hindrances ("freedom-from") and to have access to certain opportunities and capacities ("freedom-to"). In the absence of relevant limits and the presence of enough capacity and opportunity, we theoretically have the power to do whatever we wish.

Yet there are different ways that we can accomplish our objectives. "Power-over" involves control, force, domination, and manipulation. "Power-with" involves cooperation and synergy. It is the power that arises when we use our collaborative intelligence to work with others or to work with nature. The "power-of-wholeness," or holistic power, is the power at work when we bring together all those involved in a situation, organization, or community for real dialogue that includes all relevant perspectives. It is the power of self-organization present in each person or system as a whole.

How does power relate to intelligence? If we look at power as the capacity to influence or shape reality, we can look at intelligence as the capacity to enhance power in various ways and to use its influence *appropriately or well* – in ways that meet the exact needs of the moment to achieve desirable results with minimal effort and maximum elegance. Intelligence is also the capacity to learn from each departure from desirable conditions, so that efforts that are more satisfactory can be undertaken next time.

Next, we will explore how power plays out in politics. If we apply our understanding of co-intelligence, I believe we can raise the quality of power that is used in politics – and, ultimately, change the nature of politics itself and our political systems – so that the use of wiser forms of power becomes habitual.

A spectrum of political engagement

Integrating both power and intelligence, we can define politics as how a community or society reflects on its circumstances, solves its problems, envisions possible futures, makes decisions and takes action on its own behalf or in support of what it cares about. Politics also embraces the activities of citizens playing their roles in that realm, sometimes from narrowly self-interested perspectives, sometimes from "enlightened self-interest" or for the common good.

Citizenship and political culture play out in modern democracies in diverse ways that we can view as a "spectrum of political engagement." The spectrum ranges from alienated rejection of politics, through the routines of citizenship (such as voting and following the news), to the vast realm of *power politics* where lobbyists, politicians and other power players manipulate our adversarial system to win something for their cause, party or interest group. This entire realm is defined by power-over.

From the perspective of "power politics," the "common good" is supposed to emerge somehow from the fray of competing interest groups. The outcome of the struggle, however uneven, is presumed to be the "common good." Regardless of how much we may feel as activists that our efforts within the realm of power politics are on behalf of the whole, we are likely to be seen as yet one more special interest group. Our adversarial system of power politics recognizes no voice for the common good, only partisan voices.

Beyond (and overlapping) the familiar world of power politics, new forms of *cooperative politics* and activism are emerging, in which people are using "power with" to pursue shared visions and needs. At times, these collaborations include people and organizations that have traditionally viewed each other as enemies.

Also emerging are experiments in *holistic politics* and activism, which attempt to create new ways to call forth the wisdom of the whole society for the benefit of the whole through engaging creatively with the diversity of the whole. These new forms explore what politics would look like if we took wholeness, interconnectedness, and co-creativity seriously – in other words, if we engaged in co-intelligent politics.

All of us engage in most of these forms of politics at least some of the time. Since we can not handle every issue head-on, we may use one form of political engagement to deal with an issue we are focusing on, and another approach for issues that are more in our background. Organizations and movements often manifest one mode internally and another in their external relationships, for example, working with one another (cooperative politics) to win political battles (power politics).

Progress is not always linear. People who have engaged in power politics in their past and have since discovered more cooperative and holistic approaches to other parts of their lives may become dissatisfied with their political work and not know where to turn. They may seem to drop out for some time into routine politics or anti-politics, and then suddenly become engaged in cooperative politics when an opportunity presents itself.

In the next chapter, we will present a closer look at cooperative and holistic approaches to politics.

CHAPTER 11

COOPERATIVE AND HOLISTIC POLITICS

As we explore the areas of cooperative and holistic politics, it is good to remember they are part of a spectrum. Just as blue blends into violet, cooperative blends into holistic. We often find both holistic *and* cooperative modes present, with one mode predominating.

I want to also make it clear that these categories – *cooperative politics* and *holistic politics* – are themselves newly emerging. There is definitely a territory here I want to share with you, and the map is just being sketched out. I am only beginning to understand this realm.

Other adventurers and mappers are needed (and some are already at work). I am still not sure if these are best seen as two distinct but related modes of politics, or as two aspects of the same mode. Perhaps holistic politics is the leading edge of cooperative politics. This will undoubtedly become clearer as the model is used and talked about. I offer it up to the wisdom of the ensuing conversation.

In each category below, I explore what I see so far in some detail. For clarity, I will be stating things in somewhat absolute terms. Take the absoluteness with a grain of salt, but try to get a "feel" for the essence of what the statements are pointing to. After describing the two modes, I will consider a few examples of politics in this realm, and how those examples embody the two modes (and sometimes other modes as well).

Before we start, just to get oriented, let me share what seems to me to be the essence of each mode:

- The center of gravity of cooperative politics is people and high-quality relationships.
- The center of gravity of holistic politics is the life and patterns of the Whole – the whole group, community, country, world, etc.

Most of the characteristics of each mode, I believe, derive from those two different but closely related central concerns.

Cooperative politics

In cooperative politics, we work together to pursue shared visions and satisfy shared needs. We want to involve and include people, simply because they are people and they deserve to be included and we would like to have them aboard. We want people to get to know one another and to find active roles that are meaningful and satisfying and that use their unique qualities and capacities well. In our work, we usually have lots of food and conversation. There is a respectful diversity combined with a search for common ground. This search is usually done with a sense of compromise, giving slack, and grounding ourselves in our shared humanity. We help each other get involved, learn about the issues, and take action together, often supporting one another's issues in a coalition.

As noted earlier, some communities and interest groups engage in a rough-and-tumble version of cooperative politics to help them effectively promote their shared concerns in the larger world of power politics.

To the extent they become infected with the adversarial values and practices of that larger world, however, their own *internal* group relationships can become contentious. Sadly, much anti-political sentiment arises from people's frustration with the effects of power politics on political movements that start out as cooperative. It is a difficult edge to walk.

Cooperative politics seeks inclusion. However, the more diversity we try to include, the more inevitable conflict becomes. Luckily, as we move towards holistic politics, we start to see such contentiousness as a potential resource for our group. We become less concerned with keeping the peace and more concerned with utilizing that diversity and conflict well, to generate insight, energy and power.

As noted earlier, the trademark of cooperative politics is attention to individuals and the quality of their relationships. There is a sense that much power comes from people and relationships being healthy and engaged, not just as cogs in a larger operation, but as vital sources of unique life. The spirit of mass mobilization and mechanistic organization that characterize so much of power politics is tempered, if not totally replaced, in cooperative politics by attention to the interests and abilities of individuals and the quality of relationships. As a good example of cooperative politics, the consensus organizing discussed in Chapter 2 was based almost entirely on building relationships.

LIVING DEMOCRACY

Two recent pioneers of cooperative democracy are Frances Moore Lappé and Paul Du Bois. During the writing of their book, *The Quickening of America*, I had the privilege of working with them occasionally. They allowed me to edit excerpts from their drafts into an article entitled "Living Democracy." It begans with their motto: "Democracy is not what we have. Democracy is what we *do.*" They wrote:

> Only an active citizenry is both accountable enough and creative enough to address the root causes of today's crises. And millions of Americans are doing just that, creating, here at home, a new American revolution in democracy. They are discovering how to do democracy as a rewarding way of life that encompasses their schools, workplaces, community initiatives, media, government, religious groups, health care, and human services. Through living democracy, they are developing their own power, with others, to solve real problems.

Without naming it as such, the vision of Lappé and Du Bois was deeply embedded in cooperative politics. They reframed power and self-interest in cooperative terms, and spoke of people learning "the arts of democracy," most of which had to do with collaborative skills and dialogue.

POWER-WITH

Lappé and Du Bois pointed out that people can become more able to accomplish their goals if they work together. This simple fact suggests that power – the ability to accomplish one's goals – is not a limited resource to fight over, as the power politics mode assumes. It is, rather, an *unlimited* capacity that we can generate together. In the words of Lappé and Du Bois, "The concept of power becomes one of mutually expanding horizons" – or, as Mary Parker Follett said, of "infinitely expanding reciprocal relations."

These are beautiful articulations of the "power-with" concept, coined by Follett, that is the foundation of cooperative politics. Power is seen to reside at least as much in relationships as in individual people and institutions. Power becomes a matter of enabling relationships and co-creative interactions among diverse stakeholders and players, and of recognizing that everyone is always both cause and effect. From this perspective, responsibility lies less in blame and heroics than in consciously improving the dynamics among us.

ENLIGHTENED SELF-INTEREST

Likewise, *self-interest* looks different in this collaborative light. Lappé and Du Bois note in "Living Democracy" that our self-interest includes all the things we really care about:

> ...our families, heritage, country, faith, health, favorite pastimes, and personal goals. It includes our need to feel useful to others and to be respected. Self-interest also includes our strongly felt commitments to the larger world – such as to a restored natural environment or an end to needless hunger. It is related to who we are at our very core.
>
> We can't get very far with our self-interest by ourselves. Not only do we need to work with others to get what we want, but what we want evolves as we interact with others. It seems that some of our deepest human needs cannot be addressed outside of public life. Citizenship ... means learning to see our self-interests embedded in others' self-interests. Whether we're concerned about environmental health and neighborhood safety, or effective schools and job security, we can't achieve our political goals by ourselves. We each depend on the needs of others being met as well.

This is what some call "enlightened self-interest." It is so refreshing to see even self-interest embedded in a cooperative frame of reference!

So how do we pursue that enlightened, cooperative self-interest? Part of that pursuit is ensuring accountability between us, especially between those chosen to act on behalf of others and the others who are thereby served. But cooperative self-interest is primarily pursued through dialogue, through active listening, through reflection and, finally, through the exercise of "political imagination" that allows us to enter into one another's worlds and envision shared worlds together.

CREATIVE CONFLICT

Lappé and Du Bois remind us that it is often necessary, in this collaborative process, to engage in "creative conflict" – conflict where we can, in the words of Parker J. Palmer, "confront each other critically and honestly over alleged facts, imputed meanings, or personal biases and prejudices." Conflict can play an important role in collective intelligence since, as Mitchell Thomashow says, it "disrupts easy explanations" and thereby opens doors to deeper understanding. According to Lappé and Du Bois in "Living Democracy,"

> The rewards of creative conflict include clarity and learning. Each side comes to better understand how and why the other side feels as they do. And each becomes more clear about their own values and ideas in relation to the views of others. Everyone becomes more involved in and more knowledgeable about the issues. Since good solutions depend on accurately defining problems and on avoiding jumping to conclusions, conflict can increase the quality of problem-solving by helping us see the whole picture. Conflict becomes truly creative when, in addition to heat, fighting generates light and energy to find new options.

Thus, conflict has a different "feel" in cooperative politics than it does in power politics. The conflict is embraced by an expectation, not that someone will win the argument, but that everyone will be heard and greater understanding will be generated. That greater understanding – that collective judgment – becomes the common ground upon which the group can then stand while it engages in cooperative activity.

Sometimes conflict, in the form of nonviolent action, needs to be engaged in as an initial means to bring everyone to the table to participate in a collaborative process. For example, the No Spray campaign in Sonoma County, California, trained hundreds of community activists in nonviolent resistance, before the local government officials agreed to sit down to a collaborative problem-solving process for the purpose of finding alternatives to mass spraying of the population with toxic pesticides.

When engaged in nonviolent direct action, activists operating in the mode of cooperative politics see their main goal as the creation of a collaborative and holistic process in which all parties can work together to create a solution that works for all. The process is collaborative to the extent that they are interested in *working with the other parties involved.* It becomes holistic as they realize that an adequate solution can only be found if *all relevant perspectives* are brought to the table, not just the main adversaries. And it becomes even more holistic to the degree that they don't stop with one particular conflict, but *seek to establish ongoing inclusive dialogues* that can generate wise public policy for the well-being of the community as a whole.

Holistic politics –
The politics of wholeness

Normally, when we look at a community or society, we tend to see its parts, its people and groups, instead of the whole. A whole community or society seems like an abstraction to many of us. We may think of it in terms of its geographical identity, or its symbols, or its government, but we have a hard time holding the whole thing in our minds, as a living entity in its own right.

THINKING ABOUT THE WHOLE

However, groups, organizations, communities, societies, and civilizations *are* all entities in their own right. I usually think of them as *living human systems.* Holistic politics starts, first of all, with a willingness to see them as such, as living entities, about which we can ask questions such as: How intelligent, sane, and healthy is this thing we call the United States of America? How wise is the city of Eugene, Oregon – not the government, but the whole community? Where can we listen to the voice of The People as a whole, in the Indian state of Andhra Pradesh?

These are primarily questions of holistic politics. And the activities of holistic politics have a lot to do with helping these whole human systems *be* intelligent, sane, healthy, wise and heard.

One of the things I admire about that great pioneer of democracy, Mary Parker Follett, is that she embraced both the collaborative and holistic realms of politics. Her insights were prescient. We can only wonder how many people understood her when she wrote, back in 1918, these two remarkable sentences: "Democracy is the rule of an interacting, interpermeating whole ... We have an instinct for democracy because we have an instinct for wholeness."

So what does holistic politics look like? For one thing, it has to do with broad perspective. In the world of holistic politics, we realize we can never see the whole picture. Therefore, when we encounter opposition, we take that as a sign that there is more of the picture we have not yet taken into account. There is more in the situation for us to learn about.

From the holistic perspective, we see the significance of people or issues as reaching far beyond their individual legitimacy: They are meaningful because they are related. They are evocative of deeper dynamics. They are resources for the common good. They are doorways and windows into larger realms. In the holistic mode, we do not tend to think in terms of "bad guys" anymore, because everything and everyone has a place in the bigger picture, and we are trying to understand and relate to that bigger picture. We try to stay flexible, curious and open to change, seeing rich opportunities for learning in incidents others might view as failures.

Co-intelligence thrives to the extent we (and others) can transform our views and relationships through dialogue. This, in turn depends on the consciousness we bring to our dialogues, the processes we use and the culture we inhabit.

THE CAPACITY TO INCLUDE AND INTEGRATE

We also know that our "shadow," the part of ourselves and life that we push away or deny, does not stop influencing us simply because we are not aware of it. So we try to make what is unconscious more conscious, to understand more about the psychological and spiritual dimensions of life, both individually and collectively, and how these play out in our political world.

In holistic mode, we do not leave cooperation behind. In fact, cooperation is a central reality with which we work. But we also expand our view to embrace larger patterns and dynamics of the whole, many of which include cooperation. For example, we may notice that cooperation is greatly enhanced by having a shared vision or story. Or we might realize, as Gandhi did, that most social problems persist only because of the cooperation of many people, even those who are harmed by the problem. In some cases, competition is very healthy for the whole system, as long as it is contained within a larger cooperative context. Cooperation becomes one of many system dynamics we can work with.

The perspective of wholeness leads us (1) to be concerned with building the capacity of the whole community or society to reflect on itself and its circumstances – its whole circumstances – and (2) to evoke the wisdom of the whole to benefit the whole. This is why we tend to focus on such things as processes for community dialogue; quality of life indicators such as the ones introduced in Chapter 2; multiple-viewpoint drama such as Anna Deavere Smith's work in Chapter 8; systems thinking; and the creative use of media as an ongoing, perceptive "mirror" for the community. All these resources build collective awareness.

From a systems perspective, we believe that we can accomplish a lot by including all *perspectives* in a situation where we are not able to include all *people*. Since integrating diverse *perspectives* produces wisdom, we do our best to include as many perspectives as possible. This allows us to think in *qualitative* rather than *quantitative* terms when making decisions: We want the right variety of perspectives, not just lots of people.

This may show up in our attitude towards voting results. For example, if half the people vote and the majority of those vote for one proposal or candidate, normal majoritarians may be satisfied. But we might be more interested in which perspectives were lost to the decision-making process by the low voter turnout – *and* by the quantitative, non-dialogic nature of voting itself – and what was thereby lost to the community's collective intelligence.

APPRECIATING SYSTEMS DYNAMICS AND LARGER PATTERNS

A systems perspective leads us to understand that some problems and solutions persist simply because of how things are arranged, or what people believe about them, or habitual patterns of behaving or relating. We know that often simply changing certain patterns or beliefs can dramatically transform a problem, making it shrink or vanish, or open us up to some deeper understanding. We know the power of dialogue and story to generate such shifts. Thus, we attend to the capacity of a community to generate its own dialogues and stories, so it can shift and grow in ways that make sense for it.

A holistic perspective leads us to attend to "living system" dynamics, the big picture, and the long-term. We feel ourselves embedded in what Joanna Macy calls "deep time" – the extended millennia of past and future – or in what Thomas Berry has called The Great Story, the vast evolution of the Universe, Life and Consciousness. We are interested in the history behind events, the stories of people involved in a situation, the visions that give our life meaning, the dynamics pulling us from the future, the fate of the generations who will come after us and have to live with the consequences of our decisions. We sense that much more than the obvious present actors and factors are involved, right now, in what is going on. We want the bigger picture and we look for ways the whole group, community or society can access it.

The perspective of wholeness may also lead us to explore how patterns from "the new sciences" – ecology, evolutionary biology, quantum mechanics, field theory, chaos and complexity theories – apply to the human systems we are working with, living in or being. We know that we need to be aware of the larger patterns we are all part of, because we are not separate or independent. We are whole beings – within whole contexts – within a whole, living universe.

At the same time, we are interested in the dynamics of social, political and economic systems, and the ways they structure our experience and activities. We know there are all sorts of patterns within us and around us that have the power to shape our lives, and we want to participate consciously in that shaping. Our awareness of how powerfully systemic forces shape people may make us more tolerant. This awareness may also lead us to place greater emphasis on systemic solutions than on changing individual behaviors.

We feel our politics as an expression of Life itself. And we are interested in Life's ability to self-organize, to heal itself, and to transform at all levels, from the microbial to the planetary. At the same time, from a co-creative perspective, we realize that we ourselves play a part in that self-organization, and that we can choose the kind of role that we want to play.

We are always open to asking ourselves, What else is there? Who else should be part of the conversation? Where are the missing pieces? How might we call forth what is trying to emerge? We are trying to help "the whole" to pursue its agenda, rather than pushing our own agendas. Thus, we tend to think of ourselves less as leaders and more as facilitators, catalysts, servants or midwives.

A CLOSER LOOK AT HOLISTIC POLITICS: DISTINGUISHING CONTENT AND PROCESS

Content is what people talk about. *Process* is how they talk about it. Imagine that you are having a conversation about democracy in a group in which one person happens to be dominating the conversation. Obviously, having a conversation about democracy is not necessarily the same as having a democratic conversation!

I see three different approaches to holistic politics emerging in our society at present. Two of them are focused on content. The third approach, the one I have been describing so far, is focused on process. For the sake of clarity, I would like to make some important distinctions between them.

The first of these approaches to holistic politics is focused on holistic political ideology.

One of the more interesting undertakings in holistic philosophical circles is creating political ideologies that integrate diverse political perspectives, such as liberal and conservative, into one inclusive view. This, of course, is valuable in helping us understand how things fit together.

However, I offer a note of caution: such "inclusive" ideologies can be used by those who dominate an adversarial political system. They can consolidate their power by making their propaganda more appealing to a broader audience. By creating the *appearance* of a broad social consensus, such an ideology could also be used to more effectively marginalize anyone who challenges the dominant political order. I think we have seen the results of such "inclusive" ideologies in the increasing similarities between the Democratic and Republican parties in the U.S. They are each struggling to embrace a larger majority of the population with such formulations as "compassionate conservatism," while aligning themselves with the same corporate power structure.

In contrast, the approach to holistic politics we are advocating in this book consists of holistic political *processes* – systems of dialogue and participation that enhance a whole community's or society's capacity to learn and envision and create. If such holistic political *processes* are in place, then holistic *ideologies* might become one more resource for catalyzing collective reflection within a community.

The second approach to holistic politics also focuses on content. But instead of emphasizing holistic ideology it emphasizes holistic programs, including some of the programs that have been described in earlier chapters of this book. A host of other wonderful holistic programs are included in such books as Corinne McLaughlin and Gordon Davidson's *Spiritual Politics*, which catalogues a host of innovative and successful programs in education, rehabilitation, social services, etc. Many of these excellent programs are designed to bring people together, work with nature, call forth the spirit in people, redesign systems for health and sustainability, and so on. I fully support most of these brilliant solutions – and yet, I still feel that they do not address the particular need that I am trying to speak to here, the need for a holistic political *process*.

As long as such brilliant solutions for the common good have to compete in an adversarial environment dominated by self-interested powers, they are fighting an uphill battle. I believe that establishing holistic political processes is likely to support the establishment of holistic programs in all sectors of society.

For all these reasons, I suggest that holistic democratic process is the primary factor that determines how holistic our political lives will be.

AN EXAMPLE OF A HOLISTIC POLITICAL PROCESS

Perhaps the most promising holistic democratic process I know of – one that could call forth the voice-of-the-whole – is an innovation I call *citizen consensus councils*. We have already seen one example of a citizen consensus council in the brief description of the Canadian experiment, which we will be exploring more fully in the next chapter. Citizen consensus councils are one way of "helping the whole community or society see and reflect on its whole self and its whole circumstances, and evoking the wisdom of the whole to benefit the whole."

A citizen consensus council is comprised of one or two dozen citizens chosen to represent the diversity of a larger community or country. It is given the mandate of deliberating on the common good with regard to a particular issue, or with respect to the general state of its community or country. Its deliberations are facilitated to a consensus and its conclusions are publicized to the larger population from which its members were drawn.

For example, in the winter of 1997, fifteen Boston citizens were carefully selected to reflect the diversity of the larger population of the city. They included a homeless shelter resident, a high-tech business manager, a retired farmer, a recent inner-city high school graduate and eleven others. With professional help, this council undertook an intensive study of telecommunications issues.

Over two weekends in February and March, they discussed background readings and received introductory briefings. Then on April 2nd and 3rd, they heard ten hours of testimony from experts – computer specialists, government officials, business executives, educators, and representatives of various interest groups. After interrogating the experts and deliberating late into the night, assisted by high-quality facilitation, they came up with a consensus statement recommending judicious but far-reaching policy changes.

The council presented their impressive recommendations at a press conference at Tufts University, covered by WCVB-TV/CNN and the *Boston Globe*, among others. U.S. Representative Edward J. Markey, ranking Democrat and former chair of the House Telecommunications Subcommittee, recognized the political potential of this innovation, saying, "This is a process that I hope will be repeated in other parts of the country and on other issues."

Dick Sclove, formerly of the Loka Institute *(loka.org)*, was a lead organizer of the meeting. He saw it as a "first" in modern history—a *dialogue* specially organized to gather *informed* input from *ordinary* U.S. citizens. As far as he knew, there had never before been a systematic effort to provide public policy guidance on a complex technological subject using Americans who were neither experts on the policy issues they were studying nor representatives of organizations with a direct stake in the outcome.

Noting that these ordinary citizens ended up knowing more about telecommunications than the average

Congressperson who voted on the issue, Sclove said that their behavior conclusively disproved the assertion that government and business officials are the only ones competent and caring enough to be involved in technological decision-making. This lay panel assimilated a broad array of testimony, which they integrated with their own very diverse life experiences, in order to reach a well-reasoned collective judgment grounded in the real needs of everyday people. To me, this example demonstrates that democratizing science and technology decision-making is not only advisable, but also possible and practical.

As I have said, I consider this innovation to be perhaps the most powerful form of holistic politics we have available to us. It taps into one of the most mysterious characteristics of wholeness – that the whole can be contained within a part of itself. Just as you can taste a soup with one spoonful, you can tap the wisdom of a whole community through *the thoughtful dialogue of a properly diverse group of its citizens.* That fact makes possible the careful and unbiased handling of virtually any public issue. It is truly a means of tapping the wisdom of the whole, on behalf of the common good.

Citizen *consensus* councils are particularly powerful because they always involve consensus. I will explore the controversial power of consensus further in Chapter 18. However, consensus is not required to evoke wise public judgment from diverse citizens. Any good dialogue or deliberative process will do that. This fact underlies the many forms of citizen *deliberative* councils covered in the next few chapters. Some deliberative councils are consensus councils and some are not.

Although few people know these councils exist, I believe that the full spectrum of citizen deliberative councils are vital to creating a practical system of holistic politics that can bring forth a world that works for all. Read on, and see what *you* think...

CHAPTER 12

THE CANADIAN EXPERIMENT

People are sick and tired of being pitted against each other when there's already so much suffering and the Earth itself is under assault. They're ready to reconnect and honor the life we share. That is the great adventure of our time. And it's happening.
— JOANNA MACY

In June 1991 a dozen Canadians met in a resort near Toronto in search of a shared future for their deeply divided country, torn by the question of Quebec separatism among many other issues. These people were not politicians, academics or a revolutionary cabal. In fact, a more diverse group of Canadians would be hard to find: They had been scientifically selected for their differences, differences that reflected the very divisions in their nation. Within hours of meeting, they were immersed in arguments. And yet, two days later, they had all signed a detailed, visionary agreement charting a course to greater mutual understanding by all Canadians, and were hugging each other good-bye.

The gathering was sponsored and hosted by

Maclean's, Canada's leading weekly newsmagazine (the equivalent of *Time* or *Newsweek*). *Maclean's* instructed their polling firm, Decima Research, to "identify scientifically the clusters of thinking in the country that, taken together, constitute a portrait of the main patterns of thought that dominate the nation. Then, by carefully selecting individuals whose views match ... the characteristics of each cluster ... create a panel that represent[s] the collective thought patterns of the nation." After reviewing thousands of surveys and doing hundreds of additional calls, Decima and *Maclean's* staff managed to select twelve extremely articulate citizens who, among them, balanced not only the various Canadian points of view, but also the age, gender, ethnic and regional differences of Canada. They included hard-liners and moderates on both sides of "the Quebec question," as well as peacemakers – and a Tlingit Indian filmmaker.

Maclean's editors described the twelve Canadians they had brought together as "initially united only by the depth of their different convictions." The gulf was especially vast between the folks who advocated separatism for Quebec and those who advocated a strong federal government for all of Canada. The two hardline Quebec separatists in the group were lawyer Charles Dupuis and civil servant Marie LeBeau. Of the three advocates of federalism, one of the most outspoken was prosecutor Richard Miller. Reflecting the complexity of the situation, another participant was Carol Geddes, a Native Canadian, speaking on behalf of "First Nations' sovereignty."

The *Maclean's* organizers knew they had managed to obtain diversity, but how were these people going to find common ground? For that, *Maclean's* turned to law professor Roger Fisher, a world-renowned negotiation and conflict resolution expert, co-author of the classic book *Getting to Yes,* and director of the Harvard Negotiation Project. With two other non-Canadian colleagues, Robert Ricigliano and Stuart Diamond, Fisher flew to Toronto, hoping to help the participants find their common interests and their way toward a common vision.

The path they took makes an instructive and heartful story. The account below rests heavily on the report provided in *Maclean's* July 1, 1991 issue, which devoted 39 pages to different aspects of what it called "The People's Verdict," including a lengthy account of the dialogue.

Day One: Discovering differences

The weekend began on a sunny Friday afternoon, June 7, 1991, at Briars resort on Ontario's Lake Simcoe outside of Toronto. Negotiators and participants alike were nervous. In an interview, Fisher described the challenge of the coming weekend as "taking a dive off the high board without knowing if there was water in the pool yet." Miles away, on a bus heading to the retreat center, Quebec separatist Charles Dupuis felt like a Christian heading to the lions' den. Rural nurse Karren Collings arrived at Briars figuring Canada was "heading for a breakup." In fact, there was a lot of anxiety in all quarters that day. The travel-weary participants had little idea of what to expect.

Friday's opening session began with the negotiators introducing the process, framing it as "a discussion about mutual concerns and interests about the future of Canada." They appealed to the participants to try to understand how each one of them viewed their shared problems.

Participants paired up, interviewing each other and then introducing their partners to the rest of the group. The process failed to reveal much common ground. However, when they started discussing Canada's problems, they found they all shared frustration about the existing state of affairs. As they called out the things they saw as problems, Ricigliano took notes on chart pads. As their list became long and wildly varied, several participants wondered if Canada was really a coherent country at all. Few of them knew much about the other regions, identifying more with their provinces or subcultures than with Canada as a whole.

The issue of mistreated minorities arose early and poignantly. Quebec lawyer Dupuis declared, "The main cause is...having two principle cultures – the Anglo-Saxon and the French-speaking." To which filmmaker Geddes replied: "There are more than two main cultures in Canada. The First Nations are a main culture." Dupuis apologized: "I'm sorry. I forgot about you. We are intruders." Then, with both Quebec and indigenous cultures carefully in mind, he concluded, "Minorities have a fear of being eaten."

Dinner started a little before 8 o'clock. Although the less formal mealtime conversations facilitated the formation of casual friendships, the gulf between viewpoints became even more obvious – especially on the issue of Quebec. At one table Miller, the federalist prosecutor, told facilitator Diamond that he, Miller, did not understand what the folks from Quebec wanted.

"I don't understand the problem. I don't understand the threat the Quebecers like Charles perceive, or at least I don't understand how they see separation as being some solution to that problem."

At another table, Quebec separatist LeBeau told Fisher and others that she felt assaulted and insulted by the way English-speaking Canadians treated Quebec's dedication to the French language. She got irritated when non-Quebec participants complained they couldn't read French signs, saying that she had to read signs in English when she went to other parts of Canada – and no one was objecting to French signs in France!

At a third table, Dupuis and non-separatist Quebecer Robert Lalande described to facilitator Ricigliano how protesters had stepped and spat on a Quebec flag, and how the television news had played those scenes repeatedly. Ricigliano commented, "There could be 90% agreement; the media wants to cover the 10% disagreement."

As they left dinner, Karren Collings, the nurse categorized by Decima, the polling firm, as a Peacemaker, told Lalande that she was already beginning to learn something from this process. Collings acknowledged to Lalande that what Dupuis had said earlier "about being afraid of being treated like a minority was all new to me. I was more aware of the Native problem. This is what I came to find out: the other side. And I learned it tonight. It's opening my eyes." Her opened eyes would play a significant role in the process as the weekend unfolded.

After dinner, Fisher told the group, "I am surprised at how emotional and sensitive the language question is, with so few clear identifications of what is wrong and what would be right." He described what he expected the group would do the next day, and then ended the session shortly after 10 p.m. Later, he and his colleagues expressed hope that the stage of outpouring grievances, which they had expected and encouraged, was now complete and that the group could turn toward solutions on Saturday. But it turned out the group was not yet ready for that.

Day Two: Passions rise

The Saturday session started right after breakfast, and it took a while for participants to loosen up. Nationalist Miller, tired of hearing about Canada's problems, launched into a passionate defense of the nation: "We live in such a wonderful place at such a wonderful time ... because of systems that were created some time ago that have worked incredibly well over the past hundred or so years ... [We are] quibbling, and our problems are really minor problems. And we seem to want to view them as major problems. The danger in that is that we will wreck everything. We will destroy the systems that have given us what we've got, just for the sake of change."

Geddes flashed back, "Do you think it's quibbling that aboriginal people have the highest infant death [rate] and the shortest life-span, the highest poverty rates of all Canadians?" Miller said he was not suggesting Canada did not have problems, but that "we don't need to toss out our whole system of nutrition just because we have a side ache. Maybe just a little Band-Aid will work." To which nurse and social worker Viola Cerezke-Schooler replied, "We need radical surgery." Lawyer Miller rejoined, "You don't have a lung transplant if you have a chest cold." Peacemaker Collings, also a nurse, suggested, "No. But if you let a chest cold go, you get worse."

The previous night, Fisher and his crew had sorted the problems that participants had identified into three categories – the constitutional impasse, the threat of economic decline, and the lack of understanding and empathy among Canadians for one another. He created a group for each topic and put four participants in each group, according to their interest. He sent them off with instructions to brainstorm possible solutions to their respective problems.

In the "mutual understanding" group, participant John Prall noted that, although he was a teacher, he had hardly visited other provinces. Furthermore, until this weekend, he had had no idea that Native Canadians' problems were so great. This evoked ideas from the other group members about Canadians vacationing in their own country and about the need for a more well-rounded history of Canada as well as other balanced curricula. They imagined the federal government forming problem-solving groups like themselves, made up of people from different parts of Canada

In the economy group, participants shared fears that economic prospects were not good, with too much government and taxes. They wondered whether social programs should remain as universal as they were. The solutions they brainstormed included regional joint boards for economic development (which would include private citizens), more co-operation among industries, and independent audits of government operations.

Meanwhile, in the constitution group, the conversation was a bit more edgy.

"Let's call a cat a cat. Quebec needs all the powers to determine its own future," asserted Dupuis. To which Geddes retorted, "Before we talk of distribution of powers, some people are not even let in the door of the forum. We don't want to be covered by the term minorities or multiculturalism. Our identity is as a First Nation. We don't want to hear we are a minority." Ricigliano, facilitating, suggested that the group come up with some new ways to address the interests of both Natives and Quebecers. Prosecutor Miller, trying to be cooperative despite his strong Federalist stance, conceded that language and culture could be considered the responsibility of provinces. Following his lead, the group agreed that all citizens should be able to fulfill basic needs like education, but that program content should be determined locally. So far, so good.

The participants went to lunch. When they all reconvened together afterward, Fisher shared with them what he saw as the four dominant options being discussed by Canadians:

- an independent Quebec,
- a strong federal government,
- stronger provinces, and
- self-government for First Nations.

He invited the group to critique these proposals, which they did with gusto. Soon it became clear that

none of these options would be able to achieve majority support. Fisher then pointed out the obvious conclusion: Advocating these options more strongly would
not help the group – or the rest of Canada – make any
headway on the problem. Instead, it would only generate more noise. He then asked the group, "Can we create a new option that looks as though it has a realistic
chance?"

Some of the participants were not comfortable with
this way of framing the issues. During a break, Geddes
noted that no one ever listened to Quebecers and Natives
unless they shouted and screamed for their positions.

For the late afternoon session, participants returned
to working in small groups. Although consensus grew
readily in the groups dealing with the economy and
mutual understanding, the constitutional committee
was coming apart at the seams.

Dupuis and LeBeau did not want to talk about the
design of the federal government, only about the design of a government for Quebec. LeBeau told Ricigliano,
"I have already left Canada." Miller called them naive
to think they could leave Canada without producing
bad relations between the two areas. But Dupuis considered separation inevitable, and challenged Miller:
"If Quebec says a clear 'no' to Canada, would Canada
impose its views?" Miller rejoined, "You mean, would
we send in the tanks?"

The situation was at an impasse. Fisher, who had
been working with one of the other groups, adjourned
his group's discussion and came over to the constitutional group. He advised LeBeau and Dupuis to stick
with the exploration of what a united Canada would
look like, without necessarily abandoning ideas of independence. It was a nice try at compromise, but it did
not work. The level of alienation felt by the Quebecers
was not being fully understood.

Maclean's described the scene: "Miller and Geddes
sit angrily stone-faced. Dupuis, his right leg jiggling

nervously, rubs his eyes repeatedly. And LeBeau, frustrated and angry, launches into a painful, and poignant, description of how hurt Quebecers have been by what they perceive as a rejection by the rest of the country."

"The only thing I can say is that I am fed up with hurting the way I am hurting now. It is incredible. I don't have the words to say how I am hurt right now. I don't say it is right or wrong. Why have I left Canada? I don't want to hurt anymore. What lies beyond, I don't even want to know. I want to be ... not here. And I think, through the people that I meet every day, I am not alone. Friends told me: 'Go tell them. Lots of people hurt.'"

Fisher quietly pointed out that being hurt does not necessarily mean you know how to proceed, and reiterated his call for LeBeau and Dupuis to continue seeking "directions that hold some promise." The participants tried to be agreeable as they broke for dinner, but considerable tension was still bubbling away right beneath the surface.

DAY TWO DINNER: BREAKTHROUGH

At dinner, Collings suggested they combine their tables so they could eat together. But the three Quebecers sat separately, conversing in French. Undeterred, Collings slowly moved towards them until she became part of the conversation. LeBeau continued to express her upset and alienated feeling.

As they ended dinner, Fisher went to another room to figure out how to recover the shattered process. Ricigliano joined the Quebecers who were still at their table. With half the group gathered around, listening intently, he asked LeBeau to speak about the intense feelings she was experiencing. "We are children crying out for love," she said. Pointing at Collings, she said to Ricigliano: "I love her. I do. And if I told her that I don't want her to decide what happens in my daughter's school – you know what? – maybe she is not offended by the idea. But someone said she should be ... Such different people for so long and we're still together. And I bet that 200 years from now, we still will be."

Collings responded with heart: "And I want you to be with us, the way it should be. *Not* the way it is. The way it should be."

LeBeau went on: "If kids are suffering in Nova Scotia, it hurts me. And if Native women suffer in the Yukon, it hurts me. And I think we all have to shut up for some time and listen. We might not like what we hear. But we have got to listen ... It is a question of survival to me. I don't want to lose Canada."

Collings, looking directly at LeBeau, said forcefully, "And I don't want to lose you."

LeBeau heard her, and felt moved. "We are on to something here. And maybe someone should become aware that we might be losing it. Do you want to lose it?" she asked Collings. "No." "Neither do I," said LeBeau." "That's why I'm here," said Collings.

LeBeau shook her head and looked down. "God. And if you tell me the only way you can survive is *this way* [hearing each other], then I think I am ready to listen to you and say, 'Well, it's never been done this way before. But maybe it can work.'" She whispered, "Maybe we can try it."

"Tonight," she said, "I was asked to give answers. My only answer is that I am ready to try. And I would say, 'Let's get the politicians out of it.' This country is all about love and emotions, and it is the only subject we won't touch."

There was a silence. Then Ricigliano said, "Until tomorrow."

The negotiators stayed up late, finally deciding to set aside the constitutional debate and to take the time to address the group's personal conflicts. But their time was running out, so they also went over the endless sheets of chart pad notes, extracting ideas that they wove into a first draft of a possible agreement.

Day Three: Discovering common ground

Shortly after the meeting started on Sunday morning, LeBeau, her attention freed by her catharsis the night before, turned to Geddes, the First Nations member. LeBeau asked Geddes to share her own hurt, saying, "I am at last ready to listen to you. Three days ago, I might not have listened. What do you want me to recognize? Please tell me now. Talk loudly."

Geddes talked for almost fifteen minutes about how, against tremendous obstacles, Native elders had sustained their cultures and how Native people wanted to be partners in Canada. Rather than looking to get something from Canada, the elders wanted to share the treasures of their culture with others. When Dupuis, trying to be helpful and respectful, suggested that rough times can make people stronger, Geddes replied that the strength of Native peoples came from their culture, and that adversity had killed a lot of her people. While these were difficult communications, the embattled energy of the previous day seemed to have lifted.

Fisher recognized that a breakthrough had happened on the level of relationships – something that his negotiation method specifically seeks to support – and that this breakthrough had probably opened the way for agreement. Collings and Ricigliano, really hearing LeBeau after Saturday's crisis, had in turn allowed LeBeau to listen deeply to Geddes on Sunday morning. The resulting mood of mutual understanding spread to others, generating a climate of fellowship in which an agreement could at last be considered.

Fisher shared copies of the draft agreement he and his team had prepared from the input they had gathered, and asked for participants' responses. During the discussion that followed, many participants reached out to one another with healing comments.

During lunch, as Ricigliano incorporated all their comments into a second draft, Miller and Geddes clashed over Native self-government. Miller called the idea "absurd" and Geddes replied that if all Canadians had that view, that would drive the First Nations into "the same position as Quebec." The disagreement flared but did not catch fire. The group was no longer combustible.

When they convened again after lunch, the group seemed ready and determined to reach an agreement. Individually, in small groups and then together, they worked over the document. As consensus seemed near, Ricigliano tried to depart unceremoniously for an assignment in Greece. But the group stopped to cheer for him, acknowledging the crucial role he had played the night before. Ricigliano choked up, saying he felt attached to the group members. As he reached for his bags, Marie LeBeau rushed over and hugged him. The rest of the group immediately crowded around for hugs and good-byes. Many had tears in their eyes.

After Ricigliano's departure and a break for a swim, during which the final draft was typed up, all of the participants reviewed and signed their hard-won agreement. At five minutes before 7:00 p.m. Sunday night, Fisher called for "a bottle of something" to celebrate.

The next morning Fisher left early for Boston, leaving Diamond to wrap up. Erstwhile adversaries Dupuis and Miller went together to visit the grave of the famous Canadian writer and humorist Stephen Leacock. Quebecer Dupuis, who had never heard of him, wondered if Miller, who was from British Columbia, had heard of the famous Quebec singer and poet Félix Leclerc. Miller had not. The two lawyers had generated more than their share of conflict during the weekend, all too often against each other. Now, they suddenly realized that they had become friends, and that they shared the problem of their mutual ignorance, the ignorance that was tearing their country apart.

In the final session with Diamond, most of the participants acknowledged significant shifts in their feelings, if not always in their ideas. LeBeau said that while she had arrived certain about her Separatist stance, she now felt she did not know enough to have her mind made up. Miller said he had moved from trying to convince everyone of his ideas to searching for an agreement that would satisfy everyone. Dupuis was impressed with people's willingness to listen. And Geddes told Dupuis and LeBeau that, although she really understood their pain and their desire to leave Canada, she hoped that they would not.

Aftermath

In interviews with a reporter nine years later, journalists from *Maclean's* and from the Canadian Broadcasting film crew who covered the event still remembered it as a life-changing experience for everyone.

The final agreement reached by these dozen diverse Canadians took up four pages of small print in *Maclean's*. It contained dozens of policy recommendations and suggested changes in the behavior of Canadians individually, as well as businesses, governments, schools and other segments of Canadian society.

Perhaps most importantly, the document stressed what these people learned during just two and a half days together: that when the human dimension is addressed well, when people really hear each other and learn about each other's histories, lives, concerns and needs, all the other questions "will be far easier to resolve." It is this attention to the wholeness of human experience that allows us to engage deeply with diversity and reach creative consensus without compromise.

The organizers of this gathering came to the same conclusion that Rep. Edward Markey did after the Boston citizens panel on telecommunications. *Maclean's* editors pointed out in their commentary on The People's Verdict that "the process that led to the writing of the draft could be extended to address other issues." Assistant Managing Editor Robert Marshall noted that earlier efforts, which had included a parliamentary committee, a governmental consultative initiative, and a $27 million Citizens' Forum on Canada's Future, had all failed to create real dialogue among diverse citizens about constructive solutions, even though those efforts involved 400,000 Canadians in focus groups, phone calls and mail-in reporting. In stark contrast, this weekend had been a spectacular success. "The experience of the *Maclean's* forum indicates that if a national dialogue ever does take place, it would be an extremely productive process."

One might well wonder, if this process is so remarkable, why it is it not being done regularly, and why is it not part of official policy. It seems that it would be very useful for any democratic country to convene this kind of council every year. It could help both government and the public at large to learn more about what the people are thinking and feeling, if they like where the country is headed, and what they want to do together.

In this day and age, we also confront countless complex, highly technical social and environmental issues – global warming, biotechnology, resource depletion, terrorism, arcane financial catastrophes like the collapses of Enron and WorldCom. Can ordinary citizens ever hope to generate real wisdom together when the issues they face are so complex, confusing and riddled with competing experts and interest groups? The next chapter explores some of the successful experiments that have been carried out along these lines.

CHAPTER 13

CITIZENS DELIBERATE ABOUT PUBLIC ISSUES

[A]s our social, environmental and economic problems become more complex, our political system is reaching the limits of its capacity to meaningfully respond ...

Thomas Jefferson ... espoused what has been called the "politics of engagement," a model in which people work together in a spirit of cooperation to find common ground and solve mutual problems. The Jeffersonian model rests on the conviction that people are essentially reasonable, and will work to achieve the common good if they can agree on or be brought to understand what it is ...

Nowhere does our current political structure offer a place where people can come together to balance the needs of the larger community ... [T]here is a gap in our system of governance – a gap that has everything to do with our ability to create a sustainable future ... What government does not do very well ... is to bring people together to solve problems – especially when the problems are complex and the solutions require the participation of many people ...

[I]t is now time to build the structure that will give us a place to come together to solve the problems and seize the opportunities of today that our current government system cannot or will not address.

— JOHN KITZHABER, GOVERNOR OF OREGON

In the last chapter we saw a group addressing a big national conflict over the vision for their country. Such citizen deliberation has also been used to address specific social problems and policy options.

Ten years and two weeks after the *Maclean's* group completed their process in Canada, a gathering of citizens took place in India. Twenty individuals, some of whom were illiterate, were chosen to represent the diversity of their state. They met in the impoverished village of Algole to investigate development policy. For five days, they explored various scenarios in detail. Unlike the *Maclean's* group, these Indian citizens had the opportunity to interview experts on all sides of the issue. After a great deal of conversation, they finally decided on the kind of agriculture and development policy they really wanted.

Their meeting and their findings were reported in several newspapers in England, the country from which much of the money for development in their state was due to come. I have included a more detailed version of their story below, as yet another example of the thesis that *"If you give a group of diverse typical citizens a chance to learn about an issue and talk about it well with each other, they will come up with ways to handle the issue that make a lot of sense to a lot of people."*

Yet the farmers in India are not the only ones to have replicated this experiment. In the decade between the event in Canada and the one in India, thousands of ordinary people have been involved in hundreds of similar councils of various types. After learning about complex issues from each other and from a variety of expert testimony, they have been able to generate surprisingly sophisticated recommendations about how their governments and others should proceed.

What exactly are these "citizen deliberative councils," and what do they have to do with politics and government as we know it? How do they work? What sorts of issues do they cover? What different ways of doing our politics and governance do they make possible? Let us take a closer look.

Development according to whom? – A citizens' jury in India

On June 25, 2001, twenty "marginal-livelihood" farmers, small traders, small food processors, and consumers – mostly women and mostly "untouchables" – converged on the village of Algole in India's impoverished Medak District. They came from all over the state of Andhra Pradesh, whose rural diversity they embodied in their group. Some of them had never left their local villages before. Although many could not read or write, they were determined to learn and to make their voices heard about an issue that would have a profound effect on their lives: the future of agriculture in their state. They were concerned with the direction of economic development and the genetic engineering of food crops. They had come to participate in a *Prajateerpu,* a citizens' jury or "People's Verdict," organized by two UK-based non-governmental organizations – the International Institute for Environment and Development and the Institute of Development Studies – along with The Andhra Pradesh Coalition in Defence of Diversity, the leading forum for discussing different agricultural options for the state's future.

For some time the British government, the World Bank and some North American consultants had been working with state officials to develop a twenty-year strategy to mechanize, consolidate and genetically engineer Andhra Pradesh's agriculture to produce cash crops for export, and to reduce the farming population from seventy percent to forty percent, freeing workers up for industry. None of these powerful people had formally asked the impoverished Indian citizens, who were supposed to benefit from these developments, whether

they liked this new direction or not. The citizens' jury
was designed to correct that omission.

The jurors were given three scenarios to consider:
One was that official plan, put forward by Andhra
Pradesh's Chief Minister and backed by grants and
loans from the World Bank and the UK government.
The second scenario, supported by the International
Federation of Organic Agriculture Movements and the
International Trade Center (a shared project of the UN
and the World Trade Organization to promote trade in
developing countries) involved developing environmentally friendly agriculture to produce cheap organic products for domestic and Northern supermarkets. The
third vision, heavily influenced by Gandhian and indigenous ideas, involved increasing local self-reliance
and sustainability in both agriculture and economics.

Each vision was presented through videos illustrat-
ing key features of life under that vision, followed by a
summary of the policies and institutions that steered
Andhra Pradesh in that direction. Jurors then heard
testimony from, and cross-examined, expert witnesses,
including key government officials, scientists, corporate and civil society representatives from all levels –
state, national and international.

Sometimes passions ran high. Having heard from
one expert that a genetically engineered plant contained
a gene from a deep-sea fish, one juror retorted: "I think
these scientists and all their equipment should be
thrown into the bottom of the sea."

The fairness of the process, the materials and the
selection of expert witnesses were overseen by an outside panel chaired by a former Chief Justice of India's
Supreme Court. The World Bank and the UK's Department for International Development had also been invited to act as independent observers, although The
World Bank refused to attend.

The jury members – impoverished in material
wealth, but not in skills, experience or perspective –

considered the pros and cons of each vision, based on their own knowledge, priorities and aspirations. Free to choose any of the three visions, they were also encouraged to use them as raw material with which to craft their own unique vision. They explored their choices, and the likely consequences of their choices, for days, and then came to their conclusion.

THOUGHTFUL CONCLUSIONS

In their recommendations, released on July 1, they said they wanted self-reliant food and farming, and community control over resources. They wanted to maintain healthy soils, diverse crops, trees and livestock, and to build on their indigenous knowledge, practical skills and local institutions. They wanted to maintain the high percentage of people making their livelihood from the land, and did not want their farms consolidated or mechanized in ways that would displace rural people. Most of them could feed their families through their own sustenance farming. They did not want to end up laboring in dangerous brick kilns outside of Hyderabad, like so many who had left their farms. They also rejected genetically modified crops and the export of their local medicinal plants. They provided many suggestions for practical steps that could be taken by various parties to help realize their vision.

The People had spoken. Their voice was heard loud and clear by the sponsoring organizations. Whether they will be heard by the powers-that-be remains to be seen. Organizers hoped that the jury process and verdict would

> encourage more public deliberation and pluralism in the framing and implementation of policies on food and agriculture in Andhra Pradesh, thus contributing to democratic governance. Because of Andhra Pradesh's status

as one of India's model states, the outcomes of this deliberative and inclusive process should be of national
and international significance. (Pimbert and Wakeford,
2001)

Using downpour to build community

Ten weeks after the Indian jurors returned to their homes
in Andhra Pradesh, fifteen Australians in the crowded
Sydney suburb of Bronte came together for a citizens' jury
of their own. They had never done anything like it before,
they knew nothing about what happened in India or
Canada, and they had never met one another. It was all
new. They had been convened to deal with the problem of
stormwater that was eroding their lush landscape and
polluting their spectacular beaches.

Perhaps most interesting of all, many of the jury members didn't know much about the stormwater issue before they were selected for the jury. Although they had
seen the rubbish, leaves, and grass cuttings on the beach,
they knew little about the heavy metals, fertilizers and
other pollutants that washed into the popular surf with
each storm. However, by the end of the jury process, they
had all become quite expert, concerned and sure of what
was needed to handle the problem.

Sponsored by the mayor, Councilor Paul Pearce, and
the New South Wales Environmental Protection Authority (NSW EPA), the jury was organized by The Bronte
Catchment Project, part of a private consulting firm. The
Project sent out an info package to all 877 Bronte households listed in the phone book. 358 responded and participated in a telephone survey. The results were tabu-
lated and saved for the upcoming citizens' jury.

Through the poll and various community promo-
tions, The Project then recruited a pool of candidates
whom they interviewed further, finally selecting fifteen
who represented "a demographic cross-section of people

with a range of environmental views, values and involvement in the local community." They specifically
did *not* want "the usual suspects" – the active partisans who always show up at public meetings. Instead,
they wanted ordinary citizens who were "normally im-
peded from participating in civic issues, and/or not
readily perceived as effective stakeholders." They
wanted people, in short, who needed only a supportive
and structured forum to free up their creative participation in community affairs. Looking back over the
process, project organizer Roberta Ryan believes the
diversity of the participants "gave us incredible vitality."
It also supported the legitimacy of their findings in the
eyes of a diverse audience of officials and citizens.

One thing these very different citizen jurors had in
common: They all loved their community. One described it vividly as "one of the jewels of the Sydney
beach scene. It's actually quite a small enclosed valley, with a beautiful piece of remnant bushland in the
Bronte gully, flowing down to a not very large beach
with beautiful headlines and rock platforms." Another
said, "It's a very special shape, a land-form shape. It's
very sort of cradling, you know, it's cradling of its community."

After reading detailed briefing papers, going to several orientation meetings, and getting to know one another a bit, the citizens' jury formally met in the city
council chambers for three days. They read more reports, grilled expert witnesses – including a scientist,
a deep ecologist, an engineer, and a community educator – and deliberated together assisted by a professional facilitator. When they were finally ready, their
recommendations were presented to representatives
from their city council, NSW EPA and its Stormwater
Trust, and to members of their community in a formal
ceremony.

The team that organized the project worked hard to
make sure that the citizens' jury's recommendations

would be taken seriously by engaging local, state and Commonwealth officials as sponsors and by ensuring the integrity of the process. As organizer Ryan said, the city council knew "that the recommendations coming to them on this project [would] be a set of ideas that have had more rigorous scrutiny than any other form of input that they could have into their decision making."

COMMON SENSE COMMUNITY WISDOM

The jury's recommendations were remarkably creative, practical, and achievable, including many low-cost suggestions utilizing community information and participation. As a local radio reporter noted, "They cut across education, research, regulation and urban planning, and they were simple, but good ideas."

These were the sort of recommendations that I like to call "common sense community wisdom." This jury's integrated, sustainable approach, aimed at a broad range of stakeholders, was remarkably sophisticated, especially considering they knew so little about the problem just weeks before. I would like to share some of what they said, to show you what I mean by common sense community wisdom.

The jury avoided dependence on high-tech "end of the pipe" solutions. Instead, they talked about a community mulching station for clippings and leaves, a public car-washing space in which run-off could be controlled, bins and ashtrays in strategic places, using porous materials for car parks (parking lots) so water could soak into the ground instead of running off, setting up practice-display houses and businesses to model sustainable water practices, and supplying police with cameras to photograph stormwater law violations.

The jury added that their primary high-tech solution – monitoring invisible chemical pollutants – should "have a participative and educative focus, utilising local knowledge and resources," and therefore, it "needs to be conducted in partnership with community groups, such as schools, precincts, surf clubs, Beachwatch, Streamwatch, etc.; and universities linking to students doing internships and research projects." They also wanted the results of the monitoring widely and regularly publicized.

In other words, they wanted the community *involved*. The citizen jurors knew that pollution prevention ultimately would require the informed participation of everyone, from businesses to children to tourists, and so they issued recommendations addressed to them all. They even instructed bureaucrats to practice "integrated approaches" that included educational and participatory activities as well as engineering solutions.

Their advocacy of "education and participation" included "building knowledge, attitudes, skills and behaviours through involving the community with stormwater issues, from whatever starting point they are at, and through whatever means most suits their needs" – from informative signs to street festivals to school curricula to public performances to special briefings for new residents.

During the information-gathering part of the deliberations, the jury had listened to indigenous perspectives as well as others. As a result, they developed sophisticated environmental, cultural and historic sensibilities that were demonstrated by their use of the term "permanent visitors" to refer to residents like themselves. Tourists were "temporary visitors." The jurors were, in effect, saying "We're all just visiting here. We need to steward this place while we're here, for those who will come after."

Their understanding of the systemic dynamics of the problem was reflected in their admonition that the flow of water had to be not only reduced, but also slowed and absorbed, to prevent erosion. They advocated increasing the ratio of pervious to impervious surfaces in all areas of their community, including reducing the amount of ground covered by construction at any building site, so that water could soak into the ground. To contain and take up the run-off, they advocated increasing the planting of deep-rooted vegetation, as well as the installation of tanks to hold and recycle rainwater for other uses.

In other words, they had some fairly sophisticated suggestions – not the kind of shallow answers they would have given if some pollster had asked for their off-the-cuff stormwater opinions a few weeks earlier.

REAL CITIZEN ENGAGEMENT

The jury, which was originally due to dissolve on completion of its immediate task, felt spunky enough to request that the city council report to them on progress regarding their recommendations, and to attend to jury members' subsequent comments about that progress.

Mayor Pearce was worried at first about the possible consequences of sponsoring the citizens' jury.

> It might have finished up in a shambles. [But] in fact what we have seen is the capacity of your local citizen, your local resident, or your local visitor, to absorb and analyze some very detailed technical information, to think strategically and to think outside of the square, to coin a cliché, and pull in different strands of what are otherwise and all too often separate and discrete disciplines ... [Their] recommendations are ... very broad, they're also achievable, and they're extremely creative. They're not all big dollar items.

When asked by radio reporter Natasha Mitchell if he was interested in using citizens' juries to address other issues, Mayor Pearce replied, "I think this is a very exciting initiative and procedure for achieving greater levels of public involvement. I'd encourage other local governments to do it. I think elected people and those who are in a representative structure, have got nothing to fear from involving the broader community." (Mitchell and de Blas, 2001)

Citizens' juries

These stories from India and Australia are but two examples of what may be the most popular form of citizen deliberative council – the citizens' jury. In it, a group is selected to fairly reflect the diversity of a particular population. They proceed to learn about and deliberate on an issue that concerns that larger population. For three to five days, they hear and cross-examine a broad spectrum of experts and then craft their recommendations, which are publicly presented to official bodies (councils, committees, agencies, etc.) and also to the public, often through the media. Usually an advisory committee containing authorities who represent the full range of opinion about the issue being discussed oversees the fairness of the whole process.

The Jefferson Center, a nonprofit organization in the U.S. founded by citizen deliberation pioneer Ned Crosby, has organized more than thirty Citizens Juries® in the U.S. in the last twenty-five years.* The topics covered include urban solid waste, property tax

---

* The Jefferson Center has trademarked the capitalized version of the phrase Citizens Jury®, and has reserved the use of the phrase in the United States for citizen deliberative councils overseen by them. Similar efforts that do not use that phrase, or that are undertaken in other countries, do not require their involvement or approval.

reform, physician-assisted suicide policy, the future of public schools, environmental risks, at-risk children, health care reform, various budget priorities, and mayoral, gubernatorial and presidential candidates. They considered issues of a church and several school districts as well as the concerns of numerous cities, counties, states and the whole United States. They discovered that there is no collective issue, and no level of social organization, for which a Citizens Jury® would not provide useful insight and guidance.

Planning cells

A few years before Ned Crosby developed Citizens Juries in the U.S., Peter Dienel developed "planning cells" *(Planungzellen)* in Germany.* Although similar to Citizens Juries in many respects, planning cell projects are unique in that a number of more or less identical juries (or "cells") are held simultaneously, usually in different locations, each with about twenty-five members. The conclusions of the diverse cells are collected, compared and then compiled into one "citizen report" by the organizers/facilitators. After participants have the opportunity to review the composite report, it is presented to the sponsor, the media and other interested parties. Most German planning cell projects are commissioned by government bodies, and there is a

---

* Incidentally, the discovery of planning cells and Citizens Juries is a case of independent, almost simultaneous discovery reminiscent of Newton and Leibnitz's development of calculus and Darwin and Wallace's discovery of natural selection. Neither Crosby nor Dienel knew of the other when they made their innovations. They met many years later and were startled by the number of similarities, both in their process designs and in their personal lives.

contract between all of the parties involved that requires the commissioning body to publicize its response
to the final recommendations.

The largest project thus far that has used this approach was a national deliberation about a computer
networking issue that involved privacy concerns. The
process was sponsored by the federal government, and
consisted of twenty-two simultaneous four-day planning cells involving five hundred citizens in eight towns.

Danish-style consensus conferences

Denmark is the only place in the world where I have
found this sort of citizen deliberation institutionalized
as an ongoing part of the operations of government.
Once or twice a year, when the Danish Parliament decides to consider new policy to deal with some major
technological issue, they convene a form of citizen council, called a consensus conference, to review it.

The Danish government has a special office, The
Danish Board of Technology, similar to the now-abol-
ished U.S. Congressional Office of Technology Assess-
ment. When asked by Parliament, this office convenes
a panel of fifteen ordinary citizens selected to represent the diversity of the Danish population. It then
assists the citizen panel in studying and recommending policy guidelines for the particular technology Parliament is considering. In 1999, for example, a citizen
panel investigated genetic engineering of food.

The members of the consensus conference's citizen
panel begin by reading briefing papers. Then they discuss with the Board of Technology organizers the questions that come up for them. The citizen panel decides
which experts, from across the spectrum of opinion on
the subject, they want to have testify before them. A
public consensus conference is then held in which the
lay panel interviews these selected experts – who, as

Frances Moore Lappé notes, may be surprised to find themselves *on tap* to the citizenry, instead of *on top* of the decision-making process. When the testimony is over, the citizen panelists are professionally facilitated to a consensus statement about what they think should be done about the technology. Their findings are presented to the government and to the press and sometimes citizen study groups are organized around the country to discuss the report.

Like citizens' juries, Danish-style consensus conferences are remarkable for the extent to which their process ensures that the results cannot be credibly attacked as biased. This model has been successfully applied in over a dozen other countries. Consensus conference organizers usually follow the following steps (informed largely by Grundahl, 1995):

LAYING THE GROUNDWORK FOR A CONSENSUS CONFERENCE

1. Pick a salient topic, not too broad, not too narrow, that involves some real conflict and expertise. The topic chosen is one of current concern for the legislature, who may be considering formal legislation on the subject in the next six months or so.

2. Choose a steering committee of known partisan authorities who represent different and opposing perspectives; who are familiar with the full scope of the topic; and who are willing to support an unbiased effort. This steering committee will oversee the organization of the consensus conference and the fairness of its informational materials.

3. Advertise in newspapers for volunteer lay participants, requesting a one-page letter describing the volunteer's background and reasons for wanting to participate.

4. From the 100-200 replies, choose about fifteen who roughly represent the demographic breadth of the country's population and who lack prior knowledge of or partisan interest in the topic.*
5. Commission a background paper that maps the political terrain surrounding the issue. Have it screened and approved by the steering committee.

PREPARATORY WORK WITH THE LAY PANEL

1. Organize an initial preparatory weekend meeting at which you discuss the background paper with the lay group and work with them to formulate questions for experts. During this time, provide opportunities for the lay panelists to get to know one another and develop their ability to reason together.
2. Assemble an expert panel that covers the technical and scientific dimensions of the problem, as well as its ethical and societal implications. Include significant stakeholder representatives.
3. Organize a second preparatory weekend meeting in which the lay panel discusses background readings provided by the steering committee, refines their questions and revises the expert panel list to suit their needs.

---

* Note re 3 and 4: Some Danish panels have been picked by inviting participants from an age/gender balanced random selection of 1200 Danes from the central registry of the population. From the respondents, twelve to sixteen competent citizens are selected who together provide demographic diversity (gender, age, education, occupation, and geography) for the panel. (From correspondence between Lars Torres of AmericaSpeaks and Lars Kluver of the Danish Board of Technology, relayed to Tom Atlee by Torres 10/8/2002.)

4. Request that the experts prepare succinct oral and written responses to the group's questions, using language understandable by ordinary people.

HOSTING THE CONSENSUS CONFERENCE

1. Announce an open public forum – a consensus conference – in which the lay and expert panels will meet together, attracting media, legislators and interested citizens in a large public building.
2. On Day One of the actual consensus conference, have each expert speak for 15-30 minutes, then answer follow-up questions from the lay panel and, as time allows, from the audience.
3. After the public session, have the lay panel retire to discuss what it has heard.
4. On Day Two have the lay panel publicly cross-examine the expert panel, who are then politely dismissed, along with the public audience.
5. For the remainder of Day Two through Day Three, let the lay group deliberate, with facilitation available to use as they wish, and prepare a report that summarizes their points of consensus and disagreement. The lay panel fully controls the report's content, but may be assisted by secretaries and editors.
6. On Day Four give the expert panelists a chance to correct outright factual misstatements in the report, but not to otherwise comment on it.

PUBLICIZING THE RESULTS OF THE CONSENSUS CONFERENCE

1. Arrange for the group to present its report at a national press conference. Most reports are 15-30 pages long, clearly reasoned and nuanced in judgment.

2. Publicize the report and engage the public with it, using local dialogues, leaflets and videos.

SIXTEEN BRITONS WEIGH THE MERITS OF PLANT BIOTECHNOLOGY

Details of specific Danish consensus conferences are difficult to find in English. Luckily, consensus conferences have been used twenty-eight times in fourteen countries outside of Denmark, including two in the UK – one on plant biotechnology in 1994 (before any biotechnology products had reached the open market) and one on radioactive waste management in 1999. Geoffrey Lee, one of the lay panelists in the 1994 conference, described his experience in Joss and Durant's *Public Participation in Science*. His account, summarized here, gives us a provocative feel for these events.

Lee, a bank operations manager, answered an ad in his local paper, sending in a letter of interest. After being accepted, he was soon deluged with prepared information on plant biotechnology. His first preparatory weekend was held in Oxford September 2, 1994. The sixteen lay panelists were eight men and eight women, ranging in age from eighteen to sixty-five. They got to know each other over dinner amidst pleasant college surroundings. They studied hard all weekend and heard from a scientist, an industrialist, a regulator and an environmentalist – all offering different views. Although Lee found it all quite overwhelming, he also noticed he was beginning to make sense of the issues involved.

The lay panelists, who had some major differences at the start, discussed their subject incessantly, even over meals and at the pub. As their knowledge of the subject expanded, they began to wonder if they would ever get a report done in the few days they had together. They were also concerned about how much their facilitator was getting involved in the content of their discussions, rather than just sticking to the process. At any rate, as exhausted as he was, Lee returned home excited about what lay ahead.

THE HEAT TURNS ON

During the second preparatory weekend, in Abingdon, the lay panelists began to feel real pressure. Reporters and TV people were there to interview them and watch the proceedings. Some were suspicious that the panelists were biased, and that the whole thing was "an industry public relations exercise." Undaunted, the panelists heard from more experts, some of whom they had had a role in choosing. Lee reported that under questioning, some opposing experts "came very close to blows, much to the amazement of the lay-panel members." The panel seemed to have felt quite empowered, rather than manipulated. They were quite involved in many aspects of planning the final conference – to the extent that they felt they had spent too much time planning the stage layout rather than on selecting their roster of experts and on the best strategy for questioning them.

Between that weekend and the public consensus conference, many lay panelists tried to do research on the subject in their communities, only to find that hardly any of their fellow citizens were interested in plant biotechnology.

When the panelists arrived at London's Regent's College for the public consensus conference, they were all happy to see one another and eager to get on with it, but were anxious about appearing on stage before a large audience. They checked out the stage layout the night before. Bright and early the next morning, they were already being interviewed by media who were trying to predict the tone of their final report. After official introductions, welcomes and explanations to the sizable audience, the day's interrogation of experts began. All the lay-panel members asked questions, made comments, and soon started to enjoy the debate.

The experts – researchers, company representatives, environmentalists, and consumer groups – treated them well. Environmentalists in the audience, however, expressed doubt in their ability to understand the technical complexity of the subject well enough to decide on policy recommendations. Lee felt they missed the point. "We were not there to make technical judgments, or necessarily come to a decision...[but] to reach agreement as to the way that the general public...would wish the research to proceed and, if necessary, be controlled."

CONSENSUS CAN BE HARD, REWARDING WORK

By mid-afternoon the second day, they adjourned with massive amounts of information, reconvening in their hotel at 5 p.m. to write their report. This was a closed session, from which they kept even their facilitator.

Lee wrote: "None of us had any experience of how to conduct this part of the exercise and, for reasons of impartiality, we had been given very little guidance. We were given a deadline of midnight by which time we had to have our report ready for the printers." It was not to be.

Which is not to say they did not try hard. They elected Lee chair, and then made folders for each of the seven main questions they had asked the experts. Each person wrote down his or her thoughts on each question, which they filed in the folders. Then they separated into small groups, in order to have two or three panelists write a response to each question based on the notes in the folders. Afterward, they planned to circulate the responses to each panelist, "so that every panelist would have an opportunity to contribute to every section of the report." They were still working in their small groups when they adjourned for dinner at 9 p.m.

The group found that the effort to make sure there were no disagreements was exceedingly time-consuming. When it became obvious they were not going to make their deadline, they began working through each question together as a group. As the second deadline passed in the wee hours of the morning, and still progress was slow, tempers began to fray. "But we all decided we were not going to fail at the final hurdle," Lee wrote, considering it "no mean achievement" that no violence erupted from the lost tempers. "The word 'consensus' [took] on a whole new meaning for most of the panel...[T]here is nothing like finding yourself faced with a conflict of opinion at about two in the morning for testing the depth of conviction."

At 5:30 in the morning – twelve sleepless hours after convening to seek consensus – they raced their report off to the printer and, after refreshing themselves and having breakfast, "appeared on the platform looking bright eyed, bushy tailed and totally in control" at ten o'clock. Their report arrived from the printer half an hour later. Various panelists delivered various parts of the report, various experts commented on it, and various audience questions were taken before the conference ended precisely at noon.

THEIR FINAL REPORT

In their report, the panel noted both potential benefits and potential risks of the technology (including ones demonstrated many years later, such as the transfer of genes into related crops and the emergence of resistant pests). They critically noted efforts by researchers and producers to "create a market for their products, instead of the market expressing a need or desire for the products" – as well as the inability of laboratory experiments to predict potential biotech disasters, particularly long-term effects. Among other things, the panel called for:

- regulation and control of the technology, moni-tored by an independent ombudsman and inter-national safety standards;
- labeling genetically modified organisms in prod-ucts;
- controlled research in the public sector to maxi-mize benefits to all;
- support for plant biotech research specifically designed to benefit less developed countries, and the monitoring of multinational companies so they don't disrupt local farmers and their crops, acknowledging the value of appropriate technol-ogy and sharing "the profits derived from the con-tinued use of plants derived from the gene bank in the country of origin";
- more stringent monitoring of biotech patents and revision of patent law, since "the goalposts are being moved to the advantage of multinational companies";
- the use of consensus conferences as part of the parliamentary decision-making process in En-gland, as it was in Denmark.

The report was widely reported in the media. Lee's primary criticism of the process itself was that there was insufficient time for the panel to do as good a job as it wished. He recommended at least another prepa-ratory weekend.

I can imagine not only having more time, but hav-ing subsequent consensus conferences on the same topic to (a) evaluate how well legislators were handling the issue in light of previous consensus conference recommendations, (b) identify problems in the regula-tory process, and (c) make any new recommendations needed. Such an iterative process would allow the whole society to learn, over time, how to best deal with a com-plex and constantly changing issue such as biotech-nology research.

Further Questions

I consider these citizen deliberative councils to be remarkable innovations. We face daunting issues and technological developments. Many of us feel concern that unpredictably powerful technologies and social problems are developing with virtually no effective input from citizens, certainly nothing like the kind of thoughtful, full-spectrum deliberation that we've seen in the stories above. Would we not be better off if we created a strong public demand for this kind of real participation in our governance processes?

Of course, there are a host of other questions to be considered. What would a political system based on citizen deliberation look like? How would it work? How might official citizen deliberations relate to other parts of government?

And what explains the capacity of citizen councils to come forth with the kind of common sense wisdom that we have always wanted from our public and private leaders and deliberative bodies, and so seldom get?

CHAPTER **14**

CITIZEN DELIBERATIVE COUNCILS

Democracy works poorly when individuals hold preferences and make judgments in isolation from one another.

— MARK E. WARREN

The deliberative sense of the community should govern.

— ALEXANDER HAMILTON

Deliberation is a specific *form* of dialogue. Dialogue, as we have seen earlier, can include any conversation in which people explore together "questions that matter" (as World Café cofounder Juanita Brown calls them). I call these explorations "deliberative" when their intention is to produce decisions, policies, recommendations or collective action. I also call "deliberative" those explorations intended to produce at least greater understanding upon which decisions, etc., *could* be based. Deliberation involves a careful consideration of an issue, ideally weighing the full range of facts, factors, perspectives, options and consequences related to it, and often creating new options in the process.

Of course, to become wise as a democratic, collectively intelligent culture, we need more than decisions and recommendations. We need open-ended explorations, too – explorations that take us deeper into what matters to us. We need dialogues whose purpose is simply to create deeper understanding, or deeper relationships among the participants, or deeper connections to the realms of spirit and heart. We need ongoing, varied conversations that deepen our humanity and engagement with the world and with life. Such a larger culture of dialogue – which we will explore in Chapter 17 – creates a rich context in which citizen deliberation can be powerfully effective.

The citizen deliberations that I explore in this book are conversations that address the "well-being of the whole" – i.e., public concerns or the general welfare of communities or societies. Citizen deliberation involves people who hold diverse perspectives talking together about public issues in such a way that they can all be heard and their views can contribute to a deeper shared understanding. Often a facilitator, mediator or "designated listener" is crucial in helping people contribute and be heard, especially in highly polarized situations. Sometimes a well-designed structure that everyone has agreed to can serve as the "facilitator."

Although some people believe that computer dialogues are as effective as face-to-face encounters, my sense is that wise public engagement with public issues requires at least some significant measure of face-to-face communication. This opinion arises from a belief that creative deliberation involves more than the cognitive content of communication. There is more going on than just "the exchange of ideas and information." Considering the full dimensions of a public issue requires engagement with the full humanity of "the Other" – engagement which I believe is possible only in the presence of one another. That said, I believe that such face-to-face dialogue can and should be powerfully augmented by information and communication technologies, a subject I will explore further in Chapter 16.

Evoking the people's wisdom

In the last two chapters, we read stories about citizen deliberations in Canada, India, Australia and England. There are significant differences among these various efforts, but they also share important characteristics. In particular, they are all set up to use a small group conversation to promote a higher level of deliberation *throughout society.* I have chosen to call small deliberative groups that are intended to have a broad deliberative effect on a whole community or society "citizen deliberative councils." To my knowledge, this category has not been previously identified. Within the category of "citizen deliberative councils" I am including not only citizens' juries, consensus conferences and planning cells, but a number of other experiments, like the Canadian gathering, that meet a certain set of criteria I shall describe below. I have created this category to help us think about these models, understand them better and creatively apply them, because I believe they have a unique and pivotal role to play in the future of democracy.

Within the larger category of "citizen deliberative councils," I want to draw your attention to two major distinctions. The first distinction involves the purpose of the council. The second involves how it arrives at its conclusions.

Some councils, like the *Maclean's* experiment, are designed to clarify an overall vision or direction for the community or society. Other councils, like the Australian citizens' jury on stormwater and the English consensus conference on bioengineering, are designed to address some specific social or environmental problem. In the former, which we could call *visionary* citizen deliberative councils, participants may be more focused on generating shared understanding among one another and becoming creative together. In the latter, which we could call *issue-oriented* citizen deliberative councils, participants may be more focused on gathering and understanding information from briefing materials and experts, so they are all informed enough to sort out what should be done about the issue they are working on.

Councils also differ in how they make their decisions. Some approaches, such as the Canadian experiment in Chapter 12, are specifically designed to facilitate a consensus outcome. As noted earlier, I sometimes call these citizen consensus councils. Various approaches to consensus will be explored in Chapter 18.

Other citizen council models – such as citizens' juries – have not been designed with a consensus decision in mind, but instead rely on various forms of voting. They may produce a majority decision and/or articulate rationales for diverse opinions, much as the U.S. Supreme Court does. But even in these models, their process encourages some learning or shift in perspective in most or all of the participants, as they discover greater appreciation for the complexity of the situation in their considered search for "the common good."

Characteristics of a citizen deliberative council

Now let us look more closely at what all citizen deliberative councils have in common. I am defining citizen deliberative councils as having seven characteristics. I derived these characteristics from observing the similarities among a variety of models that all seemed to share a common purpose: to inform officials and the

public of what "the public interest" might be, if a diverse group of ordinary people were given some time to
really think about the issue and consider a variety of
perspectives.

Over the years, I have noticed that each of these
activities has these seven features:

1. *It is a real council.* The council is an organized
face-to-face assembly. It is not an open-partici-
pation public forum, nor is it primarily electronic.

2. *It is a fair cross-section.* The council is made up
of people selected such that their collective diversity fairly reflects the diversity of the larger
community or population from which they were
drawn. The council usually (but not always) numbers between twelve and fifty people chosen by
some form of random selection.

3. *It is very temporary.* The council is convened for
a limited number of days, usually a few days to a
week of actual meetings, sometimes distributed
over several weeks.

4. *It is made up of peer citizens.* The council's members deliberate as peer citizens, setting aside any
other role or status they may have. Although
sometimes chosen to bring particular viewpoints
into the council's deliberations, individual council members are not mandated to represent any
particular group.

5. *It is to some extent official.* The council has an
explicit mandate to address public issues or the
general concerns of its community.

6. *It is deliberative and balanced.* The council uses
dialogue, usually facilitated, to help all its diverse
members really hear one another, expand and
deepen understanding of the issues, and engage
together in seeking creative ways for their community to address the issues. Their explorations
reach beyond multiple-choice framings (unless

their mandate is to judge a set of fixed options already faced by the public, such as a field of candidates). When convened to address a specific issue, they have access to balanced information, often in the form of expert testimony.

7. *It generates a specific product.* At its conclusion, the council issues findings and/or recommendations to concerned officials and to the larger community from which its members came and to which they return. Usually there is an expectation that further community dialogue will be stimulated by the report, and sometimes this is organized as part of the overall process.

You may be familiar with many forms of deliberation—expert and blue ribbon panels, legislatures and various meetings of officials—that are like citizen deliberative councils. Like the councils, they meet face-to-face, address public issues, and issue findings or recommendations (characteristics 1, 5 and 7). What distinguishes citizen deliberative councils from these other groups are the councils' selection of typically diverse citizens, and the high quality of their dialogue as peers (characteristics 2, 4 and 6).

It is especially significant that the citizens on these deliberative councils are not selected because they have any status. Some may be important community decision-makers of some kind, but they are not on the council for that reason. Some members may be special interest stakeholders, and others may be homeless people. Some might have reputations as "players" of one sort or another, occupying some acknowledged position of power, privilege or expertise, while others may be janitors, students or store clerks.

The point is that in the council they are primarily citizens— members of their community. As peers, each is assumed to have a unique and equally important perspective on the affairs of their community.

The purpose of having a facilitator or mediator is to help ensure that everyone receives an equal opportunity to share their perspective and that each participant's views are received with respect. When differences in status are problematic, they need to be countered by the facilitator. What is central is that everyone has room to contribute their unique viewpoint and to participate in the collective effort to envision something better for their community.

Most public meetings do not qualify as citizen deliberative councils because they normally involve only an airing of views. This is not only true of the usual public hearings, but even of many collaborative "roundtables" intended to nurture relationships across community boundaries. Citizen deliberative councils, in contrast, are specifically designed to provide ample opportunity for thoughtful dialogue among the diverse participants. Each person can move towards wiser perspectives than they started out with – larger understandings that can be of use to the whole community.

Sometimes the issue which a citizen deliberative council has been asked to explore has been framed in terms of a limited set of narrowly defined proposals. In this situation, the public interest, as expressed by the council, may turn out to be "none of the above." Nonetheless, the council's feedback can help clarify directions to explore for further options, and subsequent citizen deliberative councils may then be convened based on a deeper and wider understanding of the issue at hand.

The seven features I describe above comprise the similarities in all the forms I group together as citizen deliberative councils. However, in defining this category we have only begun to understand the inner workings of these deliberative models and their social potential. How might we use these processes? What are the relative strengths of their different forms? Should we explore new forms? How might we integrate citizen delib-

erative councils into our political process such that
they would make a significant difference?

The Wisdom Council

Let us go all the way: What would happen if these citizen deliberative councils became a central feature of
our political system? What if we used them not only to
wrestle with specific issues, but also to provide the
overall common sense needed to guide our communities, our societies, our governments?

Consultant Jim Rough, the innovator who developed Dynamic Facilitation, has addressed these questions, and thinks such a use of these councils would
have a profound and positive impact. He has proposed
an annual national "Wisdom Council" for the U.S., made
up of two dozen citizens selected at random. It would
be established by Constitutional amendment. This diverse group would be facilitated to a consensus regarding what We the People are concerned about and what
we want. Rough's brilliant innovation is described in
his book *Society's Breakthrough!*.

Since these Wisdom Councils would involve creative
dialogues instead of mere discussion and debate, their
impact would extend beyond their final statements.
Their regular occurrence would spread awareness of
the value of high quality conversation. It is reasonable
to expect that, as a result, more and more people would
give such real dialogue a try. As Rough pointed out in
a 1997 draft of *Society's Breakthrough!*:

> The Wisdom Council sets up a new kind of conversa-
> tion, one that is not a special interest battle. It is a
> conversation where people seek consensus on what
> is best for everyone. First, these are ordinary people
> like you and me, not representatives. They are free
> to say what is on their mind and to change their

minds. The group does not have to agree or disagree with some predefined issue. They can seek the real, underlying issues and reach consensus on problem descriptions, as well as solutions. Second, a skilled facilitator can assure what I call a "choice-creating" conversation, one that is respectful of all views, and which encourages creativity.

This new kind of political conversation will take place on the nation's center stage, drawing attention away from the normal political and legal arguments. Schools, editorial pages, and back porch talking will continue the new dialogues, developing a more informed and involved public. In addition, over time, the conversation will build and articulate a national consensus.

In fact, Wisdom Councils could be formed in any community, county or state. Rough's Center for Wise Democratic Practices is encouraging their use wherever a coherent, visionary citizens' voice is needed. At the time of this writing, there have been several Wisdom Council experiments in both corporations and communities. To find out the latest, check out *Wise Democracy.org.*

Where does the wisdom come from?

I have repeatedly suggested that citizen deliberative councils are capable of generating wisdom – specifically, a highly developed form of community common sense. Why is that so?

As noted earlier, an important dimension of wisdom is perspective – the ability to see different aspects of a situation and how they fit together. The more different facets of a situation we can take into account, the more inclusive, appropriate, effective and benign – in other words, the *wiser* – our solutions and actions will be.

This has intriguing implications for politics and governance. The fact that different people have different experiences and perspectives suddenly becomes a resource for developing wisdom. But this will only be true if those differences can be used creatively, instead of to undermine each other, as is usually the case in adversarial political systems. That is where dialogue comes in, since it is "shared exploration towards greater understanding, connection and positive possibility." Through dialogue, the *interactions* among people's differences can bring forth greater understanding, deeper relationships and more fruitful possibilities. Much of the power of deep dialogue comes from the way it connects people to their core commons and generates resonant intelligence (see Chapter 4).

In addition, citizen deliberative councils do not just involve diversity, they involve *a particular community's* diversity. Thus the collective view of life seen through the eyes of the community's council is comparable to the collective view of life seen through the eyes of the community. This I call *reflective* diversity.

As citizen deliberative councils engage in dialogue, they draw upon their differences to produce greater understanding. In the process, they tap into their shared humanity and creativity to generate *options that make sense from all their diverse perspectives.* These options reflect the community's best "common sense," their shared sense of what is needed.

So it is *by design* that citizen deliberative councils generate wisdom. Such wisdom, while it may not be absolute or eternal, is highly relevant for that community at that particular time. Since it arises out of that community, it is readily usable by that community. Through the council process—including community dialogue—the community discovers its own common sense wisdom.

In addition to existing and proposed forms of citizen consensus council, there are a number of ways that we could experiment with the basic model to generate even more wisdom to guide our communities and societies. Citizen deliberative councils could receive expert testimony from a wide variety of sources, including leaders of diverse spiritual traditions and ecumenical efforts. They might also call upon scientists grounded in the holistic "new paradigm" sciences, including ecology, complexity theory, cultural anthropology and consciousness studies, to offer a broader perspective on the issues they are addressing. Facilitators could lead citizens in exploring possible futures, and in processes that foster systems thinking. In addition, they could help participants to honor and integrate all the diverse intelligences available within, among and beyond them—emotions, rationality, stories and the vast intelligences of nature and spirit.

Much exploration and experimentation could and should be done in all these realms—as long as we remember that we are seeking *democratic* wisdom. Thus, the ultimate arbiter must be the integrated diverse voice of the community itself. The place for expert wisdom is on tap *for*—not on top *of*—community wisdom.

Current efforts with regard to citizen deliberative councils

Would it not make sense to institutionalize citizen deliberative councils—to set things up so that we can generate the wisdom of We the People, when and where we need it in our political and governing systems?

We could use common sense wisdom in:

- articulating what We the People feel and want
- developing inspiring visions for our communities and societies
- creatively and effectively addressing specific social and environmental issues

- evaluating ballot initiatives and legislation
- evaluating our government and the candidates who want to work for us
- monitoring how well the whole system is addressing our needs and responding to our dreams.

There are many ways we could institutionalize citizen deliberative councils to perform these functions. Several current initiatives are seeking to do that.

The first two functions listed above—articulating what We the People want and feel, and developing inspiring visions for our communities and societies—are particularly well suited to the Wisdom Council format.

The other functions—addressing specific issues, evaluating proposals and evaluating and monitoring politicians and governmental systems—could be done by citizens' juries, consensus conferences, planning cells and any other citizen deliberative councils that involve studying those issues and officials in detail.

In his book *By Popular Demand*, John Gastil describes how different citizen panels could perform different functions. He envisions citizen panels rating how well politicians align with the public interest. Then he proposes that those ratings be printed on the ballot next to the candidates' names. He also provides a way for citizen panels to evaluate ballot initiatives, to reduce the influence of special interests and big-budget advertising campaigns. Ned Crosby, the creator of Citizens Juries, launched an effort to actually do this at the state level in the U.S. *(healthydemocracy.org)*. Also, a leading proposal for a national ballot initiative process, the National Initiative for Democracy *(ni4d.org)* includes a similar proposal for randomly selected citizen councils to evaluate ballot initiatives.

It is also easy to imagine a Wisdom Council calling for a consensus conference to be convened around some specialized topic of concern to the members of the Wisdom Council.

In short, there are many proposals and possibilities for placing citizen deliberative councils at various points in our democratic process to make democracy more wise and responsive to the public good. However, some people question whether we should even venture down that road. They wonder whether this whole approach can be considered participatory enough to be called "democratic."

The participation of the people

Citizen deliberative councils are small, compared to the population – with usually only ten to fifty people in each one. The chance of being chosen to be part of one is relatively small. On the one hand, some would surely see this as a blessing, in the sense that most of us could go about our lives confident that "someone else" was doing good work on our behalf. On the other hand, lack of widespread involvement in deliberations as important as these councils could suggest that the effect of the process was undemocratic, disengaging citizens from participation. I think most readers would agree that we need more participation in politics and governance, not less.

Although these concerns are valid, they are unlikely to be a problem with citizen deliberative councils. In fact, just the opposite would most likely be true.

People turn away from politics *because their involvement does not make much difference.* The government rolls on, the politicians do what they do, and the citizens feel they have little influence on it all.

But citizen deliberative councils demonstrate that ordinary people can have a profound effect on public policy. *When citizens see that voices like their own actually count,* participation in all forms of active citizenship will most likely increase. In fact, many *new forms* of active citizenship may well arise from the lively political culture generated by citizen deliberative councils. For example, because council members are citizens themselves, they often recommend citizen involvement as part of the solution to the problems they're addressing. The Australian citizens' jury described in Chapter 13 did this very creatively.

Another approach to participation uses large numbers of citizens to augment council deliberations. Ned Crosby's Healthy Democracy (*healthydemocracy.org*) proposes including a large "televote audience" of 600-1000 people in the deliberations. While a citizen deliberative council of two dozen people would be deliberating about some issue at a central location, the televote audience would be studying briefing materials about the same issue, either individually at home or in small study circles in their communities. At a particular time, the citizen deliberative council and the televote audience would be brought together in a videoconference in which anyone in the televote audience could see and hear the council, and the council could talk to members of the audience by phone. The council would describe their deliberations so far and explain what sort of decisions they were leaning toward. They would take questions and comments from the televote audience. Then the televote audience would do an instant vote indicating their preferences, and that information would be given to the council to inform their final deliberations. The teleconference could also be viewed by a wider TV audience (including on the Internet) – and that audience could cast their own instant ballots on the issue, using high-tech means or just their phones.

Danish consensus conferences use another approach. As we saw, they include a day or two of open public hearings in a public auditorium, with legislators, activists, media and ordinary people in the audience. Then, after the consensus conference is done and their findings published, the sponsors often organize widespread public dialogues about those findings.

Media coverage is vital. *Maclean's* magazine arranged for significant media coverage of the Canadian People's Verdict meeting, both in their own July 1, 1991 issue and on television. The Internet, call-in shows and live drama provide further possibilities for interactive engagement.

Citizen deliberative councils draw together diverse viewpoints from the full landscape of public opinion, put them through a wisdom-generating process, and send the resulting wisdom back into the flow of public conversation. However, while citizen deliberative councils are at the center of my co-intelligent vision of a wise democracy, it is clear that they can only flourish within a larger "culture of dialogue." The conversations that happen in citizen deliberative councils arise out of and feed back into the eternally flowing river of public and private conversation that wends its way through every nook and cranny of society. Conversations are not just a tool for change. They are the medium through which all of us, together, understand and create the realities we live in. The more high-quality conversation a culture supports, the more vibrantly co-creative it will be.

There is a significant side effect of all this. The task of building a co-intelligent culture is different from many other kinds of social change and utopian vision because there is no arrival, not even in our dreams. The "final" result is a culture that can keep going – a sustainable, co-evolving culture that can learn from its experience and adapt and create in harmony with its circumstances. Such a culture will always be changing. It will never arrive at utopian "perfection," and none of us can predict how it will proceed.

Of course, our culture is already changing, faster and faster. But from the perspective of co-intelligence, we want that change to be accompanied with, and consciously co-created by, people who are learning and visioning together as a whole – as whole communities, whole states, whole societies.

Section IV

Citizenship

Toward a Wiser

Civilization

CHAPTER 15

CITIZENSHIP MEETS COMPLEXXITY

Scale, complexity and greater quantities of information impose ever-stronger demands on citizens' capacities. As a result, one of the imperative needs of democracy is to improve citizens' capacities to engage intelligently in political life.

— ROBERT DAHL

How will robust common understandings and the intelligence that builds upon them survive in a regime of virtually unlimited channels [of information] in which immediacy overwhelms memory and reflection?

— SEYMOUR J. MANDELBAUM

Note: In this chapter – and throughout the book – I use the word "citizens" to refer to all of us who live in and participate in co-creating our communities and societies. When I speak of our "citizenship," I am not referring to any official privileges and protections bestowed by the state, but rather to our active role in our communities and societies, whether we are "official" citizens or not.

In previous chapters we explored how citizen deliberative councils allow a diverse microcosm of a community to arrive at a sense of the public interest with regard to public issues.

Now let us take a closer look at why this is so important in our world today. My thesis in this chapter is that we, as a society, have reached the limits of our atomistic approach to citizenship – in which individual perspectives simply add up when we agree, or cancel each other out when they do not. In order to deal effectively with the world around us, we need a different kind of citizenship – one in which our differences can contribute to the creation of the common good through the creative use of diversity and the enhancement of collective intelligence.

Individual citizenship

There are many factors that point to the need for a different kind of citizenship, beginning with the decline of individual citizenship. Individual citizenship involves voting, staying informed, doing our recycling, speaking out about important issues, and so on. Many of you reading this have done a lot of these things, even while finding it hard to believe they make much difference. No matter what we do, things seem to get worse in very important and scary ways. We feel guilty. We just cannot keep up with all the issues and developments. It becomes harder and harder to muster the energy to do traditional forms of citizenship. So we shut down and focus where we think we *can* make a difference – at home, at work, with friends or family, in our private lives and through local volunteer work. We abandon the larger realms of political vision and action, especially at state, national and global levels.

This decay of individual citizenship is not the fault of individual citizens who drift way from active involvement. There are real forces seriously undermining the ability of citizens to make a difference. Most of those forces are not part of any conscious conspiracy.

Beyond individual citizenship

The crucial fact is that our shared world has become so complex and speedy that keeping up with it is quite impossible for any individual citizen. Thus, each of us cannot effectively exercise our *individual* citizenship in any but the most narrow sense. More and more, it looks like the only way we are going to be able understand and effectively, creatively engage with our rapidly evolving world is through interactive, holistic forms of citizenship like citizen deliberative councils. These forms of citizenship are designed to generate collective intelligence – the capacity to come up with effective responses, as a group, to the challenges that affect our collective well-being.

When individual citizens can no longer be well enough informed on all important issues to vote wisely for candidates or to speak out intelligently on the many problems and proposals they face, the idea of isolated citizens running the country (especially through non-dialogic activities like voting and polling) is like blind men controlling a car.

However, the alternative most people think of – having elites, bureaucrats and technocrats controlling the country – would mean abandoning democracy.

These are false alternatives. We now have the means for interactive, whole-system citizenship. We can design a society where microcosms of the community – temporary groups made up of ordinary citizens – can become *at least* as competent (and *at least* as wise) on any given issue as the elites, bureaucrats and experts. They can articulate truths of and for the whole community.

This means that we can now move to a higher level of democracy. It is a level of democracy that has never been possible before, a bright firebird rising from the ashes of our old, sorrowfully inadequate political culture.

To institute these new forms of citizenship, we will need leadership. Leadership is most co-intelligent when it increases the capacity of the led system to lead itself. In communities and societies, the most effective leadership involves creating institutions and cultures that help people self-organize wisely together. This is leadership we need, we can demand – and we can provide.

I think it is clear we are not talking about tinkering with the system – although it could use a lot of creative tinkering, and I support such tinkering. What I am proposing is a radical shift in the way we think about and do democracy.

I am not advocating such transformation because I think radical change is inherently a good idea. Sometimes it is and sometimes it is not. I am advocating serious transformation because I think it is absolutely necessary and I see no other choice. I believe democracy may well be *impossible* without citizen deliberative councils. We'll need citizens' juries, consensus conferences, Wisdom Councils and even forms that have not been developed yet. This realm of political innovation is vital to our future.

I feel this is true because what is wrong with citizenship now is something far deeper than the oft-cited problems of low voter turnout, corporate control of media and elections, and lack of time for citizenship. It is not that these recognized problems are not real and important. But the more profound problem is both relatively new and growing fast. It would continue to cripple effective individual citizenship even if we managed to deal with all the other forces corroding our democracy.

For lack of a better term, I am calling this problematic factor *complexxity*. (Yes, with two x's.) That is what is going to force us to change our democracy or lose it.

Complexxity

The double-x in this coined term refers to a higher level of complexity, a more complex complexity, that has come into being through the interaction of an increasing number of factors, some of which are listed below. Each of these factors is itself increasing in complexity and intensity, and together they create a situation in which it is not only impossible to become a truly informed citizen, but most people are so overwhelmed they don't even want to try. *Under these circumstances, it is impossible to generate society-wide collective intelligence using the existing political structures.*

Our collective problems are growing rapidly, with increasing crises. Clearly, we need society-wide collective intelligence more than ever before – and new political structures to generate that collective intelligence. Although I am open to other democratic innovations (and promote them on the *democracyinnovations.org* website), I am convinced that we especially need democratic structures like those I've been describing. I am also convinced that we can create them, since so many of them have been in use for years outside of mainstream political processes.

But to make this crystal clear, we need to understand complexxity. A short list of complexxity factors would include at least these three complexxity "megatrends":

1. OUT OF CONTROL VOLUME, QUANTITY, SCOPE AND SCALE

Cities are becoming bigger and more crowded with people, buildings, messages, and vehicles. Information and knowledge are exploding into infoglut, crowding out reflection and wisdom. The media are filled with incomprehensible numbers – billions of dollars, megawatts, gigahertz. The broad application of popular and powerful technologies is leading to the ubiquity of cer-

tain threats such as global warming, nuclear prolif-
eration, antibiotic resistance, environmental toxicity,
etc. As technologies grow more powerful and economic
systems become more interconnected and computer-
dependent, we become increasingly aware of our vul-
nerability. There is a growing sense of unease, a feeling that we are seriously out of our league here. As
Dorothy observed in *The Wizard of Oz*, "We're not in
Kansas anymore."

2. FRAGMENTATION

Increasingly, people are handling infoglut by custom-
izing the information they get, cutting out the information they do not want. An unfortunate side effect of
this is that it further undermines our common pool of
shared knowledge, our sense of a shared story and
destiny. Meanwhile, every field of human inquiry and
endeavor is becoming increasingly specialized and com-
partmentalized, usually with its own language, priorities, and sources of belief and confusion. Science, which
is supposed to provide objective common ground, has
proven almost as multifarious as religion, riddled with
competing theories, experts, and constantly shifting
assertions. Our senses of stability, reality, belonging
and meaning are under constant assault.

3. PACE AND NOVELTY

Most things – transport, communications, computers,
images on video screens, our lives, our children's lives
– are moving faster and faster, demanding that we keep
up or get ahead. The speed of change is phenomenal,
not just out in the world, but in the structure and content of our lives. The amount and speed of flow, of
motion, of things, of novelty, of demands on our attention is increasing with each new turn of events. Stock
market crashes, terrorist attacks, layoffs, new technologies – we cannot know what the next day will bring.
We only know we have to keep moving.

And all this is in addition to: the intrinsic and growing complexity and abuse of economic and natural systems upon which we are totally dependent ... the collapse of distance ... the dogged persistence and unbelievable interconnectedness of so many social and environmental problems ... and the stressful dissonance between our growing sense of impending disaster and the constant reassurances of political, economic and media authorities.

Interactive whole-system citizenship

So how, exactly, is a citizen supposed to deal with all this? How do we exercise "informed consent," to say nothing of real deliberation, in the face of such complexxity as this? And where does real, usable wisdom fit into this picture? Isn't it incredibly simpler just to turn away and work at our own lives, with maybe a bit of community service and charitable donations on the side? And if most of us do this, isn't it clear that our communities and countries will become rich soil for the invasive weeds of demagoguery and greed, for random acts of chaos, and for predictable, avoidable catastrophes? If we cease to care for the Commons we share, then the Commons will cease to care for us.

That is why I think these interactive, whole-system forms of citizenship (in particular, citizen deliberative councils) are so important. Although as individuals there is less chance that we would be selected for a citizen deliberative council than for jury duty, our most effective form of citizenship may be our support for and engagement with such councils. For those of us ordinary people who are chosen to serve on such councils, we will be able to take the time to fathom the issues we face, explore their connections, weigh diverse perspectives, and consider where we as a whole community or society should head next. Then the rest of us would have the opportunity to deliberate on a local level on these councils' findings, and to take political action that made sense to us. Furthermore, wherever these councils were held regularly, all of us – the whole citizenry – could start to learn from our collective experience and persistently pursue our shared visions of where we want our community or country to go.

All this is not just a great idea. It is an entirely new kind of citizen participation that is *required* by the new situation in which we find ourselves. As troubled as they were, previous democratic cultures faced nothing like our complexxity. Democratic citizenship in ancient Athens was practiced by propertied free men. They had time on their hands and only a city to think about. Democracy was reborn in a predominantly rural America where town meetings made sense. People knew each other and shared the immediate experience of their problems and the consequences of their collective solutions. Their lives were busy but far slower paced and less cluttered than ours.

It is becoming painfully clear that things have moved light years beyond that. Those early communities are now fragmented, populations have exploded, and we are left with hundreds of millions of isolated citizens plugged into mass media and vast systems functioning partly on automatic and partly through the manipulations of elites and multinational conglomerates.

An example of the crisis in complexxity

Here is a particularly provocative example to show why we – We the People – need the innovations described in the last section:

Among the many issues raised by the 9-11 attacks on the U.S. are some that were raised earlier by high-tech guru Bill Joy. Joy – whose credentials include co-founder and Chief Scientist of Sun Microsystems, co-

chair of a presidential commission on the future of information technology research, and co-creator of Java
and Jini – published a widely discussed article in the
April 2000 *Wired* magazine entitled "Why the Future
Doesn't Need Us." He pointed out that we are developing technologies – biotechnology, nanotechnology, robotics, and others – that will probably enable individuals or small groups in the near future to effectively
(and affordably, and perhaps accidentally) wipe out
civilization or higher forms of life on earth. He asked
the question: "If our own extinction is a likely, or even
possible, outcome of our technological development,
shouldn't we proceed with great caution?" He went so
far as to suggest that we should limit our pursuit of
certain kinds of knowledge in order to prevent breakthroughs that, once made, would make our extinction
virtually inevitable. I summarize his inquiry as,
"Shouldn't we have second thoughts about developing
these technologies in the first place?"

This is a very thorny question, very charged, with
profound significance for virtually every aspect of our
society. But take another look at the question:
*"Shouldn't we have second thoughts about developing
these technologies in the first place?"* It raises some
other very disturbing questions:

- Who is the *WE* that needs to reflect on Bill Joy's
  question?
- What exactly would such reflection look like?
- How do you suppose decisions would be made
  on such a question?

WHO IS THE "WE" THAT CAN DEAL WITH ALL THIS?

We need to become more sensitive to what we mean
when we say "we" are doing this, or "we" should be
doing that. We need to shift our thinking from a vague

"lots of individuals" sort of WE, to a very specific organic, systemic sort of WE – in other words, institutions that embody the best collective wisdom, voice and
will of We the People.

In our own heads and in our families and workplace conversations, we can reflect on Bill Joy's question. However, our *individual* responses to that question are more or less irrelevant unless there is a way
for our entire society, or even the world, to come to a
wise judgment on this amazingly complex issue. Failure to have a *collectively intelligent* response would
constitute failure to have *any* intelligent response.
Since the self-destructive capabilities we are talking
about are collective, the response must be collective.

Any political system is an attempt to create collective coherence, to create a "we" that can respond to
this kind of situation. One approach is for one sub-
group to have the power to reflect and act *as* the whole
community. In a dictatorship, for example, that is usually done by suppressing all perspectives that differ
from the dictator's. The dictator acts *as if* he were the
whole country – a phenomenon associated with "the
royal We" with which monarchs refer to themselves.

In a representative system, by contrast, the representatives reflect and act (at least theoretically) *on behalf of* the whole community or country. If their system is majoritarian, authority is given to the majority.
Diversity is framed in terms of minorities, who strive
to become the majority – or to be part of a majority
coalition. They can then act *as if they* are the whole
society, marginalizing *other* minorities that they disagree with.

Collective intelligence is undermined to the extent
that social coherence is achieved by suppression or
depowerment of diversity, dissonance and minority
perspectives. On the other hand, collective intelligence
is enhanced by the creative use of diversity. Any system – any collective entity – that utilizes its diversity

creatively will most likely have a high degree of collective intelligence.

Part of intelligence is not making the same mistake twice. Another part is not making a predictably disastrous mistake, such as destroying civilization, even once. Bill Joy and others are announcing to the collective consciousness where critical danger lies.

Do the institutions exist to help these warnings sink into our collective awareness, our collective behaviors, and society's policy-making activities? Or are these vital warnings lost in the eddies and cyclones of information swirling every which way in a thoroughly distracted collective mind?

What would we have to know and do in
order to avoid this ultimate collective folly?

By now, you know many of the answers to that question. I have described them in this book. They are not all the answers, but even those answers you already know would, if instituted, take us quite far in addressing not only Bill Joy's question, but all our other collective problems, as well.

The needed breakthrough

I'd like to distill into a two-step program what we have already explored as a path to breakthrough:

1. **Escape the divide-and-conquer box of individual citizenship, and ground ourselves in interactive, whole-system citizenship.** Individual intelligence can no longer grapple with the complexxity of modern life. Nor, in fact, can specialized interest groups – even public-interest nonprofits – solve our problems for us through their political battles. Interest group arguments are almost inevitably one-sided. Raging partisan battles – and the over-

whelming cacophony of information that results from them – breed and encourage co-stupidity. Hopes for democracy, survival and a decent civilization lie primarily in enhancing and exercising *the collective intelligence potential of the whole community or society through processes that allow us to respectfully and creatively engage with our differences regarding public issues.*

2. **Generate and access collective intelligence by effective dialogue among diverse viewpoints.** We are not talking here about diverse *people*. We are talking about diverse *viewpoints*. In addition, we are talking about *effective dialogue* – high quality powerful conversations. The extent and effectiveness of both diversity and dialogue are the keys to the kind of public participation that can generate or access collective intelligence. Partisan arguments between "both sides" will not cut it anymore. This form belittles the complexxity we are dealing with, which involves far more than two sides.

None of the above is meant to suggest that there is no role for individual citizenship. We are, among other things, individuals, and we still face individual choices and are called to exercise our individual leadership – i.e., our conscious, responsible participation – in co-creating our communities and our world.

What this *does* suggest is that more individual citizenship needs to be focused not on isolated issues but on implementing new forms of democracy. We need to focus on developing collective intelligence at community and societal levels. Luckily, we do not have to reinvent the wheel. Most of the pieces are available and ready to be assembled into wheels and put on the cart so it can get rolling.

Public dialogue + citizen councils = a coherent WE to bring collective wisdom to society's collective power

Part of the huge crisis we are facing is a result of the imbalance in our development as a society. As we know from our experience with individuals, intelligence can be very high in one part of one's life and very low in another. We have all heard the stereotype of the mathematical genius who is not very smart when it comes to his personal life or relationships. Well, we could say that modern societies are like that, exhibiting extremely high collective intelligence when it comes to scientific research (an enterprise which often uses diversity creatively), and low-to-mediocre collective intelligence when it comes to politics (where majoritarianism, manipulated media, political parties, and scarcity of real dialogue restrict the creative use of diversity).

This imbalance creates a perilous situation. We have rapidly developed our power in the world, without a parallel development in our wisdom in using that power well.

In this book we have been exploring ways to effectively address the critical problems we face, including the ones Bill Joy points to so clearly. We know, for example, that we could create a wiser WE by convening a citizen council about biotechnology (or any of the challenges we face). This council would be randomly selected to be a microcosm of the rest of us. Not influenced by special interests, it would cross-examine experts and engage in facilitated dialogue to come to the sorts of conclusions the big WE – all of us – would come to if we had a chance to really study the issue together.

This is not the ultimate answer, but it is a good place to start, and it is *way ahead* of what we have now.

Of course, such councils don't just happen. They must be envisioned, established, empowered and convened. In doing so, we must distinguish between citi-

zen councils and broader public dialogue. Official citizen deliberations – thanks to a combination of microcosm structure, special resources (good information,
facilitation, etc.) and formal mandate – are empowered
to evoke a legitimate community-wide or society-wide
WE – an authentic, coherent, informed and wise voice
of We the People. This is distinct from the many broadly
dispersed public and private conversations in which
we as a society continually reflect on our collective situation in all our homes and communities.

Both kinds of conversation are vital. There is synergy between them. The thousands of broader conversations generate a field of "distributed intelligence" that
constitutes both the matrix for the emergence of a coherent voice of We the People and the vehicle that car-
ries that coherent voice into the everyday life of our
society. The citizen councils – as official, recognized
forums carefully designed to accurately reflect the larger
diversity present in our society and given a privileged
level of support for their deliberations – "ratchet up"
both the content and process of the broader public dialogue, making it wiser and giving it a coherent voice.

Furthermore, in order to institutionalize citizen deliberative councils, we will first need a whole host of
informal conversations – widespread citizen dialogues
– to help build a movement calling for such collective
forums. Once the forums are in place, we will need a
higher level of informal conversation throughout our
society to explore, debate, digest, refine, and apply the
insights generated by citizen deliberative councils.

In short, we need all the citizen deliberation and
dialogue we can get. Fortunately, we have a rich sup-
ply of additional methods and resources that can
complement the use of citizen deliberative councils and
help us exercise our collective, interactive, whole-system citizenship deliberatively and creatively. This larger
toolbox of resources is the subject of the next two chapters.

CHAPTER 16

MORE APPROACHES TO DELIBERATIVE DEMOCRACY

Citizen deliberative councils are part of a larger movement in the United States and throughout the world promoting deliberative democracy. At heart this movement is about faith in the power of real dialogue and deliberation to help us address our common problems.

As noted earlier, deliberative conversations are ones where our intent is to produce decisions, policies, recommendations or collective action – or at least, greater understanding upon which decisions, recommendations, or actions could be based. Deliberation involves a careful consideration of an issue, ideally weighing the full range of facts, factors, perspectives, options and consequences related to it, and often creating new options in the process.

Deliberative conversations are a vital part of the interactive, whole-system citizenship needed to deal with the complexxity of twenty-first century problems. There are currently many efforts underway that promote deliberation in a variety of ways. Up to this point, I have focused on citizen deliberative councils as I believe them to be an overlooked but extremely promising form of deliberation. Now I want to provide an overview of some other significant approaches to deliberation on social issues.

Broad public deliberations

One significant approach involves organizing widespread opportunities for the public at large to participate in small group deliberations. Among the institutions promoting and practicing this approach to citizen deliberation in the U.S., perhaps the most established is the **National Issues Forum** (NIF at *nifi.org*). It regularly asks Americans what issues concern them and then – with Public Agenda *(publicagenda.org)* and others – produces nonpartisan briefing booklets about selected critical issues. These booklets are widely used by civic organizations around the U.S. in a variety of local citizen forums and study groups to generate deliberative insights that are shared with the larger public and elected officials. The National Issues Forum provides a network of forum organizers, and sponsors workshops (**Public Policy Institutes**) to train people to be forum organizers in their own communities. Since its founding in 1981, NIF has worked closely with the **Kettering Foundation**, one of the United States' leading democratic research institutes.

A parallel activity is the **study circle** movement, involving small groups of people studying issues together. Although not all study circles deal with public affairs, issues like race, education, terrorism, youth problems and healthy neighborhoods are at the heart of the current rapid expansion of study circles in the U.S.

A study circle is a voluntary, self-organizing adult education group of between eight and a dozen people who meet several times to explore a subject such as a critical social issue. Each meeting commonly lasts two to three hours and is facilitated by a moderator who is also a group member, and whose role is to promote a lively and focused dialogue in which everyone has a chance to talk. Between meetings, participants read materials they were given at the end of the last meeting. These materials, usually provided by the organizers, are used as springboards for dialogue rather than as authoritative conclusions.

Leading the resurgence of study circles in the U.S. today is **The Study Circle Resource Center** *(study circles.org)*. Not only do they provide information packs and training, but they have pioneered the use of community-wide study circle programs in which citizens from many concurrent study circles convene together to form teams to take action to improve the situation they were studying. And since study circles are small, inexpensive, democratic and non-expert, they can be adapted to virtually any issue, and organized by any group.

Leonard P. Oliver's classic *Study Circles* tells the fascinating history of how study circles evolved. They were invented in New York in the 1870s, and hundreds of thousands of Americans participated over the next fifty years. Before they faded from the U.S., they were carried to Sweden by union and political activists, where they flourished. Today millions of Swedes participate in study circles every year, often subsidized by their government. Study circles were transplanted back into the U.S. first by Norman Kurland of the NY State Education Department in 1978, then in the mid-1980s by the NIF and the Domestic Policy Association, and finally – and most dedicatedly – by The Study Circle Resource Center starting in 1989.

Meanwhile, down in the grassroots, hundreds of other citizen deliberation and issue-study activities are being sponsored by religious institutions, nonprofit advocacy groups, civic organizations, salon networks, community colleges and others around the country who believe that citizens can best engage in public life when they talk together to reach deeper understandings about the issues they face.

Stakeholder Dialogues

When many people think about public participation these days, they tend to think about **stakeholder dialogues**. Stakeholder dialogues do not involve the general citizenry, per se, but rather engage selected representatives of diverse parties who have a particular stake (or interest) in a situation. Often this involves some controversial public issue. For example, environmentalists, loggers, ranchers, recreation professionals, community leaders, government regulators, and businesspeople are often brought together to address rural land use conflicts. They are helped to hear one another's perspectives, to get a big-picture view of the situation, and to then search together for common ground solutions. This popular approach emerged from the field of negotiation and **alternative dispute resolution (ADR)** *(acresolution.org and adrr.com).*

Many "whole system" stakeholder dialogues go far beyond negotiation. These include Future Search and Holistic Management:

Future search participants are chosen to represent the interests of significant portions of the organization or community concerned, including outsiders who have dealings with it. These fifty to a hundred stakeholders explore their shared past and the big forces that make up their current environment. They do not attempt to work through their differences, or to create a common statement for the generic guidance of the whole community or organization. Rather, they come up with shared visions, values and projects that they work on after the conference in volunteer teams, often creating notable effects on the whole organization or community. Their effectiveness is enhanced by the fact that they come from all over the system and – through the future search process – build ongoing relationships across social and institutional boundaries. See *futuresearch.net* and *Future Search* by Marvin Weisbord and Sandra Janoff.

Holistic management gathers decision-makers from all aspects of a situation, who then identify available resources – which includes everyone who will be affected by their decisions. They explore the quality of life needs that their decisions should address (including those of the people currently involved, of future generations and of ecosystems). All these are woven together into a short statement of purpose intended to embrace the needs of the whole and all its parts. This broad holistic goal is then used by all parties as a benchmark against which to measure their future decisions. A subsequent testing phase reaches back to often ignored considerations to make sure that none are being forgotten. See *holisticmanagement.org* and *Holistic Management* by Allan Savory.

An emerging form of *official* stakeholder dialogue is the **Consensus Council** *(governing.com/2assess.htm)*. In this approach, the Consensus Council is not the stakeholders themselves, but a government office that convenes stakeholders to address "issues that have proven immune to conventional legislative solution." The Council chooses a representative from every significant interest group with a stake in the issue and then helps them come to agreement on recommendations. The Consensus Council then passes this resolution on to the legislature.

An early success of this approach involved a 1995 effort to address the thorny problem of who should pay for polluted Superfund site cleanups. Existing state

laws assigned "joint and several liability" – which meant
that the current resident of a site could be liable for
pollution caused by a long-dead corporation. Although
obviously unfair, it was clear that someone had to pay,
or the sites would never be cleaned up. When industry tried to push through a bill abolishing "joint and
several liability," the legislature turned to the Department of Environmental Quality, who called on the
Montana Consensus Council (MCC).

The MCC convened a collaborative study group con-
sisting of representatives of four stakeholder groups –
local governments; state and federal agencies; public
and environmental advocacy groups; and potentially
liable businesses. This group met monthly for a year,
delving deeply into the complex issues involved and
exploring how other states dealt with the problem. They
finally came up with the idea of having an official "allo-
cator" hear the facts on each case and apportion liability according to twelve specific criteria, ranging from
whether a party caused the toxic release to how dangerous the release was. They also proposed an "orphan
share fund" to cover clean-up costs not included in
the liability apportioned for that site. Money for the
fund would come from taxes and fines related to toxic
industries. The group formalized their proposals into
two bills that they shepherded through the legislature.
The bills passed with extremely wide margins and the
issue has not shown up in the Montana legislature since
then.

Montana's experience with Consensus Councils
suggests that the idea may be good politics. Former
governor Marc Racicot was elected in 1992 on a con-
sensus-building platform. As soon as he took office,
he created the Montana Consensus Council by executive order. The success of his official Consensus Council in Montana *(discoveringmontana.com/mcc/css/
default.asp)*, and of a comparable one in North Dakota,
has led to an effort by a major mediation group, **Search**

for Common Ground, to have Congress establish a national Consensus Council (search *sfcg.org* for "United States Consensus Council").

Comparing and contrasting two complementary approaches

As I have described above, stakeholder councils are a valuable facet of deliberative democracy. I would like to compare them with citizen deliberative councils to better understand their diverse strengths and possible synergies – and to emphasize the unique and special contribution of the less well-known and used citizen deliberative councils.

In stakeholder dialogues the participants are already intimately connected to much of the relevant information regarding the issue being considered. This means no briefing papers need to be commissioned and no experts brought in. Furthermore, the fact that participants are quite conscious of their stake in the outcome means that they usually don't have to be paid to participate. Both these factors make stakeholder dialogues cheaper to convene than, say, a citizens' jury or consensus conference.

If there is conflict involved, a stakeholder dialogue is a powerful way to resolve it. Since the conflict is not between individuals but between broad stakeholder sectors, creative, well-publicized negotiations between respected members of each group can have a profound effect on real-world relationships among widely scattered individuals from all groups involved.

(Note that stakeholder dialogues are different from negotiations between unions and management, or between nations, in which participants are *officially* answerable to their constituents and procedures exist to make any agreements binding on all members of all groups. In stakeholder dialogue, on the other hand, participants only *informally* represent the people in their group, so broad support for any resulting agreement or legislation among like-minded people will be voluntary. Because of this, the selection of specific respected participants can be one of the most important tasks in organizing stakeholder dialogues.)

The ability of stakeholder dialogues to resolve polarized stakeholder conflicts has another interesting dimension. Stakeholder dialogues such as consensus councils are often very attractive to politicians trying to navigate between passionate partisans on both sides of a hot controversial issue. When a consensus council comes up with policy proposals that satisfy all sides, most politicians are more than happy to sign on, simply because of the political safety these proposals provide. Along with the cost savings, this factor can make stakeholder dialogues quite attractive to potential sponsors.

For more general social or environmental issues, however, or to consider the general state of a community, state or country, stakeholder dialogues may not be as suitable as citizen deliberative councils. In particular, to the extent stakeholder dialogues are made up of partisans, the general public may be interested in observing them, but may not identify with them. This can be a significant factor.

Most people do not have strong feelings about an issue until they learn more about it and/or until it has a significant and immediate impact on their personal lives. They may have opinions on all sorts of things, but most issues do not loom large in their busy days. Such people are more likely to identify with one or more citizens on a randomly selected citizen deliberative council than with the specially selected partisan advocates in a stakeholder dialogue.

So, for the purposes of generating a legitimate voice for "We the People," citizen deliberative councils may prove to be more potent than stakeholder dialogues, especially to the extent the former uphold the values, interests and life experiences of "ordinary people." Furthermore, the fact that these ordinary people – the members of a citizen deliberative council – *become* experts on the issue under consideration can serve as a role model, a message to other ordinary people that they, too, are able to become experts if they put a little time into it. At the very least, the ordinary person usually feels they can trust what these non-elite citizen council members come up with, simply because the conclusions of a council sound like something they'd have come up with themselves, if they'd had a chance to participate.

Although stakeholder dialogues often include community leaders or ordinary people representing the interests of the person-on-the-street, their positioning as "a stakeholder group" among other stakeholder groups may be seen to provide weaker advocacy for "the common good" and "the general interest" than a fully random selection of citizens – at least in the eyes of the general public. I expect this would be especially true where that random selection is "stratified" to make sure that the most visible and politically hot forms of diversity – such as gender, age, race, socioeconomic status, etc. – are adequately represented on the council.

In designing a new democratic order that will (a) engage people and (b) increase their sense of being heard and taken into account while (c) generating wise solutions and visions that (d) the broad public considers legitimate, it is vital to actually *research* how people perceive various council designs. In politics, perception is at least as important as reality. We want both the reality *and* the perception of both fairness *and* wisdom in the councils we institutionalize.

Finally, I would like to consider some possible synergies. The role of a citizens' jury or consensus confer-

ence is normally to evaluate and recommend the best
option(s) for dealing with an issue. Sometimes they create new options as well, but their central role is evaluation. It would seem, then, that a citizens' jury or consensus conference considering some issue might value
having, among all the options they are considering, at
least one option that is agreeable to all the stakeholders
involved. That doesn't guarantee that that option is the
best for the whole community or its average citizens.
But that is what a citizen deliberative council is convened to consider. What are the likely consequences of
these proposals *for the average citizen?* How do they
align with the values of our community?

One approach to a wiser democracy, then, could
involve various panels convening other panels. Not only
might a Wisdom Council call for a citizens' jury to fully
investigate some issue that the Wisdom Council doesn't
have sufficient expertise to address, but a citizens' jury
(or a Wisdom Council) might call for a stakeholder dialogue to generate a whole-system, conflict-resolving
proposal for them to evaluate on behalf of the larger
community.

My instinct is to keep citizen deliberative councils
central to all such processes, because most of those
who will be affected by any community decision will be
ordinary citizens, not just partisans and vocal stakeholders. Furthermore, average citizens are more likely
to view the problem-solving activities of a randomly
selected citizens council as more democratically legitimate than those of a select group of partisan stakeholders.

Ensuring the primacy of citizen deliberative councils over stakeholder dialogues also ensures that power
elites don't simply use stakeholder dialogues to calm
the waters of specific controversies, thereby maintain-
ing their control without addressing the broader, deeper
issues that tend to surface in certain citizen deliberative councils, including questions of power.

In closing this section, I want to stress that much of what I've said here derives more from my general understanding than from research data. This could and should be the subject of field research — and that is true for many of the possibilities described in this book. I can imagine few more productive lines of inquiry than discovering which kinds of dialogue and deliberation best serve which aspects of a wise democracy.

Still More Approaches to Deliberation

Several productive forms of deliberation and dialogue have arisen to explore the question of how people are influenced through their participation in these processes. Does respectful engagement with others who hold very different views result in a hardening of partisanship or a softening or even transformation of opinions and feelings? – or no change at all?

There is now good evidence that ordinary people change their views and grow much more sophisticated through relatively simple education and deliberation programs. In a practice called **Deliberative Polling**, a broad random sampling of several hundred participants are convened at a central location. They are polled on a selected public issue, and then exposed to broad-spectrum information on that issue, including written materials and panels of opposing experts and politicians, with whom they can interact. They deliberate together and then are polled again, with the before-and-after differences noted *(la.utexas.edu/research/delpol)*. In *The Voice of the People*, deliberative polling founder James S. Fishkin describes the first major experiment of this type, done in Manchester, England in 1994. He found that the changes were significant – but not always in the same political direction! His write-up makes fascinating reading.

Technology has enabled us to involve large numbers of people in deliberation. Some large-scale deliberative approaches use computers to link facilitated small groups. **AmericaSpeaks** *(americaspeaks.org)* organizes such well-publicized electronically augmented town meetings. They bring hundreds or thousands of diverse citizens together to publicly deliberate on selected issues and to develop shared agreements for future action. At various points in the process, ideas and votes are collected from the smaller groups by computer and votepad and integrated into summary statements by the organizing team. The findings are then projected on a large screen so everyone can see their collective ideas and opinions.

This process was used in a project called "Listening to the City," sponsored by New York City's Civic Alliance. This diverse coalition of business, community and environmental groups was formed to assist in rebuilding downtown New York City after the 9-11 World Trade Center attacks. It invited over six hundred diverse New Yorkers to work collaboratively to create guidelines for rebuilding downtown New York. The results of their deliberations called for a memorial, mixed-use buildings, a transportation hub, affordable housing and tree-filled open spaces, as well as planned next steps. These collaboratively created guidelines were posted at *civic-alliance.org.*

The February 2002 conversation was followed up in July with an even more ambitious conversation involving over four thousand New Yorkers – ten citizens and a volunteer facilitator at each of more than four hundred tables! Leading decision-makers from the Lower Manhattan Development Corporation and the Port Authority of New York and New Jersey were put one to a table, immersed in this sea of citizens where they remained in conversation for the entire day. (I see this immersion as one of the great strengths of the AmericaSpeaks approach.)

As a mark of their independence even in so structured a setting, the citizens turned down all the site plans and memorial proposals they had been asked to evaluate, urging planners to be more bold in creating a lively, affordable, diverse community with residential, cultural, educational, recreational and commercial functions including many green spaces and an appropriate memorial. Eight hundred people who missed the in-person event participated in twenty-six small group discussions online over several weeks, and their input was also included.

Such experiments suggest there is tremendous positive potential in combining high technology with large group deliberations. As we travel that road, however, we need to proceed with care. When technology is applied to support a culture of voting, we can be tempted to limit conversation to choosing among a few options or solutions. That could seriously dilute or constrict the potential productivity of the dialogue. Awareness of this can help us choose and use our technologies wisely to enhance, not hinder co-intelligence.

Technology can also inspire us to create larger and larger forums. We need to stay aware that, above a certain number of participants, we hit a point where the more people we add to the dialogue, the more challenging it becomes to sustain high quality engagement and open-ended exploration. At the same time, the journey to deliberative democracy supported by high technology can be a very productive one, in which there is a lot of experimentation with different approaches. For example, the Healthy Democracy proposal that we mentioned in Chapter 14 shows how we could complement a citizen deliberative council with a large televote audience using advanced teleconferencing technology.

There are, of course, far more deliberative initiatives in the U.S. than I have described here. But I hope

this brief introduction gives you a taste of some remarkable developments that are seldom adequately
covered by mainstream media. Above and beyond them
are the many deliberative activities taking place all over
the world. Here are a few highlights of that work.

Innovative deliberative efforts in the developing world

Two approaches used often to raise community consciousness and capacity in developing countries are
Technology of Participation® (ToP) and **Participatory Rural Appraisals** (PRAs).

Technology of Participation is a package of tools
developed by the Institute of Cultural Affairs *(ica-
usa.org)* to help a community or organization become
more aware of the whole situation they are dealing with,
create visions and strategies they can all say "yes" to,
and track the implementation of what they decide to
do. An example of this was described in the Chapter 2
story, "Awakening the power and wisdom of a community." ToP was originated in the U.S. and continues to
be used by consultants in the U.S., but has spread
very widely in the developing world and elsewhere.

Participatory Rural Appraisals are a family of approaches that enable poor people to express and analyze the conditions of their lives, and to come up with
shared understandings and actions to improve those
conditions. These conversations are initiated by outsiders who enter into mutual learning with the local
people. (Chambers and Blackburn, "The Power of Participation: PRA and Policy"). Approaches like this owe
much to the pioneering work of people like Brazilian
grassroots educator Paolo Friere, described in his classic *Pedagogy of the Oppressed.*

Perhaps the most remarkable and effective *official* participatory deliberation process I have heard about, short of the Danish consensus conferences, is the **Participatory Budget** of Porto Alegre, Brazil. Porto Alegre is a big city, the capital of its state, with over a million inhabitants. Every year, thousands of citizens and NGOs (non-governmental organizations) participate in deciding how to allocate the discretionary portion of their municipal budget – and to review how the previous year's budget was handled and what effects it created in their city.

Not only are big meetings held for this purpose in each of the city's sixteen regions, but public gatherings are also convened to review specific areas of the budget – city organization and urban development; transportation and mobility; health and social services; education, culture and leisure; and financial development and tax planning. These meetings establish priorities and elect representatives whose deliberations weave the priorities into an "Investment Plan" for the next year. The Plan is forwarded to city's elected executive council, who can modify it but not make any fundamental changes.

Since the program began in 1990, tens of thousands of households in poor neighborhoods have been connected to water and sewage systems, 25-30 kilometers of roads are paved each year in the poor and suburban areas of the city and there have been major improvements in education. Perhaps even more remarkable: More than seventy other cities have adopted the process. For a good overview, see "Popular Participation in Porto Alegre" by Szilard Fricska (see Bibliography).

For more detailed descriptions, see Jos Verhulst's "Orcamento Participativo" and Boaventura de Sousa Santos, Gianpaolo Baiocchi and Leonardo Avritzer's papers on "The participatory budget experiment in Porto Alegre, Brazil" (see Bibliography).

We can all look forward to the day when more cities around the world find the courage and sense to do this.

Ways to deepen our understanding about the future

Much of deliberation involves exploring our visions and weighing the consequences of our choices. Therefore, tools that help us deepen our understanding about the future are very important in deliberation. Among these tools are scenario work and visioning work.

Scenario work involves exploring alternative pathways to the future and how the future might turn out – and how we might respond – if we assume certain things will be true or if we play with certain variables. The idea is not to predict the future, but to get familiar with the possibilities. Although the future probably will not look exactly like any of the scenarios we explore, it will likely contain elements of them, and we will have developed a certain savvy flexibility and made some wiser decisions because we have already become familiar with them.

Scenario work can be used to better understand which future it makes sense to focus on. One of the most famous scenario projects occurred in 1991 in South Africa, the year after Nelson Mandela was released from prison. The country was abuzz with conversations about how to handle every sort of social problem and where the country should be headed. In the small town of Mont Fleur, Adam Kahane of the **Global Business Network** facilitated three three-day meetings of a multi-racial group of twenty-two respected leaders from across the political spectrum – from the radical African National Congress and the Pan African Congress to the dominant right-wing National Party and leading businessmen. The meetings were informal, members participated as individuals, and no decisions were made. Nevertheless, they had a profound effect on official negotiations and public discourse at the time.

As described in a major report on the effort, *The Mont Fleur Scenarios* by Pieter le Roux, et al.:

> The team analyzed South Africa's social, political, and economic crises and compiled 30 possible 'stories' about the course of events during the next decade. These included stories of revolution, economic growth through repression, right-wing revolts, and free-market utopias. The 30 stories were carefully scrutinized [by the team] and sifted in terms of criteria such as plausibility and internal consistency. Nine stories survived and these were pared down to four by the end of the second meeting.

Significantly, the scenario process itself did not challenge anyone's highly charged positions, values and commitments. It simply explored possibilities. The group did not even have to agree on how various possibilities might turn out – only that they were credible possibilities.

The four scenarios that all participants agreed, in the end, were most plausible were given flight-related names:

- Ostrich - failed negotiations leading to continued non-representative government;
- Lame Duck - unwise compromises leading to a constrained, indecisive majority government;
- Icarus - a quickly formed populist government pursuing unsustainable socialist economic policies; and
- Flight of the Flamingos - a majoritarian government pursuing inclusive and sustainable middle-way strategies.

Interestingly enough, even though the group was not attempting to make a decision among these four options, in the process of exploring the options they evolved considerable consensus about the likely failure of the first three. The group ended up being left with the "obvious truth" that the final option was the one that made the most sense.

These stories were made into an insert distributed through a national newspaper, as well as a video shown by the participants and discussed in presentations to over fifty civic organizations, political parties, trade unions, corporations and academic forums. The team members – and most of those who came in contact with their findings – came to more nuanced understandings of South Africa's complex situation, which caused them to shift their assumptions and open up to each other as colleagues in co-creating a future that would work for all of them. The exercise influenced the policies of the elected majority government that ultimately took office in South Africa in 1994.

Visioning work is a somewhat different co-creative act of imagination than scenario work. While scenario work asks us to imagine what kinds of different futures are possible, in visioning work we ask "What kind of future do we want?" Various exercises help us get clear on that. Visioning work is especially important to democracy because shared vision has a profound effect on self-organization: When people share a vision, their actions tend to align to a certain degree even without coordination. This is perhaps most dramatically illustrated by a practice I call **imagineering**. My definition – using the imagination to directly or indirectly shape reality – includes but goes beyond imagineering in the Disney tradition, which is the act of imagining something and then engineering it into reality, or David Johnson's "the imaginative application of engineering sciences."

My favorite examples of imagineering are two novels – Edward Abbey's *The Monkeywrench Gang* and B.F. Skinner's *Walden Two.* The first inspired hundreds of independent imitators who later coalesced into the environmental group Earth First!. The other inspired the creation of several long-running intentional communities.

My own effort to apply imagineering involved creating a small journal called *The Ecotopian Grapevine Gazette,* which contained imaginary news stories about events or innovations that had not happened yet, but which I and others wanted to have happen, written *as if they had happened.* At the end of each article, I put the contact name of someone readers could call to participate in making that story a reality. This imagineering approach to networking could be used at conferences, in publications and on websites.

Another interesting approach for including an exploration of the future in creative deliberation is **the Widening Circles Exercise.** In it people are invited to explore an issue that they are already familiar with, looking at it from four very different perspectives: (a) their own, (b) that of a person with very different views, (c) a non-human being involved in the issue and (d) a future human who will be affected by people's choices on that issue. This fascinating process is described in *Coming Back to Life* by Joanna Macy and Molly Young Brown and at *co-intelligence.org/P-wideningcircles.html.*

The term "futures work" often refers to a category of exercises that help improve people's relationship to the future, such as the tools I have described in this section.

For additional examples of future work, see *co-intelligence.org/P-scenario-visioning.html.*

* * * *

There are hundreds of methods that could be used to further effective citizen deliberation. Most of them were actually developed to assist corporations, although many arose in community work. We can only wonder what it would be like if all these tools were gathered and studied with the explicit intention of creating a wise democracy. What role would each method play? How would it relate to the other methods? What might it contribute to our overall ability to exercise effective interactive, whole-system citizenship?

In other words, we need to explore how all these deliberative approaches fit into a broader culture of dialogue – because that culture of dialogue is the matrix in which public deliberation will ultimately add up to collective intelligence.

CHAPTER **17**

THE EMERGING
CULTURE OF DIALOGUE

*In human societies there will always be differences of
views and interests. But the reality today is that we
are all interdependent and have to co-exist on this small
planet. Therefore, the only sensible and intelligent way
of resolving differences and clashes of interests,
whether between individuals or nations, is through dialogue. The promotion of a culture of dialogue and nonviolence for the future of mankind is thus an important
task of the international community.*

— THE DALAI LAMA

As we saw in Section Three and in the previous chapter, citizen deliberative councils are a significant innovation within the larger field of citizen deliberation. At
the same time, to be maximally effective, citizen deliberative councils and other forms of citizen deliberation
need to take place within the broader context of a vibrant culture of dialogue.

In the midst of all of the challenges and difficulties
we are facing, I believe that we are witnessing the emergence of this larger culture of dialogue. This phenomenon includes many forms of dialogue – from therapy
sessions to open space conferences, from Internet chat
rooms to conflict resolution work, from workplace team

meetings to private heart-to-heart talks, from interracial dinners to creative radio interviews to weekly salons and café conversations. Some people are even exploring interspecies communication. Our culture is rapidly developing better understanding about how to have a good conversation, and millions of people are practicing it. It is beginning to change the quality of our culture – for the better.

The Dalai Lama's vision of a "culture of dialogue" is one in which people gather together to explore their lives, their differences, their dreams. Such behavior can be an expected, natural part of life. Every facet of such a culture can contribute to people learning together, building healthy relationships with each other and the natural world, and co-creating better prospects for their shared future.

We need widespread, high quality dialogue to generate shared understandings about environmental problems, diversity, future alternatives, and countless other issues. We need dialogue to get to know each other better – especially as our cultures interweave and our diversity grows. Most of all, we need dialogue to co-create the kinds of meaningful, satisfying, beautiful lives and communities we would really like to have.

However, we are unlikely to read much in the newspapers or see many TV reports about all of the efforts that people are making in this regard. Unfortunately, the news tends to foster what Deborah Tannen has aptly termed "The Culture of Argument." Conflict, tension, and polarization are often aggravated by news organizations, political campaigns, and other social institutions, whereas the multitude of efforts of people all over the world to create better understanding and reconcile differences goes too often unreported. We need to hear the good news as well as the bad, if we are to take heart in the efforts of others and redouble our own.

There are many efforts currently underway to promote dialogue in our culture. In the rest of this chapter, I will explore some of these efforts as well as looking at how we can increase both the quality and the power of public dialogue.

A spectrum of approaches to public conversation

Public conversation can range from circles in salons and cafés to studying together, from listening that changes a community to engaging creatively with conflict. Public conversation can expand as it engages the Internet and television. Here are some of the some creative initiatives I have encountered in each of these areas – a few of the many buds that are flowering forth from our emerging culture of dialogue.

CONVERSATIONS FOR LEARNING AND TRANSFORMATION

Café conversations and salons are small, voluntary, informal, intentionally convened, often periodic group conversations about topics that matter. They are usually held in homes or public places such as libraries or cafés. Sometimes larger groups (even several thousand) convene around a topic and break up into smaller groups to talk about it. Among the many forms of café are **World Café** (*theworldcafe.com;* see Chapter 7), Vicki Robin's **Conversation Café** *(conversationcafe.org)* and Sharif Abdullah's **Commons Café** *(commonway.org/ cafes).*

  From the Four Directions *(fromthefourdirections.org)* organizes intentionally diverse circles around the world "to foster the rising of a global voice." These ongoing local conversations help citizens and leaders clarify their hopes and challenges, learn from one another, and take courageous action. In *Turning to One Another: Simple Conversations to Restore Hope to the Future,* Margaret Wheatley, one of the co-founders of this effort, offers a series of provocative questions for conversations, including:

- What is my faith in the future?
- What do I believe about others?
- What am I willing to notice in my world?
- What is the relationship I want with the earth?
- What is my unique contribution to the whole?

See *turningtooneanother.net/world.html* for a linked list of several dozen world-concerned conversational initiatives.

   Listening projects create change by asking questions. Most involve trained interviewers going door-to-door asking powerful questions about local issues. Once people become convinced of the interviewers' sincerity, they tend to share their knowledge, needs and concerns – and that brings issues to life in their own minds and hearts. Often both interviewers and interviewees gain understandings or possibilities they had not noticed before, and people volunteer to take action. Information gained is often fed back to the community from which it was gathered, sometimes by subsequent waves of interviewers, so that the community comes to know itself over time in a way it never did before. Listening projects have also been used by activists trying to better understand and empathize with those they have opposed, and to lower the emotional tension of certain conflict situations. It turns out that listening itself has tremendous potency for all sorts of uses. For more information on listening projects, contact Rural Southern Voice for Peace (RSVP), 1898 Hannah Branch Rd, Burnsville, NC 28714, (828) 675-

5933; email: *rsvp028714@yahoo.com* or *hwalters@
yancey.main.nc.us.*

MAKING A BUSINESS OF FOOD, CONVERSATION AND COMMUNITY

Interestingly enough, the spirit of conversation on behalf of a better world can become a business opportunity. **Judy Wicks' White Dog Café** *(whitedogcafe.com)*
gives us an idea of what a restaurant might look like in
a culture of dialogue. In addition to great food, the White
Dog features lively conversation, activism and involvement with all sorts of people. Here are her formal dialogue programs:

- Lectures and discussions with prominent people
  on public concerns, several times a month during breakfast or dinner;
- Meals at "sister restaurants" in inner-city and
  ethnic neighborhoods – where mainstream din-
  ers can overcome media-driven fears and discover
  the vitality of Philadelphia communities they have
  never been to;
- A weekly after-dinner storytelling at which
  "underrepresented people" – the homeless, refu-
  gees, ex-convicts, gays, immigrants, youth, se-
  nior citizens – tell their life stories and everyone
  can exchange personal perspectives on experiences such as war, protest marches, parenting
  and illness.

In addition, Wicks brings people together for monthly
community service work. She encourages bringing se-
nior citizens to lunch every Saturday (at reduced prices),
and holds annual multicultural banquets including
Noche Latina, Native American Thanksgiving Dinner,
Rum & Reggae, Dinner in Memory of Dr. Martin Luther

King, Gandhi Birthday Dinner, and a Freedom Seder. She also hosts dinners with inmate gardeners, and tours of inner city community gardens and wall murals. There is ample conversation in all of these activities. Wicks' quarterly newsletter tracks all this for over fifteen thousand loyal customers.

The White Dog Café makes a good profit using the shared joys of food and fun to help diverse people get to know each other, to break down barriers and to build bridges of understanding between people of all classes, races, and persuasions – and ten percent of that profit goes to activist nonprofits. What would the world be like if most of its restaurants were like that?

CONVERSATION AND CONFLICT

Some conversations are especially designed to deal with conflict and polarization. **The Public Conversation Project** *(publicconversations.org)* sponsors conversations among people involved in opposite sides of public issues, such as abortion and environmental conflicts. They help activists from both sides listen to each other's life stories – what happened that led them to believe in their cause so strongly. They also talk about those unacknowledged gray areas that exist in any politicized issue: Most political activism requires that people set aside their personal complexities to promote an oversimplified, highly polarized view of a problem and its solution. In confidential conversations, both pro-life and pro-choice leaders share those aspects of their side's "party line" that they, as unique individuals, are not fully comfortable with.

These conversations are profoundly transformative. Leaders on both sides of the abortion issue who have been in such conversations for years have ceased to cooperate with media efforts to magnify their conflict. They treat each other with respect in public. One pro-life leader confidentially warned her pro-choice friends to increase their security since a particularly virulent anti-abortionist was coming to town. An environmental leader and a paper company executive who had participated in a Public Conversation Project about a forestry conflict began sending each other their Letters to the Editor before publication to see if the other felt there was any misinformation or unnecessary polarization in them.

An earlier approach to abortion battles was pioneered by **Search for Common Ground** *(sfcg.org),* which went on to deal with dozens of other conflicts. They help polarized leaders learn about one another's views using a process called **mediated dialogue**. It looks like a debate, but is anything but. Person A speaks. Person B listens and, before responding, feeds back what he or she heard, to Person A's satisfaction. Then, after B speaks, A has to mirror back what B said, to B's satisfaction. Then A can speak. They go back and forth like this several times. Search for Common Ground helps them to transform their conflict into cooperative action by understanding their differences and acting on their common ground. Sample programs: Pro-life and pro-choice leaders have agreed to work together on pregnancy prevention and adoption services. Arab, Israeli, Iranian and Turkish security experts have agreed to launch an initiative for cooperation to monitor, prevent and respond to attacks using weapons of mass destruction, even among countries that do not recognize each other.

Another conflict pioneer, **Mark Gerzon,** works through the Mediators Foundation *(mediatorsfounda tion.org)* on a number of fronts, from helping polarized people and organizations bridge between their differences to helping elected officials bridge the different values, belief systems and interests among their constituencies. He has helped filmmakers in polarized cultures end their stereotyping of each other's people, and worked with emerging leaders to find their own authentic voices. In 1997 and 1999, he was selected to design and facilitate the U.S. House of Representatives' Bipartisan Congressional Retreat. His book, *A House Divided: Six Belief Systems Struggling for America's Soul,* maps the diversity of America's worldviews and describes some fascinating efforts by members of all of them to reach out to the others. His approach to conflict neither eliminates differences nor focuses on similarities, but rather transforms people's relationship to their differences, using a wide variety of communication techniques.

Arnold Mindell is a very different conflict pioneer who brings his background in Jungian psychology and nuclear physics to his work with highly charged "group fields." In his **Process Worldwork**, people in large community forums are helped to welcome conflict by bringing polarized voices out into dialogue, often in highly emotional exchanges. By using experiential approaches to increase people's understanding of abuse, power and history, Mindell and his process facilitators hope to transform the destructive potency of social fields such as racism. Mindell says, "The fire that burns in the social, psychological and spiritual dimensions of humanity can ruin the world. Or this fire can transform trouble into community." He sees his work as profoundly democratic, wisely suggesting that "Deep democracy is based upon the realization that everyone is needed to represent reality." For more information, see *worldwork.org/home.htm* or Mindell's books *Sitting in the Fire* and *The Deep Democracy of Open Forums.*

A broadly useful deep conflict dialogue approach is **Nonviolent Communication** (NVC; see *cnvc.org*). It strengthens people's ability to respond compassionately and to inspire compassion from others. NVC can and has been used individually, in relationships, and in group settings, including political and ethnic trouble spots around the world. NVC helps people in conflict become clear on what happened, explore the emotions underlying the conflict, and identify the unmet needs that stirred up those emotions. It then helps participants find ways to satisfy those needs that serve everyone involved. NVC can be somewhat successful even when it is applied mechanically. But when done with real empathy, it can work miracles, even if only one of the parties to a conflict is familiar with the practice. If you can help someone opposing you feel fully heard and cared about, their conflicted feelings may even melt away as they suddenly find themselves opening into far deeper connection with themselves *and* with you, their erstwhile adversary. For more information see Marshall Rosenberg's *Nonviolent Communication.*

DIALOGUE AND TELECOMMUNICATIONS

Conversation is not always face-to-face. Communications media allow conversations to spread everywhere. Among the initiatives valuable for building a culture of dialogue are efforts to improve the content and responsibility of mass media and new forms of online dialogue and networking.

For three decades **New Dimensions Radio** *(new dimensions.org)* has broadcast around the world hundreds of **Michael Toms'** dialogues with leading-edge thinkers, spiritual leaders, change agents and indigenous voices. All are archived and made available to the public — including some free via streaming audio on the Web — and are occasionally edited into books. Toms' latest, *A Time for Choices: Deep Dialogues for Deep Democracy,* challenges Americans to delve more deeply into their national spirit for responses to the September 11, 2001 attacks. New Dimensions is a leader among the new genre of quality talk shows that go deeper than the conflict-ridden stereotyping of so much mainstream talk radio and TV.

Duane Elgin is a planetary evolution visionary probably most famous for his ground–breaking book *Voluntary Simplicity,* although he has written several more since then, notably *Promise Ahead: A Vision of Hope and Action for Humanity's Future.* When it comes to conversation, Elgin focuses on the use of television and the Internet as media for conscious collective evolution. He sees these as our social nervous system – our collective mind or social brain – and points out that television, in particular, needs to be reclaimed for the health of the whole society and world.

Elgin asks, "How can we best evolve the culture and consciousness in a way that really serves our collective awakening?" His main answer is lots of good local face-to-face conversation about the dangers and opportunities we face, supported by conversations through the mass media, especially television, extended worldwide by the Internet. If we actually empowered such "local-to-global conversation," he says, "we could rapidly reach a working consensus for moving along a very different track towards sustainability and a much more satisfying future for ourselves."

He offers two provocative proposals along this line. Both depend on the establishment of nonpartisan, nonprofit "**community voice**" organizations in metropolitan areas. These groups would find out what issues concerned the public and then arrange televised conversations – "electronic town meetings" – between experts and studio audiences about those issues. The programs could also include mini-documentaries and periodic polling of randomly selected viewers during the show. As Elgin points out, tying such programs in "with the Internet, radio, newspapers, and other forums such as study circles" offers tremendous potential for educational, interactive dialogue. This proposal has strong resonance with one made by Ralph Nader in his 1992 **Concord Principles** (*co-intelligence.org/ CIPol_ConcordPrinciples.html* and elsewhere), calling for, among other things, "Audience Networks" which would arrange an hour of prime-time and an hour of drive-time radio and TV programming on every licensed channel on subjects that "the audience believes [are] important to them and their children."

Like Nader's proposal, Elgin's second innovation rests on broadcasters' legal responsibility "to present a balanced diet of relevant programming that serves the public interest." The community voice organizations would use scientific polling to get an accurate sense of how well various programs were serving the public interest, and then turn that data over to the stations involved at the end of each program. If stations persistently ignored this information, further actions would be taken to encourage their responsiveness.

His work to integrate these two ideas has taken form in the **Our Media Voice** campaign *(ourmediavoice.org)* for media accountability.

Online dialogue is another challenge. There are thousands of listservs, chat rooms and discussion groups of all kinds which are definitely part of the emerging culture of dialogue. However, I am particularly interested in forms of online dialogue that help people make coherent meaning together. This usually requires a higher level of responsible engagement, but the rewards can be substantial. Many forms of computer-enhanced dialogue (both online and off) are promoted by companies like **CoWorking** *(coworking.com)* and **Big Mind Media** *(bigmindmedia.com).*

One form of online shared exploration, **Wiki** *(c2.com/cgi/wiki),* involves a set of webpages which can be changed in any way by the participants. Imagine a shared online chalkboard or whiteboard, designed to create hyperlinks easily. Wiki participants build richly-interwoven hyperlinked documents together, made of dozens or hundreds of related pages. For full how-to information see Bo Leuf and Ward Cunningham's *The WikiWay.* Or visit and participate in one of the most amazing Wiki projects: the collaborative creation of an encyclopedia from scratch at *wikipedia.org.*

A very different approach to online dialogue is "**Practicing Our Wisdom Together in Cyberspace,**" found on Peter and Trudy Johnson-Lenz's **Awakening Technology** site, *awakentech.com.* This is a moderated, elegantly organized online inquiry into the nature and pursuit of wisdom. Intricately organized multiple layers of meaning and inquiry are presented in accessible graphic form, creating a stimulating treat for mind and heart. This site is a provocative window into a future in which technology actually would be used to support serious dialogue into questions that matter, so that high-quality collective intelligence and community wisdom could be produced online by any group for the benefit of the whole society.

The Web is also being used to network people into conversations and larger patterns of understanding that can inform conversations. **Barbara Marx Hubbard**, one of the first to popularize the notion of conscious evolution, sees it as something we do together through conversation, networking, innovation and community. She is among a number of networking visionaries who are working to create contexts in which people can find one another for creative conversations and collaborations. See the **Center for Conscious Evolution** website at *consciousevolution.net.*

Similar sites with powerfully comprehensive (and in this case eco-centric) views of transformative activities and resources include **The Bioneers** *bioneers.org* and Ecotrust's **"Pattern Language for a Conservation Economy"** *conservationeconomy.net.* While these are not conversational methods, per se, their inclusive, insightful maps of transformational issues support the power and fruitfulness of conversations among people who wish to make a difference in the world.

And so we find that a culture of dialogue involves not just creative deliberations, but also people learning together, celebrating together, and working through conflicts together. A culture of dialogue also involves weaving conversations through television and the Internet. And, again, all that you see here is just the tip of a very large iceberg.

The more that we can share information with one another about these various initiatives, the more we can encourage one another and support one another in our various efforts, the more this emerging culture will grow and flourish.

Ultimately, I think, a culture of dialogue will regard almost everything as conversation. As Michael Bridge says, "Dialogue is the dance that goes on between the soil and the seed, the wind and the sail, the meaning and the word, a question and an answer."

Attending to the quality and power of conversations

We can look at democracy as an effective conversation of "We the People." In a healthy democracy, people talk about their common affairs, and their conversations make a positive difference. Yet in order for our conversations with one another to make a significant difference, I believe we must attend to both the *quality* of conversations and their *power*.

We can identify many kinds of conversational quality. Most people, for example, would consider a conversation good if it produced results they were hoping for. So the productivity of a conversation is part of its quality. People also value conversations that are meaningful, and that engage participants by calling forth their life energy and full capacities, including both head and heart.

The quality of a conversation also increases the more that the full range of relevant information, factors and perspectives are taken into account. This is especially true the more that participants are able to include and integrate these relevant factors into new insights about the issue(s) being explored.

The openness to diversity and dissonance in a good conversation allows people to go deeper, to explore assumptions, stories and issues that lie beneath the surface. People's thoughts and feelings change through good conversation, so some of us call these conversations "transformational." At best, participants in a transformational conversation experience a deep connection with one another, with deep parts of themselves and with what is really important in life. In general, we could say that the more these factors are present in a conversation, the higher its quality will be.

For the purposes of co-intelligence, the capacity to produce wisdom is perhaps the most important aspect of the quality of a conversation. Wisdom is generally enhanced by the interaction among the various aspects of quality that we have already mentioned, including meaningfulness, openness, inclusiveness and depth.

Often, however, only the direct participants (and perhaps their close associates) benefit from the wisdom found through high-quality conversation. This is not enough for democracy. If we are exploring the role of conversation in a wise democracy, we need to ask how group-generated wisdom can be of benefit to a broader population. In other words, we need to understand the ways conversations can be powerful.

There are many sources of such power. A dialogue may derive special power from influential participants, for example. What people learn in a conversation, individually and collectively, impacts what they say and do outside the group. This has special impact when participants already play influential roles in the world.

However, this is not the only kind of power a conversation can have. A conversation can also have power because it involves many people – either directly or vicariously. In order to exert vicarious influence, a conversation needs to be very visible and to include enough diverse participants so that a broad range of observers can easily identify with the conversation. If citizens can "see themselves" (i.e., their kind of person) among the participants in a public conversation, they are more likely to be interested in its process and outcome. The ability of such a conversation to resonate with others increases when its quality is high enough to produce solutions and stories that clearly reflect a deep understanding of the broad population's perspectives and needs. Such resonance naturally increases the conversation's power to influence people.

Of course, the social significance of a conversation is magnified if it has an official mandate to report back to the public or to official decision-makers. In some cases the decision-makers agree in advance to implement the report's conclusions. Such conversations are even more powerful if they happen on a regular basis, becoming a normal and expected part of political culture, such as an annual Wisdom Council.

Finally, some conversations may have numinous power, as well. For example, there is some evidence that conversations may influence the collective unconscious of humanity, or that shared, focused attention can affect real-world events.

Social conditions that support a culture of dialogue

In closing this chapter, I would like to briefly mention a few factors that create the conditions needed for a successful culture of dialogue. Perhaps most basic is that people recognize dialogue as a special and desirable form of communication. Only then will they create, demand and expect it in all aspects of their lives. We see the beginnings of this in many quarters, as people demand "respect," "authenticity, "interactivity" and "participation."

But taking time for good conversation is hard, especially as so much time is taken up with the economic activities of voluminous production and consumption. When people simplify their lives and shift their focus from "quantity of stuff" to "quality of life," they tend to take more time for good conversation. Many approaches to community-based, sustainable economics can help this happen on a broader scale. I suspect that the creation of a culture of dialogue will require a change in our economics to free up time for deeper communication – and that changing our economics will require a culture of dialogue that allows us to reflect deeply upon our current economic system and its consequences. So these two developments will probably co-evolve, step by step.

Other important factors in building a culture of dialogue include:

- accessible full-spectrum information which embraces the complexity of public issues;
- abundant diversity and freedom to stimulate broader vision and greater creativity;
- peace – because the violence, fear and conformity associated with war undermine dialogue; and

- a sense of peerness and partnership, for dialogue is a shared exploration among equals.

Anything done to further any of these will enhance our evolution into a wisdom-generating culture of dialogue.

Perhaps the jewel in the crown of that culture will be a special way of exploring our differences with one another. In the next chapter, we will take a closer look at the path that some call "living consensus," where diversity and unity dance like fingers on a loom, joyfully weaving the deeper truth of our larger community with all life.

CHAPTER **18**

CONSENSUS:
MANIPULATION OR MAGIC?

The consensus process strips away all the extrane-
ous issues and allows people to speak to each other.
Most of the time, people learn that the other side is not
as "wrong" as they initially thought.
> — KARL OHS, MONTANA LIEUTENANT GOVERNOR

Social process may be conceived either as the oppos-
ing and battle of desires with the victory of one over
the other, or as the confronting and integrating of de-
sires. The former means non-freedom for both sides,
the defeated bound to the victor, the victor bound to
the false situation thus created – both bound. The
latter means a freeing for both sides and increased
total power or increased capacity in the world.
> — MARY PARKER FOLLETT

Two of the most significant obstacles to implementing
citizen deliberative councils, as well as a culture of dialogue, are people's misgivings and misunderstandings
regarding consensus. When I first began exploring citizen deliberative councils, I was quite surprised to find

that some people regard consensus and even deliberation as oppressive processes. They feel that any effort
to reach agreement necessarily involves *suppressing*
differences.

Until recently, I did not know that consensus had
negative connotations for many people. In my years in
Quaker meetings and then in activist groups, I learned
about "consensus process" *(co-intelligence.org/P-
consensus.html).* This term loosely referred to the idea
that a group would not act on any decision until everyone agreed on what the group should do. My friend
and consensus trainer, Randy Schutt *(vernal
project.org),* gave me some of my best insights about
consensus. He defined it as "a co-operative, loving,
nonviolent process in which people share their best
ideas and come up with superior decisions." He noted
it was most effective in a group that shared experience, values and trust. The Quakers were more spiritual in their approach, hearing the guidance of God in
what everyone said, and deliberating prayerfully until
that guidance cohered into something that felt right to
the whole group.

Of course, I also knew that sometimes consensus
process could be a long drawn-out affair and therefore
feel inefficient – although the resulting decisions were
often much easier to implement, thanks to the broad
agreement about them. And, when there is not a clear
understanding of the process, consensus process can
sometimes degenerate into a "tyranny of one," where
the person who decides to block consensus in effect
has "veto" power over the rest of the group.

These are valid concerns. So I think it is important
to explore this issue further, since I believe consensus
is a profoundly important resource for the generation
of community wisdom. First, I want to explore some of
the mainstream views of consensus. Then I want to
distinguish the conventional uses of the word "con-

sensus" from the kind of consensus I have been talking about in this book.

Most people understand consensus as a general state of agreement. In the larger political world of adversarial politics, "consensus" usually means that a significant majority of people – perhaps two-thirds or more – support a particular proposal. In small group situations, people usually think of consensus as unanimity – that is, that everyone agrees about something. In both cases, an agreement is often called "consensus," regardless of how it came about, how deep it is, or what it is based on. If it was derived from shallow understanding, mutual fear, reluctant consent, backroom deals, threats or negotiated compromises, it is often still called "consensus."

The dark side of consensus

In *The Heart of Conflict,* Brian Muldoon suggests that consensus refers to "the consensual grant of authority to 'leaders' by the governed ... Consensus protects the system from change ... The dark side of consensus is that it results in *homogeneity.*" Here Muldoon is pointing to the kind of conformity-based consensus that politicians try to manipulate in a population, usually through mass media, and often by making dissenting voices feel too unwelcome to speak up.

The same thing can happen in a group. An atmosphere of conformist "groupthink"* gets in the way of real debate or exploration. It may well be the case that

---

* The term "groupthink" was coined by Irving Janis to refer to the way a group's desire for unanimity can undermine their ability "to realistically appraise alternative courses of action." (Janis, 1982). He identified eight groupthink dynamics: feelings of invulnerability, rationalization, ste-

the people who have dim views about consensus and deliberation have gained that perspective as a result of such negative experiences. All too often, agreement-oriented processes have achieved their goal by squelching disagreements and pressuring people toward an uneasy unanimous vote.

Tim Holmes and Ian Scoones of the Institute of Development Studies in England write in *IDS Working Paper 113: Participatory Environmental Policy Processes: Experiences from North and South,*

> The search for consensus...[can] silence rather than give voice to those already marginalized. This is particularly likely where the values and interests of some parties are subordinated, knowingly or unknowingly, to those of more powerful, articulate or persuasive actors in the participatory process ... The pressure for consensus has the potential to inhibit the argumentative process ... intimidat[ing] participants to produce a "consensus" that [is] largely rhetorical or based more on grudging compromise ... that does not rise above a low common denominator.

As it turns out, this has too often been the case with interest-based negotiation and mediation as well. In the desire to achieve a "settlement," mediators often direct the process towards the settlements they feel will be easiest to achieve, and use their role to place subtle pressure on people to agree to a compromise. Furthermore, some research shows that those who are less powerful often end up with the short end of the stick as a result. No wonder "consensus" has such a bad reputation among so many people.

---

reotyping, moral arrogance, illusions of unanimity, conformist pressure, self-censorship and self-appointed mindguards. The subject is a vital dimension of what I call co-stupidity and deserves more research to expand on Janis' excellent initial insights.

A spectrum of consensus

I hope to make it clear in this chapter that such manipulated consensus is an entirely different animal than wisdom-generating consensus. As I have described throughout this book, wisdom comes from the inclusion, exploration, acceptance, celebration, creative use, integration and/or transcendence of our differences, not from their suppression. **Manipulated or forced conformity or consent** results in agreements that are usually more apparent than real, and that have been achieved *at the expense of* diversity, creativity, and integrity, instead of *as a result of* diversity, creativity, and integrity. In consequence, they are only a pale shadow of the real thing. Any agreements that might result from an engineered process are not nearly as powerful, solid, or long-lasting as those that emerge from openly and creatively exploring both our differences and our common ground.

I also want to make further distinctions between real consensus and **conformist "groupthink."** While groupthink is not usually the result of manipulation, it is also a dysfunctional form of agreement that arises out of psychological and group dynamics. In certain group situations, the need to be liked, power relationships, rapid-fire conversation that discourages less assertive voices, politeness and other factors can contribute to participants holding in check their impulses to disagree, without calculated manipulation or domination by anyone. Such a situation would not give rise to wise consensus.

By contrast, many of us have experienced what I am defining here as "real" consensus: that is to say, **comfortably agreed-to outcomes achieved through real dialogue** that creatively and collaboratively explores differences as well as noting common ground.

Such dialogue usually evokes and works through conflict. It may conclude with clarifying statements of both points of agreement (consensus) and points of disagreement (sometimes called "dissensus," as are the minority opinions of the Supreme Court). Or, the consensus may even consist of a shared recognition that the issue is still unresolved or needs to be set aside to further "ripen" or "season."

On the most powerful end of the spectrum is the experience of real "magic" in group process. Beyond the laborious process of hammering out fair and square working agreements, many of us have experienced this magic, a transformational "flow" state, a **process of "co-sensing" together the ever-changing "whole picture"** as it emerges during a shared exploration of a problem or topic. In this kind of process, agreements are usually experienced as shared discoveries, and arise naturally and almost incidentally out of a deep exploration of diversity, as they did in the "Fertilizer Factory" story in the prologue of this book.

Co-sensing is the most potent form of consensus for generating shared wisdom. It is evoked more easily by non-linear processes (such as Dynamic Facilitation, transformational mediation, listening circles, Bohmian dialogue) than by more linear forms, such as certain types of traditional consensus process or interest-based negotiation. However, it can happen in any process, to the extent that people really listen to each other and the process does not actively stifle their emergent energies.

Furthermore, once we have had the experience of co-sensing, something in us is transformed. We realize that creative consensus without compromise is a real possibility for any group no matter how strong the differences, whenever we are able to create a situation where participants are truly able to speak and listen from the heart.

Beyond Agreement

As we explore co-sensing, we come to understand consensus in ways that are not rooted in agreement, per se. For me and many others, that alternative conception of consensus has to do with shared insight or awareness: it is not so much that we agree on some conclusion, as that we are looking at the same territory together. This is what I mean by "co-sensing," or sensing together. What we are seeing and feeling together may just as likely be filled with acknowledged differences as with discovered common ground.

For example, after we have talked for hours, it may become quite clear *to all of us* what it is that we each, individually, believe. Not only do we all understand that we each believe very different things, but we have all come to deeply understand *why* it is that we each believe those different things. We have not arrived together at a single unified, shared belief, but we may nevertheless experience a shared "ah-ha" realization that these particular diverse beliefs of ours form a meaningful pattern. We may understand better the diverse cultures or life experiences that led us to our differences. We may suddenly realize how our different beliefs all serve to keep a shared problem alive. We may not know what to *do* about that, but we can clearly *see* it.

An experienced, non-directive facilitator will seek out and welcome divergent ideas in order to help us see the whole "map of the territory." He or she will bring all our differences out into our shared space, often by writing them down on papers in front of the room, or having us do that. Most people familiar with deep forms of consensus know that welcoming divergence is an extremely important step, and one that often needs to be taken over and over again in the process of consensus-generating dialogue. The point is that we each want to move together, through this process, to a more inclusive vantage point from which we can see not only our own perspective, but also how our perspective fits in with other perspectives. At least, we want to generate a shared reality that includes all of these various perspectives, even those we do not agree with. Notice that it is not agreement we have found, but shared understanding. It is an important distinction, and a key to dialogue and consensus.

Although most people associate consensus with the product of a conversation – a formal statement that everyone can agree to – we can also think of consensus as a process, as *a way of being together* as we talk and explore. We might benefit by shifting our focus from getting a final agreement, a consensus statement. Instead, we could practice our capacity to sense together, to be aware of the collective pictures we are painting with our differences, to see things through all our eyes, together, and to feel things through all of our hearts. This is a new way of understanding "consensus process" – consensus as a way of being in inquiry with each other rather than any of the products that emerge from that inquiry.

Underlying such consensus is the assumption that greater truth emerges *through* the inclusive interactions among all our differences. So any consensus statement, anything we all agree on, is likely to be a temporary resting point. If we are to be realistic, we need to acknowledge that eventually the situation will change and views will shift. We will stumble on new information, or some other change will happen, such that some new perspective, some new voice, will need to be heard by all of us, if we are to continue to co-sense what is going on. At its best, consensus involves living through our changing experiences together.

Seeing consensus as a process is not unlike seeing science as a process. Each theory science "discovers" is indeed a valid discovery. But it is also just one more hypothesis. Experienced scientists know that all theories end up being modified and even overthrown when their useful time is up. Science is not so much a body of knowledge as a way of seeking knowledge.

Living Consensus

So it is with consensus, **living consensus.** Living consensus is a way of seeking understanding, clarity and coherence together. To see consensus as mere agreement is to reduce and impoverish it, to undermine its aliveness. If we do that, we risk sliding into the seduction of agreement, which soon leads to the tyranny of agreement, which soon lands us all in "groupthink" and co-stupidity, not wisdom.

The antidote to an obsession with agreement is a spirit of inquiry. The dance between inquiry and agreement, between convergence and divergence, between knowledge and uncertainty, is dialogue – especially the kind of dialogue that leads to "co-sensing."

Living consensus is a kind of group coherence that arises from everyone seeing, feeling or understanding things together as they explore a subject. Again, what we are co-sensing could be the landscape of our differences: our consensus might be a coming to terms with the need to do something different than any of us would choose by ourselves, simply because it is has become clear that any of our isolated approaches would be a disaster, given where everyone else is at.

Usually, living consensus unfolds as people explore not only their differences, but also tap into their commonality. When we humans are able to share our deeply felt emotions, our individual predicaments and needs, we paradoxically are also able to touch the common ground of our shared humanity – what I called in Chapter 4 "the core commons." Exploring outward creatively from the core commons, we are generally able to discover some understanding or option that really meets all of our needs and deeply excites every single one of us. We saw this in the story of the *Maclean's* conference in Canada.

We must not forget that this process is grounded in real human diversity. The diversity in the group sets up a tension that, if well engaged, becomes a creative, not a destructive, force. The energetic potential in that creative tension can lift people out of old ways of thinking and seeing the world, into totally new understandings and options. It can also link people to a deeper common source of intelligence and wisdom. When these things happen in a group, it can be a very powerful experience that is felt quite vividly by all involved.

Facilitation can help this experience occur simply by creating a space where everyone can be heard. Many indigenous cultures relied on elders who filled the role of simply listening to all parties until the "co-sensing" process began to unfold. It is helpful to understand the role of the facilitator as that of "designated listener," someone whose work it is to listen deeply to all participants and to "take all sides," in order to support the natural self-organizing process that leads to "co-sensing."

Just like any diverse group of people with good facilitation support, citizen deliberative councils have the potential to generate creative wisdom, options that lift us into new realms. Given the challenges we face in the twenty-first century, we could use all the creative wisdom we can find or make.

This brings us back to the community orientation of citizen deliberative councils. The creative tension that generates the creative wisdom *needs to be* the same tension that already exists in the community among its various perspectives regarding a particular situation. Those different perspectives *contain* the larger information and various energies that need to be taken into account.

When the interaction among the various participants who reflect those diverse perspectives results in a wise consensus that thoroughly and creatively takes all those different aspects into account, something very significant has taken place. We now have something that the whole community is likely to accept and recognize, both as deep truth and as "common sense."

In summary

Reflective diversity – small-group diversity that reflects the diversity of the whole community – provides a creative tension that is appropriate to the community and its circumstances. Dialogue, especially creative consensus process, provides the means to use that creative tension productively. Non-directive *living consensus* helps a group arrive at deeper levels of shared understanding and direction in a manner that fully respects and *depends upon* the full expression and valuing of all of the diversity that is present within the group.

Through the combination of reflective diversity and high-quality dialogue, citizen consensus councils have a unique wisdom-generating power. If institutionalized into our political process and tied into whole-community conversations, this innovation would qualify as a true breakthrough in democratic politics and governance.

This new form of democracy does not overthrow traditional adversarial and representative systems. They have tried-and-true roles to play in democratic political culture. However, they have proven unable to provide the wisdom we need to make it through the twenty-first century. And so we turn to the many cooperative and holistic approaches to politics that have been developed in recent decades.

Our evolving democracy can and should use these approaches to call forth and empower the common sense wisdom of whole communities and societies to navigate our collective future. Citizen deliberative councils offer a particularly flexible way to institutionalize this new form of democracy. Embedded in a broader culture of dialogue, they could make all the difference in the world.

CHAPTER **19**

CO-INTELLIGENT
CITIZENSHIP AND ACTIVISM

We are caught in an inescapable network of mutuality,
tied in a single garment of destiny.

— MARTIN LUTHER KING, JR.

At the beginning of this book, I referred to The Great Peace March in 1986, which started me on this exploration of co-intelligence. I want to tell you about the moment the peace march was born.

> *A man asked his seven-year-old niece what she was going to be when she grew up. She replied, "I'm not going to grow up. I'm going to die in a nuclear war." The uncle, David Mixner, was so stricken by her statement that he set aside a lucrative political PR business to create the Great Peace March for Global Nuclear Disarmament, which ultimately involved thousands of people for over a year.*

And what was the impact of all that? What happened when the march was "over"?

No one will ever know the full story. However, I know a part of it. I am writing this book, for one thing. But the book you are reading is only one of the many off-spring of the Great Peace March. There were several other books, as well. And hundreds of lives were radically changed – including mine, in many ways. And several Russian-American peace marches were carried out, some in the U.S., some in Russia. And the people who kept the mobile kitchen that fed the marchers not only served food at other peace demonstrations for years afterwards, but also fed rescue workers in the devastating 1989 earthquake where it had collapsed a section of freeway in Oakland, California. And another marcher organized a "March for a Livable World" across the U.S. and has now built an ecovillage in Ithaca, NY, with people she met on her march (*ecovillage.ithaca.ny. us*). And the list goes on. It could easily fill a book all by itself. All from a seven-year-old's response to her uncle.

David Mixner's niece, in her wildest dreams, could not have imagined the impact her comment would have. She was like the proverbial chaos-theory butterfly whose flappings, under the right conditions, can trigger a hurricane.

Sometimes, when I imagine you reading this book, I get the vivid feeling that each of you has done something which led to its being written. At the very least, you have played some role in creating these exciting and terrifying times. We are all creating it all.

Intrinsic participation

Our impact in the world unfolds, often without us knowing it is happening.

This insight can be overwhelming or wondrous, depending on how you look at it. We are all playing roles in the development of gravitational fields, children, economies, planetary weather, the health of people in Tasmania in the year 2053. Every single person in the world unknowingly conspires with every single green plant to maintain the right mix of oxygen and carbon dioxide in the atmosphere to sustain life. Every citizen who stays home on Election Day participates, along with every voter, in electing their President. Everyone who picks up trash on the street, or leaves it lying there, plays a role in determining whether the next piece of trash falls on the street or not.

We are active participants in everything that happens, even when we think we are "doing nothing," even when we are totally ignorant of what's going on. We are never merely irrelevant observers, spectators or bystanders. We are – each of us, right now – actively participating in the unfolding of the world into its future. I think of this as "intrinsic participation." We cannot avoid participating.

But it is not just us. Everything and everyone is co-creating everything and everyone else. Everything is bringing the next moment into being. As David Spangler says in his book *Everyday Miracles*, we live in "a co-incarnational universe." It turns out that this assumption – this way of looking at the world – has profound implications for who we are, how we are in the world, and how the world is.

Among the most intriguing implications – and the most useful for activism – is that there is no *single* source or cause for anything. This means that no one is totally to blame – nor are they (we!) totally innocent. Usually a close look will also uncover systemic factors that make certain behaviors and outcomes *much* more likely. When unemployment goes up, so do alcoholism and spousal abuse. When the only places to shop are at malls to which no busses go, even those who are aware of the dangers of a "car culture" will drive. When a group process is based on a fast-paced agenda, few dissident voices or emotional concerns will be raised. The structures and circumstances we live in have a powerful influence on our lives. But neither the structures nor the powerholders nor the crazy people (nor their parents) are in control of what happens, nor are any of them the ultimate cause of any problem we face. Nor, as many people claim, is it "up to each of us" individually to correct these social ills.

All of us *together,* dancing to the tunes of the structures we create and cooperate with, are co-creating what happens. Although any one of us can, with luck and courage, stop dancing to at least a few of the destructive tunes, real cultural change can only happen when we *together change the tune.* This is a valuable insight for activists and citizens of all kinds.

But the question remains: How do we apply that insight to actually influence real change?

New forms of power to influence change

To play activist roles more effectively, we need to develop new kinds of holistic and participatory power that transcend adversarial power and fragmented, individualistic modes of thinking. Among the many interrelated powers that the co-intelligence perspective has to offer – powers which suggest new forms of citizenship and activism – there are four I want to focus on:

- the power of systems thinking
- the power of conversation and self-organization
- the power of co-creativity
- the power of holistic spirit and aliveness

THE POWER OF SYSTEMS THINKING

The co-intelligent vision can increase our ability to understand and engage with whole social systems. By system I do not mean a machine, with parts that need fixing or manipulating, but rather a living organism that has needs and is capable of intelligence and healing on its own behalf.

A living system can also be viewed as a field of living energy that can be impacted by evocative energies, such as those found in stories, in archetypal images and in love and compassion.

The co-intelligence perspective gives us a place to stand that is beyond issues, a place from which to understand why social issues are (or are not) handled well by society. Virtually every social change group could benefit by helping to increase the collective intelligence of the larger culture. This would help *their* favorite issues be better addressed by that culture. Someday, I hope that coalitions will be organized around this larger issue, the need to increase our society's collective intelligence.

THE POWER OF CONVERSATION AND SELF-ORGANIZATION

The co-intelligent vision can give us a better understanding of the power of process, dialogue, listening, facilitation and inquiry. Ultimately, this awareness opens the door to a truly democratic activism that has no agenda of its own, beyond the facilitation of a truly participatory, collective voice, intelligence and will of the people. This is what I called in Chapter 5 "social process activism."

Activism that honors self-organization enables, frees, links, enlightens and empowers all existing and emerging energies toward a better community, society and world. The self-organization of human life has been, after all, the evolutionary mission of democracy.

Co-intelligent citizenship, activism and community participation recognize that an underground river of life energy and potential wisdom runs through every person and community – a river of values, needs, visions, purposes, things that matter or have "juice." This river offers an almost infinite resource for motivation that can evoke self-organizing energies and help people creatively work through conflicts along the way. Even former adversaries can become collaborative partners in the healthy self-organization of the whole system.

When we move beyond advocacy into co-creating forums and institutions for effective dialogue, we might explore situations with questions such as these in mind:

1. Where is the passion, the energy, the motivation here? What juicy topics, pressing issues or "questions that matter" are associated with this situation? Who can tell us more about this?
2. What conversation is needed? Who should be included in it? Who else? How can this conversation best evolve to include everyone concerned?
3. How can we facilitate a high quality of dialogue? How can we improve it? How can we sustain, even institutionalize, a truly high quality of conversation in this arena, on this subject, in this community or country?
4. What difference could this conversation make? What can we do to increase this conversation's potential to improve conditions? Is there a different conversation that needs to happen? Among whom? (At this point, we could start over with Questions 1 and 2.)

THE POWER OF CO-CREATIVITY

The co-intelligent vision can give us the understanding that participation is an intrinsic, inevitable part of life. There is no one in control, and no one on the sidelines. This realization can help us flow with the co-creative dance of cultural transformation. As activists, we can be more invitational and evocative, and less aggressive and frustrated, as we dance with individuals, populations and institutions.

We can also see that this dance necessarily engages our own and others' whole selves – body, mind, emotion, heart, spirit, passion and all our unique sensibilities. These human capacities are both part of the change that we want to create and also tools to use in creating that change.

There is no One Way. Everything and everyone has a role. The more of the Big Picture activists can see, the more we will appreciate the dance of change and the necessity of diversity. We will find greater respect for people with different viewpoints, different gifts, and different ways of being in the world.

This shift may lead us to greater creativity in *using* that diversity – a creativity empowered by the many tools the co-intelligence perspective brings to light. The diverse forms of politics and dialogue listed in this book can be seen as tools for co-creative citizenship and activism.

THE POWER OF HOLISTIC SPIRIT AND ALIVENESS

From the high energy of open space conferences and dynamically facilitated meetings, to the multi-modal engagement of street theater and interactive websites, to the dedicated fellowship of activist communities and the reemergence of spirituality, earth wisdom and a sense of magic in political activity, co-intelligence calls forth a spirited activism. At its best, co-intelligence helps us act, as Vicki Robin says, "from that place where our joy meets the world's need."

Co-intelligent citizenship and activism seek an integration of what is most alive with what best serves life. Ultimately, co-intelligence is about the many ways in which life goes about nurturing its own greater aliveness.

When that is happening among us or through us,

there is a sense of spirit and energy and depth to our lives. We sense we are part of a great story unfolding through the work we do together, which seems called into being from the very heart of the world. In the poem "Grace and the Great Turning," Buddhist scholar and activist Joanna Macy speaks of this.*

> When you act on behalf
>   of something greater than yourself,
>   you begin
>   to feel it acting through you
> with a power that is greater than your own.
>
> This is grace.
>
> Today, as we take risks
>   for the sake of something greater
>   than our separate, individual lives,
>   we are feeling graced
>   by other beings and by Earth itself.
>
> Those with whom and on whose behalf we act
>   give us strength
>   and eloquence
>   and staying power
>   we didn't know we had.
>
> We just need to practice knowing that
>   and remembering that we are sustained
>   by each other
>   in the web of life.
> Our true power comes as a gift, like grace,
>   because in truth it is sustained by others.
> If we practice drawing on the wisdom

---

* Edited into verse by Tom Atlee from an interview in *Yes!* magazine (available at *futurenet.org/ 13new stories/ macy .html*) and approved as a poem by Joanna Macy.

and beauty
  and strengths
    of our fellow humans
    and our fellow species
we can go into any situation
  and trust
    that the courage and intelligence required
    will be supplied.

Exploring the special concerns of co-intelligent activism

Let us explore how all this applies in realms normally covered by traditional activism. Here are some questions that characteristically concern various activist movements when they confront a situation or a society:

- "Are things fair and free? Is power decentralized – or at least constitutionally answerable to the people?" *(pro-democracy advocates)*
- "Is the environment respected? Is nature's wisdom followed in society's activities?" *(environmental activists)*
- "How do these people (or nations) handle conflict? How much do they resort to violence?" *(peace movements)*
- "Does everyone have enough? Who is oppressed? Who owns the means of production?" *(socialists)*
- "Are people creative? Does this society support individual self-realization?" *(the human potential movement)*
- "Is this society compassionate? Is there due attention to consciousness? Do people behave mindfully?" *(spiritual activists)*
- "Are people taking moral responsibility for themselves and their families? Is our country secure? Are the rights and needs of businesses respected?" *(conservatives)*

- "Is this society using the absolute minimum of government? Are problems addressed by evoking the self-organizing capacity of the society, rather than through regulation?" *(libertarians)*

These are all very important questions. Co-intelligence-oriented activism addresses the context within which the above concerns are raised:

- "Are people aware they are co-creating their shared world? Are they creating together consciously and wisely? What about their culture and their institutions helps or hinders them in doing that?
- "Does their culture nurture diversity and support positive interactions among diverse people and perspectives?
- "Does it embrace change and challenge with elegant imagination, in creative partnership with the world, using the diverse capacities of its people?"

In the process of exploring these questions, co-intelligent activism often encounters many issues central to more traditional movements. Oppression, concentration of power, the erosion of democracy, environmental degradation, violence, materialism, consumerism and poor education, for example, all degrade a culture's ability to function co-intelligently. Since collective intelligence includes a group, community or society's ability to handle any issue well, we could define co-intelligence as a "meta-issue" – an issue above and beyond most issues. This meta-issue issue embraces most social concerns, yet reaches beyond issue-focused activism into the realm of *conscious social evolution.*

But even if we define co-intelligence as a meta-issue, we still have to present our proposals as "issues" which we want to bring to the world's attention. If there are no citizen deliberative councils, the lack of empowered citizen deliberation becomes an "issue" and the councils, themselves, become a "proposal" battling for attention in the political marketplace. Suddenly our co-intelligence-oriented questions become "just another set of issues." How, then, should we proceed?

Here are some general guidelines, which apply to all of the forms of activism and the diverse questions that concern them:

- To the extent we are engaging in traditional activism, we will have decided on the answers to our questions, will have worked out the solutions and will be promoting those solutions to the public and the powerholders, usually using partisan language and adversarial means.
- To the extent our activism is co-intelligent in its approach, we will have brought our questions to the community concerned, brought together the various stakeholders and advocates with divergent perspectives, and/or convened conversations around these issues. In some cases, we will need to take action to increase the community's capacity to deal with such questions well, usually through creating or improving certain institutions such as public forums, media, and governance structures.

Such activism is, of course, not easy. Efforts to rise above partisanship are difficult and become more so in situations and systems that are set up to promote conflict. However, through the lens of co-intelligent activism, dialogue stands out as a fundamental, vital antidote to the ultimate futility and alienation of most win/lose processes. Therefore, as co-intelligent activists, we do what we can to build bridges to those we think of as "them." This is a growing edge for many of us. It does not mean giving up our values, but rather creating a context where different values can be respected.

Time and again, we may backslide into avoiding, ignoring, or fighting "them" or "the Other." However, through the lens of co-intelligence, we are continually reminded of the hopeful evidence that it is possible to creatively encounter "the Other." As activists, we wonder how this phenomenon can be harnessed so that citizens can encounter one another regularly to solve their collective problems together. If the systems were set up better, those encounters would be routine and productive, and those of us trying to make such encounters happen would not have to be struggling upstream to make them work.

If we want to address a traditional issue co-intelligently...

Much co-intelligent activism is likely to be activism on traditional issues, done co-intelligently. Much of this work will also help build a wise democracy. It might be useful to explore how we might approach certain traditional issues, trying to understand how different strategies could enhance or undermine co-intelligence.

Consider union activity. When unions fight for better wages, benefits and working conditions, this work can enhance co-intelligence by countering the dominating power of large, irresponsible corporations and bringing members of the community together in collaborative activity. But union efforts can actually undermine co-intelligence if adversarial relationships are promoted to the degree that win-win solutions become virtually impossible, or if unions focus on the material prosperity of their members to the exclusion of other factors, including the effects their company has on other human and natural communities. Interestingly, unions in Europe have focused more on gaining shared control of their companies than on wage demands. In the political arena, they have managed to increase vacations and shorten work weeks, thus providing time for community and political life. This supports co-intelligence.

Let us consider ethnic minority groups fighting for educational curricula that honor their perspective and history. This work tends to enhance co-intelligence when it nurtures respect for diversity and uniqueness, and provides young people with a sense of cultural grounding and empowerment. But these efforts can undermine co-intelligence if groups repress dissent and diversity (or promote conformity and groupthink) within their own group, or deny their common ground with other groups or with the larger human or natural communities in which they live. Dialogues about oppression can support powerful learning and compassion when people's stories – all people's stories – are fully heard.

Peacemakers in communities torn by violence serve co-intelligence when they help polarized people work through their differences to greater understanding and teach people how to make creative use of conflict. This is especially true if they see (and help others see) that violence always has both personal and systemic causes that need to be understood and transformed. But peacemakers can undermine co-intelligence if they resolve conflicts by denying or suppressing differences, or pushing aside people's stories, or taking an unnecessarily managerial role in conflicts. It makes a difference if they acknowledge both personal responsibility and oppressive power relationships and systems. And it makes a difference whether they attend to smoldering pre-violence conflicts or only come in when there is an explosion. This goes for international and civil wars, as well as domestic conflicts.

It makes a difference if homeless services bring people together to help care for themselves, or simply sustain individual dependence on agencies and charity. It makes a difference whether organizational development consultants help corporations whose activities and products respect and serve the world around them, or those whose actions damage and degrade the people and environments they deal with. It makes a difference whether protesters are pressuring power-holders to give in to their demands, or demanding to engage with them as peers in genuine dialogue, as Gandhi did.

NONVIOLENCE

This last point bears further emphasis since nonviolence plays such a significant and complex role in activist movements. Direct action advocates can serve co-intelligence by using the tactics of nonviolent power politics – protests, strikes, sit-ins, lawsuits, etc. – not to force their own favorite resolution of the issue at hand, but to advocate for a co-intelligent process. Direct action can be used, when all else has failed, to demand a process where the full diversity of views can come together to find and implement solutions for the whole community or society.

Of course, Jesus himself said that we should be "wise as serpents and peaceful as doves." As long as institutional power imbalances exist in our society, we need to be ready to resume direct action whenever government agencies or corporations stop engaging in serious dialogue, and instead begin to withdraw or renege on their agreements or to undermine or manipulate the dialogue process itself.

However, we activists must also stay alert to ways we may be impeding or manipulating the process, and change our behavior accordingly. Co-intelligence cannot be faked. It involves real inquiry, real openness and real integration of diversity. If there is no co-intelligence, it is not "their fault." Both co-intelligence and co-stupidity are co-created. And sometimes circumstances may call us to exercise more creativity than we anticipated.

For dialogue to be effective, everyone involved needs to be participating in good faith. The generative dialogue that characterizes so much of cooperative and holistic politics requires a certain level of peerness, of direct person-to-person creative engagement, not playing political one-up games, lying and manipulation.

However, until the whole political system is set up with intrinsically dialogic structures (such as citizen deliberative councils), many powerholders will naturally tend to use power politics and domination whenever they think they can get what they want. They manipulate the process and public media to keep power in their hands. As long as this is true, grassroots activists will tend to assert their own special forms of coercive and manipulative power, particularly wild media events, nonviolent action and lawsuits.

Unfortunately, both activists and powerholders can become so habituated to adversarial strategies that they cannot stop even when there is ample evidence and opportunity for collaborative progress. So, as noted earlier, one test of co-intelligence in a nonviolent campaign is whether its demand is for peer dialogue to resolve the issue in ways everyone can honor, instead of simply demanding an outright victory for the activist position.

In those situations in which we believe dialogue may result in compromises harmful to the larger community, life or future generations, we are called to deepen our understanding and practice of dialogue. Dialogue is *not* about compromising our deepest values. It is about seeking to fully hear and understand those who feel and think differently, even if no immediate solution seems apparent. If we are fully open to others and our interactions are deeply informed by love and respect for all life – our adversaries included – we may find that our actions invite widespread resonance and transformation. From that place of resonance we may find new options together.

If we are able to meet that standard, then our efforts will always be dialogic and peer-based – heart to heart, spirit to spirit, creature to creature – even while we are engaged in nonviolent protest. And in the process, we ourselves will be willing to change if we are called to by resonance with our erstwhile adversaries.

THE DIALOGUE OF LIFE WITH ITSELF

In this case, we are not so much issuing demands as witnessing and crying out on behalf of injured life, calling out to the unconscious parts of life to wake up and move towards healing and wholeness for all. Any resistance that we encounter, we meet openly, dialogically, empathically, in a search for greater truth and wholeness. We become part of the body politic's collectively intelligent struggle for greater understanding and wisdom, helping all parts of the whole to deepen into common ground.

Thus, it is in our interest as co-intelligent activists to establish the most effective dialogues possible, to facilitate the emergence of practical and healing wisdom, and to work collaboratively to implement the outcomes that emerge.

To the extent we are grounded in wholeness, we will not exclude any relevant party or viewpoint from consideration – not powerholders, not adversarial activists, not the community, not nature, not future generations. All play a role. Our job as co-intelligent activists is to support all beings in playing their roles as creatively as possible, by helping everyone recognize that enlightened self-interest requires our collective well-being. And in turn, our collective well-being depends upon the respect we offer to each individual person and part that makes up the whole.

It may not be easy. But, as Joanna Macy points out, Life is our companion, and there is no shortage of helpful tools and guidance.

HANDLING ISSUES CO-INTELLIGENTLY WHILE INCREASING OUR COLLECTIVE CAPACITY TO DO SO

Here are some broad guidelines to handle any social issue co-intelligently and – at the same time – to enhance the co-intelligence of groups and communities who are struggling with that issue.

HELP ISSUE-ORIENTED ORGANIZATIONS AND COMMUNITY GROUPS FUNCTION WELL AND HOLISTICALLY.

All too often, the adversarial stance of so much political activity infects relationships within and between issue-oriented organizations and communities. Our focus on "the bad guys out there" can blind us to ways we manifest social patterns we despise. Our deep commitments and values can make us judgmental of potential allies, and leave us with little energy or time to deal with our own dysfunctions or needs, until we burn out. It is ironic that for-profit corporations generally do more internal organizational development and staff enhancement work than non-profit and activist groups. Among the general actions that can help: Building group self-organizing capacity; training, using and sharing facilitators and mediators; developing support groups, affinity groups and peer counseling groups for hard-pressed activists; promoting the use of dialogue processes like those described in this book – circles, world café, open space, etc. – at every opportunity.

HELP BUILD BRIDGES, COALITIONS AND DIALOGUES AMONG STAKEHOLDERS.

Build common ground that honors and creatively utilizes diversity. Facilitate shared respect, understanding and coordinated action among diverse players addressing any particular aspect of the issue. Deal creatively with polarization. Promote equity, peerness, and the sharing of both suffering and benefits through any crisis related to the issue, and through the implementation of any proposed solutions. Above all, help people feel really heard. Learn, use and promote communication methods like nonviolent communication and group processes such as Dynamic Facilitation that can help everyone do these things.

FACILITATE THE COMMUNITY'S (OR STATE'S OR COUNTRY'S) COLLECTIVE INTELLIGENCE AND LONG-TERM WELL-BEING.

Use controversial issues to stimulate greater inclusive consciousness, inclusive motivation, inclusive competence and inclusive activity. Arrange things so that expertise, leadership and media are creatively on tap, not on top. Catalyze collective learning by improving information flows, feedback systems, and comprehension of the alive complexity of issues in general. Facilitate the emergence of community wisdom. In particular, advocate empowered, official citizen deliberations to increase the ability of the society to fruitfully deal with *all* issues, including the one on the table now. Wonder aloud what else might be done to use people's work on this issue to increase the health of the community, community engagement, and the quality of life of the people and groups involved.

USE THE ISSUE AT HAND TO EDUCATE PEOPLE ABOUT CO-INTELLIGENCE — WHETHER OR NOT YOU NAME IT AS SUCH.

Advocate collaboration and partnerships (with each other, with nature) as fundamental approaches to dealing with the issue, no matter what it is. Create stories that address the issue by promoting collaborative values and positive engagement with life. Stress the power of dialogue. Share the methods, ideas and possibilities explored in this book and elsewhere. Advance people's understanding of interconnectedness, wholeness, co-creativity, living systems, co-intelligence, etc., at every opportunity.

EMBED THE ISSUE IN ITS ACTUAL COMPLEXITY AND RESOURCES TO ADDRESS THAT COMPLEXITY.

Contextualize it. Explore how the issue is related to other issues and realities, and what people and institutions on all "sides" are doing to keep the problem alive. Promote increasingly inclusive definitions of "who is a stakeholder," e.g., the disfranchised, future generations, the natural world, etc. Call for the engagement of our full human capacities in dealing with the issue in life-enhancing ways, individually and collectively. Embrace and facilitate the inclusion of clear perception, reason, emotion, intuition, imagination, story, good articulation, body sense and action, musical and artistic capabilities, practical sensibilities, guidance by higher powers, and all the rest. Help people find comfortable ways to deepen into resonance with each other and greater life or spirit.

It is good to remember that when you combine co-intelligence-building with issue-based activism, you cannot control the outcome (as if you could with any strategy!). A high-quality public dialogue may or may not arrive at the conclusions favored by a given set of activists. However, it *will* arrive at outcomes that are right for that particular community or society, at least for the moment.

Ideally, the outcomes of co-intelligent activism – for example, greater public awareness of the existence and value of participatory deliberative processes – will have increased the public's capacity to continue to see clearly and learn well from the results of their collective decisions. For example, if we have consensus conferences that publicly review the field of biotechnology every 3-6 months, noting the impact of earlier consensus conferences and any new developments, we have created a way for the whole community, as a living system, to respond intelligently to its changing circumstances. If such long-term collective capacity-building has been done – and if activist positions are, indeed, the wisest choices – then the community will naturally evolve towards them.

Done well, co-intelligent activism generates increased awareness that **building collective intelligence and community wisdom facilitates the resolution of all other issues.** People begin to realize that if we deal with this one all-embracing issue – our capacity for co-intelligence – every other issue will be addressed more intelligently.

I like to envision the day when all issue-oriented public interest and transformational movements invest just a small part of their resources on increasing the capacity of the society to reflect on and deal with the many problems and solutions we all know about. That will be the day the unstoppable, benign giant of Democracy wakes, stretches, chuckles confidently and climbs powerfully out into the world to make it fit for Life.

Whether or not we call our work "co-intelligence," we are busy waking the wise giant that is us all. You are part of that giant – as am I – as are we all.

I believe that any action taken to wake this Wise Democracy giant constitutes co-intelligent activism. It may be issue-oriented activism of the sort described in this chapter. Or it may be work to increase the co-intelligence capacity of communities and societies directly. Both dimensions of co-intelligent activism – co-intelligence capacity-building activism and co-intelligent issue-oriented activism – are intimately connected. Understanding them can help us realize the full scope of co-intelligent activism and citizenship.

Capacity-building activism

Most of this book has described ways to increase our collective capacity for co-intelligence. But since this chapter has focused on issue-oriented activism, I want to quickly review those sorts of activity that constitute co-intelligence capacity-building activism.

Perhaps the central focus of co-intelligence capacity-building is the creation of a culture of dialogue – promoting the widespread understanding and use of dialogue – in all its variations – at all levels and in all sectors of society. I believe that establishing official citizen deliberative councils, in particular, can provide forums in which the potential wisdom of the citizenry can emerge to ensure the responsible functioning of our democracy and the long-term well-being of our communities and societies.

Co-intelligence capacity-building activists may promote such dialogues and deliberative institutions directly or they may create conditions that make creative democratic discourse more likely and effective. For example, productive public deliberations need accessible, high-quality information, including responsible mass media, balanced briefings on issues and up-to-date quality of life statistics. Cultural changes – such as a shorter work week or voluntary simplicity – can provide people with time to talk. Democracy-minded city planning and architecture can provide appropriate places to gather. Research can develop better approaches to deliberation, and training can make more facilitators available. Most of us could also use more training and opportunities for collaboration, systems thinking, creative use of diversity, and accessing the deepest parts of ourselves, our core commons, individually and together.

Any and all of these constitute co-intelligence capacity-building activism. It is vital that we build our collective capacity to address all issues wisely in the future, even as we work to handle individual issues co-intelligently now.

This co-intelligent citizenship can deal with the complexxity of our times and – step by step – create a decent, sustainable world that works for all.

Some of the many ways you could participate in this emerging movement are listed on page 276.

For many of us, this feels like the most interesting and important enterprise on Earth.

CHAPTER 20

THE TAO OF DEMOCRACY

This book is entitled *The Tao of Democracy.* It talks about co-intelligence, dialogue and activism. What does all this have to do with the Tao?

In his famous little book, *The Tao Te Ching,* the sage Lao-Tzu voiced tremendous respect for the self-organizing power of Nature. He called that power the Tao, the Way of Nature.

The Tao operates in the natural world, he said. The Tao also operates in human affairs. It operates everywhere that there is life.

Taoism advises us: To the extent we tune in to the Tao and work with it, we will not need to use force, effort or control. We will recognize the illusory, temporary, counter-productive nature of these domineering strategies.

Given a little calm attention, respect and care, things will work out harmoniously.

The last chapter of the *Tao Te Ching* (Chapter 81) suggests that

> Nature has a way of creating benefits elegantly,
> without forcing things.
> Likewise, the Master calmly assists life's
>   unfolding
> unselfishly, without striving, competing or
>   harming anyone.

Taoism advises us: Live simply, be generous and empty, bend with the wind and flow with the currents of life, welcome with detachment whatever comes your way, respect limits and avoid extremes, and you will be happy. Rather than fighting what is bad, simply make mindful space for natural goodness, and then let life take its course.

The *Tao Te Ching* is famous for saying that the Tao that can be described is not really the Tao. Perhaps that is because the Tao is not a thing, but simply the natural inclination of things, a way things have of working themselves out. We can become aware of how the Tao works, but we can never describe it. It is not something to use, but rather a way to follow and, ultimately, to be.

Or perhaps our task is to become more conscious of the Tao operating in and around us – of our *being the Tao already* – since it is always present in everything we do or don't do, no matter what that is.

The Tao and Co-Intelligence

There is much resonance between this vision of the Tao and co-intelligence. Co-intelligent metaphysics and spirituality see life as an interactive, co-creative, dialogic dance – even to the point that things "dance each other into being," a phenomena David Spangler calls "co-incarnation." This deep existential co-creativity and interdependence is epitomized by the famous Taoist circle-symbol of the Yin-Yang.

But Taoism – at least as commonly understood – may differ from the co-intelligence perspective in one significant respect, and that is how it addresses the question "What should people do, given the self-organizing inclinations of nature and people?"

The oversimplified Taoist answer is, "Don't do anything. Stand aside. Let things take their course."

Inspired by Taoism, some people take that seriously, glorifying inaction of any sort. Others suggest that action or inaction are not really the issue. The issue is one's mindful presence in the flow of things – in which case whatever one does is not one's own "action." It is just part of the flow.

Others, like Aikido masters, are moved by Lao-Tzu's admiration for the liquid power of water. They stress a kind of receptive, flowing, participatory, space-making action. They seek not so much lack of action as a lack of force, resistance or solidity. They move with the energy of any attack, leaving nothing to hit or harm.

The Aikido approach is an example of actively participating in the co-creation of *mutual action* – a view very resonant with co-intelligence.

The co-intelligence approach applies this insight to the design and facilitation of processes – and the building of structures – that *evoke and encourage the co-creative engagement of all involved.* This serves to "nurture the capacity for self-organization."

But some Taoists may see that description as not fully accurate. They could justly point out that self-organization is happening all the time. What *is* being nurtured is the capacity to self-organize in ways that serve the well-being of all parties involved, with minimal negative impact on the life around them. So perhaps we could more correctly say that co-intelligence acts to nurture *positive self-organization.*

This values-based, action-oriented dimension of co-intelligence work is arguably Taoist (since it engages the self-organizing energies of nature) and arguably non-Taoist (since it intervenes in life, using designs and facilitation). Naturally, I believe in the former viewpoint – especially since an open-eyed examination of life reveals that we are intervening whatever we do, so we might as well intervene consciously, and in ways that "work with" and enhance the natural self-organizing capacities of the living systems for which we are responsible.

Taoism, Co-intelligence and Democracy

This brings us to my favorite resonance between the Tao and co-intelligence. In his famous Chapter 17 of the *Tao Te Ching*, Lao-Tzu says:

> The masterful leader governs so well
> that the people are hardly aware she exists.
> When she has completed her work,
> people say "That happened naturally" or
> "We did it ourselves."

So it seems that Lao-Tzu is one of the earliest democratic theoreticians! Democracy is, essentially, collective self-governance. *Co-intelligent* democracy is *wise* collective self-governance. Not only are The People directing their own individual and collective affairs, but they are doing it well.

Since they are doing it for themselves and embracing the full diversity of their communities, they are not inclined to use any more force (or energy or money) than is absolutely necessary to do a good job.

They co-create their communities' futures and their society's institutions and infrastructure in such a way that good things seem to just "happen naturally."

Their leaders are more numerous, less alienated, more service- and facilitation-oriented, less inclined to issue directives and more inclined to "create space" and "build capacity" for good things to happen "by themselves." As these co-intelligent leaders succeed, *leadership* begins to manifest less as a characteristic of individual people and more as a characteristic of groups and communities, and the processes and structures they set up to guide themselves. Leadership becomes distributed and responsive, showing up when and as needed, or shaping the unfolding of things in a quiet, constant hum in the depths of the community itself. Chapter 68 of the *Tao Te Ching** says:

> The most effective leader serves humbly and
>   compassionately.
> Knowing the power of not competing,
> he effectively engages the desires and talents of
>   others.
> This is called working with natural harmony
> and becoming part of it.

In a co-intelligent democracy, everyone becomes a leader in co-creating and utilizing high-quality conversations that wisely shape their shared destiny. That is what citizenship is all about. When it is exercised co-intelligently, good things happen naturally because of the caring attention and wise collective intelligence that went into setting things up so that good things would be naturally evoked.

And all this happens not because The People are individually enlightened Taoist masters, but because they honor their diversity and the good conversation that comes from engaging creatively with that diversity. Thus, they can manifest a wisdom greater than any of them possess individually. This allows them to learn together, to explore together, to create together, and to evolve together into whatever seems better ... and better ... and better – step by step by step, forever.

Just like everything else in nature, they do it themselves, naturally, evolving as they go. And they do it consciously.

---

* The passages from the *Tao Te Ching* given here were integrated by me from ten diverse translations by Stephen Mitchell, C. Ganson, Tolbert McCarroll, John H. McDonald, Charles Muller, Stan Rosenthal, Peter Merel, Sanderson Beck, Tormod Byrn, and Aleister Crowley. Comparing such translations is an adventure I encourage any lover of the Tao to undertake, if only for the surprises it offers.

EPILOGUE

For more information on books mentioned here and elsewhere in The Tao of Democracy, *or used in the development of co-intelligence, see the Bibliography on page 286.*

In this book, I have mentioned many of the activists working on the issue of co-intelligence. However, I could not possibly cover all these remarkable people. People like Benjamin Barber, author of *Strong Democracy* and founder of the Walt Whitman Center for the Culture and Politics of Democracy at Rutgers University *(fas-polisci.rutgers.edu/wwc),* and the thousands of others who are working directly to enhance democracy. People on the team of mostly organizational consultants who researched a booklet called *Centered on the Edge: Mapping a Field of Collective Intelligence and Spiritual Wisdom (centeredontheedge.com),* a pioneering effort to understand how groups can dependably connect with deeper wisdom. And people like Peggy Holman and Tom Devane (co-editors of *The Change Handbook: Group Methods for Shaping the Future*), who promote many diverse ways people can interact creatively together on behalf of the whole.

How could I fail to mention people like Christopher Bache, author of *Dark Night, Early Dawn: Steps to a Deep Ecology of Mind*, who has been pioneering the realm of collective consciousness. People like Sharif Abdullah, whose *Creating a World that Works for All* not only lays out the politics of inclusivity, but whose very title is a breakthrough in understanding where we need to go — and who gave me permission to use it in the subtitle of this book. Cognitive scientists like Mark Johnson *(Moral Imagination)* ... pioneers of spiritual politics like rabbi Michael Lerner (*Tikkun* magazine and his book *Spirit Matters*) and Buddhist monk Thich Nhat Hanh (who believes the next Buddha may be not an individual, but a compassionate group) ... and passionate truth-tellers and invokers of engaged divinity in song, sound and word like Rachel Bagby *(Divine Daughters)* – all of these are activists of co-intelligence.

There are so many who have laid the foundations for everything in this book. Feminist intellectuals like Riane Eisler who, in books like *The Partnership Way*, has made partnership an accepted focus for theory and practice in all aspects of life ... utopian novelists like Marge Piercy *(Woman on the Edge of Time)*, Charlotte Perkins Gilman *(Herland)*, Starhawk *(The Fifth Sacred Thing)*, Ursula K. LeGuin *(The Dispossessed)* and Aldous Huxley *(Island)* who have explored the nature of collaborative societies ...

And I have been profoundly influenced by M. Scott Peck's *A Different Drum: Community-Making and Peace*, Marilyn Ferguson's *The Aquarian Conspiracy*, Peter Senge's *The Fifth Discipline: On the Art and Practice of The Learning Organization*, Margaret Wheatley's *Leadership and the New Science*, M. Waldrop's *Complexity*, Jay Earley's *Transforming Human Culture*, Charles Johnston's *Necessary Wisdom*, and Robert Ornstein and Paul Ehrlich's *New World, New Mind* ...

And then there are the organizations — The Center for Group Learning *(cgl.org)*, the Dialogue to Action Initiative *(thataway.org)*, the Deliberative Democracy Consortium *(deliberative-democracy.net)*, the Civic Practices Network *(cpn.org)*, the Mary Parker Follett Foundation *(follettfoundation.org)* and the Canadian Centre for Analysis of Regionalization and Health *(regionalization*

.org/PubPartCollect.html) — all dedicated to a wide range of participatory dialogue and deliberative forms and methods ...

The list goes on and on and on. There are so many I cannot come close to listing even the ones I know of. There is no category to embrace them, since their issue is not one issue but the world where all issues live. So I have created a word for their issue, for our subject, a word that, for me at least, embraces them all: co-intelligence.

> *But there are no words to describe the range and depth of their contributions, the powerful flood into which all their rivers run, and the sea to which we are all heading.*

Even so, those of us called to serve this new emerging culture of wisdom are yet grateful for those speaking out for the trees, for the homeless, for the end to war, for some semblance of sanity in our current affairs, which cannot wait for all these new institutions to be born, for time is short and the need is great. The *whole* job must be done, somehow – hopefully as co-intelligently as we can do it. And it is all part of the birth of the next civilization, which we are all inside of, not outside.

Moving towards a wisdom culture involves as many of us as possible thinking in terms of wholeness, interconnectedness and co-creativity. It involves seeking co-intelligent solutions to social problems and co-intelligent strategies for promoting those solutions. And it will involve, above all, improving the capacity of organizations, movements, communities and societies to *be* co-intelligent – a development that will change the world for the better, very thoroughly and forever.

Because then Life will be able to change itself, learning as it goes, through us all, towards greater Life.

WHAT YOU CAN DO

The possibilities described in this book are so new and so real, that any movement to realize them will be something we create together. Various strategies, plans and possibilities will emerge over time, so check in regularly at *taoofdemocracy.net.* In the meantime, here are things you and your friends can do right now.

- Spread the word. Tell other people about this book, about this effort, and about such exciting innovations as the consensus conferences in Denmark.

- Get together with some friends to talk about co-intelligence and wise democracy.

- Organize Open Space Conferences, World Cafés (and other cafe conversations), Listening Circles, Listening Projects, or Dynamically Facilitated sessions on topics that have meaning for your community or group. The first three you can easily do on your own, using information in books and websites.

- Get trained in co-intelligent processes — especially Dynamic Facilitation.* There are also trainings in Open Space Technology, Listening Projects, Nonvio-

---

* Jim Rough has a 4-day training in Port Townsend, WA four times a year, and other trainers are starting to teach this skill, as well. *(tobe.net)*

lent Communication and many other great methods. The more capable facilitators we have, the sooner a culture of dialogue will flourish—especially if they work together to build that culture through organizations like those highlighted below.

- Contribute to the following organizations who are promoting wise deliberative democracy—or help arrange substantial funding. There is no issue that would not benefit by having the creative networks, co-intelligent institutions and culture of dialogue that these people are furthering.

    Co-Intelligence Institute
    co-intelligence.org

    National Coalition for Dialogue and Deliberation
    thataway.org

    Deliberative Democracy Consortium
    deliberative-democracy.net

- Talk with an activist group you are associated with. Share with them how co-intelligent processes could be useful for them in their work.*

- Contribute to and/or gather signatures for the National Initiative for Democracy's effort to set up an

---

* You can tell them about:
  a) how some of these processes could help them internally;
  b) how some of these processes could help build coalitions;
  c) how they could use these processes to engage the public in dialogue on their issues;
  d) how citizen deliberative councils, in particular, could be used to create political and governance systems that could make reasonable, common sense, wise decisions about the issues that concern them.
     Encourage them to use and support the use of co-intelligent processes in all aspects of their work.

initiative process for the whole U.S., with a system that includes randomly selected citizen panels reviewing all proposed initiatives before they get on the ballot. *(www.ni4d.org)*

- Start a local co-intelligence or wise democracy group. If you want help connecting with other readers of this book, email the Co-Intelligence Institute cii@igc.org.* Tell us:
   a) Your name
   b) Your city
   c) The name of your nearest large city (if it isn't the one you're living in)
   d) Your email address
   e) What you'd like to do in the world of co-intelligence with others.
   f) Whether you want to be on my free email list.

- Study co-intelligence—by yourself or together as a study group.**

- Encourage your local university or community college to offer courses on this material, or to include some of it in their existing courses.

---

*   We will try to connect you to others in your area, as they send us similar requests. You can then correspond by email with them until you find enough nearby people to create an in-person group that meets 1-4 times each month. You can then do a listening circle exploring why you came together and which activities on (or off) this list you'd like to do together. If there is a diversity of interests in your group, you may want to break up into smaller interest-activity-work groups, while keeping the larger group for socializing and deepening together.

** You can use all or part of this book, and/or some of the books, articles and websites I have referenced here or on the Co-Intelligence Institute's websites. You can create study projects that suit your individual or group interests. The Co-Intelligence Institute is planning to create a study guide for this book, as well,

- Support activities to democratically oversee and reform the media, such as Duane Elgin's "Our Media Voice" campaign described on page 227.

- Do research on co-intelligence subjects. Web searches will uncover important organizations, books, articles and activities not currently covered on the Co-Intelligence Institute's websites. You can submit 100-500 word summaries of work that you feel should be on the sites, which we will consider for posting (with credit to you).

- Organize actual Wisdom Councils or Citizens' Juries in a group or organization you are connected with, or in your community or, if you are very ambitious, in your state. Get in touch with the Co-Intelligence Institute if you'd like to work on this.

- If your city or state has a ballot initiative process, explore with Ned Crosby, founder of Citizens' Juries and Healthy Democracy *(healthydemocracy.org)*, the possibility of sponsoring a "Citizen Initiative Review"

---

and may create online courses. These will be announced when they are ready. But don't wait for them before reading, discussing and exploring this realm. If you wish, you can get information on how to create a study circle from the Study Circle Resource Center. Any study of co-intelligence, citizen deliberative councils and wise democracy will better prepare you for whatever else you may decide to do. Among the many topics you could study are:
- Moving Beyond Issues and Positions
- Building a Wiser Democracy
- Intelligence, Co-Intelligence and Wisdom
- Innovative Group Processes
- New Forms of Leadership
- What is Wholeness?
- Community-Building
- New Forms of Activism

ballot initiative (similar to the national one above) in your city or state.

- Support efforts to reform our economic indicators to show how our quality of life is faring (see pages 16-18 and 89-92). To the extent we only attend to the immediate monetary costs and rewards of our activities, we will do ourselves in very quickly. New indicators will help us see "where we *really* are at."

- Explore this realm with each other using group processes and group awareness exercises you can do with little training or experience. One organized way to do this would be to start a CASPER Group, a group awareness exercise activity described at *co-intelligence.org/I-CASPER.html*.

- Choose an issue and create an unbiased website about it.*

- Be creative. Democratic wisdom cultures will not be created from any central location, but through the creative initiatives of hundreds of thousands of people – We the People. Think about who you have personal or work relationships with that might further building a wiser democracy. (Note: This can be fun to brainstorm with friends. See *co-intelligence.org/ CIPol_engagedCI.html* for ideas.) Use your networks to build the movement. Feel free to contact the Co-

---

* Show the full range of people's ideas about that issue, in a form that ordinary citizens can really understand and use (like Robert Theobald's idea for a "possibility/problem focuser" described on pages 95-96). Or search the web for models of such sites. A good one on campaign finance reform was unfortunately taken down, but is available in the Internet Archive at *http:// web.archive.org/web/20010606141152/www.destination democracy.org/intro.html*.

Intelligence Institute to explore any significant possibilities you see.

- Let the Co-Intelligence Institute know about your activities. Share your news. When we start hearing lots of good news we may be able to start a new section on the Co-Intelligence Institute's website. (In the meantime, don't miss the great dialogue and deliberation news at the National Coalition for Dialogue and Deliberation's site *thataway.org.*)

- Check with the Co-Intelligence Institute about internship possibilities.

- Check at *co-intelligence.org/CIInvolved.html* and *taoofdemocracy.net* for more details and new actions and programs that are developed over time.

ACKNOWLEDGMENTS

This book has been in process for ten years. I am especially grateful to my partner Karen Mercer for being such a deep companion during it all, to Eryn Kalish for insisting I write a book on co-intelligence back in 1992, and to Rosa Zubizarreta who got me to actually finish it over the last two years. Rosa supported the book financially, developed the content with me and, with help from Sally Tomlinson and John Flanery, did a remarkable editing job. Tree Bressen did some edits and taught me how to do an index. Grá Darjeeling performed magic with the cover (with suggestions from Kennett Payne and David Thompson). And Adin Rogovin has helped during the last two years of this project in more ways than I can count. They are great friends and I can't thank them enough.

My parents, John and Elinore Atlee, my brother Dick Atlee and my daughter Jennifer Atlee have all been tremendously supportive of me, my work and this book project for many years. I am grateful and lucky to have such an exceptional family.

The people from whom I learned about co-intelligence are way too numerous to list. Fortunately, many of their names are scattered throughout this book, and I will let that be their acknowledgment. Yet some of them have been profoundly supportive and stimulating at a personal level, as well. I want to especially thank certain friends and companions on this journey who, like Karen, Eryn, Rosa, Adin and Jennifer, have played significant roles on the horizons of co-intelligence and my work with it: Bob Stilger, Doug Freeman, Eileen Palmer, Halim Dunsky, Jay Earley, Jeff

Groethe, Jim Rough, John Abbe, Juanita Brown, Ken Lebensold, Kenoli Oleari, Meg Wheatley, Miki Kashtan, Ned Crosby, Rachel Bagby, Robert Theobald, Tom Hurley, Vicki Robin and one anonymous friend of many years. And I always enjoy my beyond-the-horizon explorations with Cynthia Beal.

Some people have stood at crossroads pointing the way, often unaware of their impact. I want to thank Diana Brooks for giving me a copy of *Maclean's* magazine that changed my life. Marilyn Ferguson's *Aquarian Conspiracy*, M. Scott Peck's *A Different Drum,* Robert Ornstein and Paul Ehrlich's *New World, New Mind*, M. Mitchell Waldrop's *Complexity* and David Spangler's *Everyday Miracles* were all watershed books in my life. David Mixner created the 1986 Great Peace March where I had my first profound experiences of co-intelligence — which were followed in the early 1990's by experiences I had during two years in Jeff Groethe's weekly dialogue group. My most important breakthrough in understanding wholeness — wholeness is not the same as unity — came from Charles Johnston. And I discovered the phrase "using diversity creatively" in the writings of Peter and Trudy Johnson-Lenz at the home of Frances Moore Lappé. I am so very grateful to all such people who triggered major turning points or breakthroughs in my journey.

I am also grateful for the profound and heartful support and companionship I've received from Adrienne Borg, Alisa Gravitz, Anne Dosher, Anne Henny, Bev Ramsay, Bill Veltrop, Caspar Davis, David Isaacs, David La Chapelle, David Sunfellow, David Vanini, DeAnna Martin, Diana Morley, Dick Strong, Doug Carmichael, Earl Johnson, Irene Hurd, Janet McFarland, Jean Rough, Jeff Schwartz, John Steiner, Judy Laddon, Kaliya Young, Kim Welty, Larry Shook, Leonard Joy, Linda Lu, Lois Jones, Lynn Nadeau, Lynne Swift, Margo King, Marilyn Trail, Mary Ann Gallagher, Michael Dowd, Michelle Mercer, Miki Kashtan, Milt Markowitz, Molly

Hamaker, Nancy Schimmel, Nina Youkelson, Paul Ray, Peggy Holman, Peter Chabarek, Richard K. Moore, Rick Ingrasci, Serena Burroughs, Sharda Miller, Sherry Ruth Anderson, Susan Partnow, Susan Strong, Tina Lear, Toby Hemenway and Wink Franklin.

I am thankful for the support of Barbara Wood, Dan Robinson, Doug Stewart, Edward Alpern, Frank Nuessle, Grant Abert, Ian Thierman, Jackie Lanum, James Edward Pryor, Joe Kinczel, Kirk de Ford, Margaret Kallsen, Marilyn Welker, Michael Jones, Myron Kellnor-Rogers, Sally Templeton, Shirley and Bill McGrath, Stephanie Moulton Peters and Suzanne Walker. They and dozens of other individuals supported the work out of which this book was born, both financially and with kind words. I am deeply grateful to them and to the following institutions, which also provided generous support: The New Road Map Foundation, The Fetzer Instititue, The Tides Foundation, The Nathan Cummings Foundation, The Joseph and Marjorie S. Steiner Foundation, The Berkana Institute, and The Real Change Network.

Living as I often do in group houses and co-ops, I am so grateful to my current and former housemates for their patience as I holed up to work on this book — and for the tenacious enthusiasm of Eugene's Sunrise Facilitation Collective. Among these folks, I especially want to thank Adin Rogovin, Debby Sugarman, Elliot Shuford, Grá Darjeeling, John Flanery, John Moriarty, Tree Bressen and Win Swafford. Their engagement with the co-intelligence work and ideas during the last two years has been a real joy. They are my local learning community, much as the Bay Area's Center for Group Learning was during the 1990s. I am grateful for the caring explorations of both groups.

I want to thank Jane Deer and Rhodes Hilemann, and Carolyn Shaffer and Sypko Andrei, for many things, but most memorably for sponsoring manuscript critiquing sessions in their living rooms. This was back in 1993, when dozens of bright friends and critiquers passed through their homes, leaving their mark on this work from the very beginning. I thank each of them.

I also want to thank the first board of the Co-Intelligence Institute — Eileen Palmer, Karen Mercer, Kevin Reidy, Mary Ann Gallagher and Miki Kashtan — all good friends and truly remarkable people, who played a key role in critiquing several subsequent manuscripts, and in urging me to focus on the book during the late 1990's. They persistently valued the work and encouraged me.

There are so many friends, colleagues, contributors and acquaintances who have supported this work during the last decade, that I am sure I have failed to name them all. I want to extend my deep thanks and apologies for any who I have have overlooked here, for surely you deserve to be included.

I also thank those whose manipulative abuse of democracy is bringing to light the limits of our current political culture and arousing more and more people to envision truly deep and fundamental changes on behalf of Life. Those pushing the limits of greed and power are essential parts of the dynamics of transformation. And (we must never forget) so are the rest of us.

Which brings me to my deepest gratitude of all. I want to express my appreciation and awe for the Spirit of Life that moves through me, this work, and all the people mentioned here and in this book — and through the entire world in all its vast and minute unfoldings. For years I have felt that Spirit calling us insistently towards a wiser, more profound and joyful way of being in the world and with each other. Without that calling — which is so remarkably manifested in each and every person, activity and idea noted in these pages — this book would never have been born. May its birth serve well the remarkable future that awaits our partnership with that Spirit.

BIBLIOGRAPHY

Abdullah, Sharif M. *Creating a World that Works for All* (Berrett-Koehler, 1999). Clearly the world doesn't work for the under-dogs. It doesn't even work for the elites who seem to be in charge. Abdullah shows how a deeper understanding of inclusivity can help us make a world that actually works for all. See also *commonway.org.*

Ableson, J., et al. "A Review of Public Participation and Consulta-tion Methods," excerpted from *Deliberations About Deliberation: Issues in the Design and Evaluation of Public Consultation Pro-cesses* (McMaster University Centre for Health Economics and Policy Analysis Research Working Paper 01-04, June 2001). This chart describes and analyzes five deliberative and twelve non-deliberative public participation and consultation methods, and offers an extensive bibliography on each one. Downloadable at *regionalization.org/PPTableeng.pdf.*

Armstrong, Thomas. *Seven Kinds of Smart: Identifying and Devel-oping Your Many Intelligences* (Plume, 1993). An accessible, use-ful popularization of Howard Gardner's theory of multiple intelli-gences.

Atlee, Tom. "Wisdom, Democracy and the Core Commons," *Earth-light: The Magazine of Spiritual Ecology,* Fall/Winter 2002/03, Issue 47, Vol. 13, No. 2, pp. 22-26.

———. "A Call to Move Beyond Public Opinion to Public Judgment" (2002). A well-referenced summary of the co-intelligence vision of deliberative democracy. *co-intelligence.org/CIPol_public judgment.html.*

———. "Can Citizen Deliberative Councils Legitimately Claim to Generate a 'People's Voice' on Important Public Concerns?" (2002) Looks at sources of legitimacy in small groups that represent the public, particularly exploring number and diversity of council members and the role of dialogue quality in citizen deliberative councils. *co-intelligence.org/CDCsLegitimacy.html.*

———. "Using Synergy, Diversity, and Wholeness to Create a Wis-dom Culture," *Talking Leaves: A Journal of Our Evolving Ecologi-cal Culture,* Vol. 11, No. 3, Winter 2002, pp. 26-29. *co-intelligence.org/I-SynDivWhol.html.*

————. "How to Make a Decision Without Making a Decision," *Communities: Journal of Cooperative Living,* Winter 2000, pp. 26-30. *co-intelligence.org/I-decisionmakingwithout.html.* Contains the Fertilizer Factory story from this book's Prologue, and a description of Dynamic Facilitation.

————. "Co-Intelligence and Community Self-Organization" and "A Co-Intelligent Toolkit for Working with Groups," *Permaculture Activist,* December 1999, pp. 4-10. *co-intelligence.org/ CIPol_permacultureCI.html.*

————. "The Politics of Understanding," *Yes! A Journal of Positive Futures,* Fall 1996, pp 37-39.

————. "The Conversion of the American Dream," *In Context* No. 26, Fall 1990, pp. 15-19. *context.org/ICLIB/IC26/Atlee.htm.*

Bache, Christopher Martin. *Dark Night, Early Dawn: Steps to a Deep Ecology of Mind* (State University of New York, 2000). Consciousness has both individual and collective dimensions and we face its accelerated transformation in imminent eco-crises. Transpersonal therapy may involve collective healing.

Bagby, Rachel L. *Divine Daughters: Liberating the Power and Passion of Women's Voices* (HarperSanFrancisco, 1999). Rachel Bagby speaks the "vibralingual" voice of Life. Her passionate book fills the void in that incomplete holy family of Divine Father, Divine Mother and Divine Son. She tells the story of the Divine Daughter as she finds Her in her own life—earthy, spirited, and real.

Baldwin, Christina. *Calling the Circle: The First and Future Culture* (Bantam, 1998). Fully explores peer-led, spirit-centered circles.

Barber, Benjamin. *Strong Democracy: Participatory Politics for a New Age* (University of California, 1985). We are more than atomized citizens. We are part of communities that can address their problems through dialogue, through which we grow as citizens.

Bellah, Robert N, et al. *Habits of the Heart: Individualism and Commitment in American Life* (University of California, 1985). A classic study of the nature of American community.

Berry, Thomas. *The Dream of the Earth* (Sierra Club, 1988). Science may have reduced nature to a machine in earlier centuries, but now it tells us the universe is a self-organizing miracle. One of the foundational documents of "The Great Story," the emerging cosmology uniting spirit and science. See *thegreatstory.org.*

Bohm, David. *On Dialogue.* Ed. Lee Nichol. (Routledge, 1996). The foundational document of the "dialogue movement."

Bourland, D. David, Jr., and Paul Dennithorne Johnston. *To Be or Not: An E-Prime Anthology* (General Semantics, 1991). General Semantics calls English with no "to be" verbs "E-Prime." Using E-Prime, our language becomes more precise and our thinking clearer. See also *generalsemantics.org/Articles/E-Prime_intro.htm.*

Briggs, John, and David Peat. *Seven Life Lessons of Chaos: Time-*

The Tao of Democracy

less Wisdom from the Science of Change (HarperCollins, 1999). An introduction to chaos theory and how it applies to life.

Bush, Robert A. Baruch, and Joseph P. Folger. *The Promise of Mediation: Responding to Conflict through Empowerment and Recognition* (Jossey-Bass, 1994). Conflict is not so much a problem as a source of growth. See also *transformativemediation.org*.

Callenbach, Ernest, and Michael Phillips. *A Citizen Legislature* (Banyan Tree/Clear Glass, 1985). Should we create a legislature by random selection? Callenbach and Phillips make a strong case—and then include others' critiques of the idea.

Capra, Fritjof. *The Web of Life: A New Scientific Understanding of Living Systems* (Doubleday, 1996). My favorite all-around introduction to the new sciences.

Carson, Lyn and Katharine Gelber. *Ideas for Community Consultation: A Discussion on Principles and Procedures for Making Consultation Work* (New South Wales Department of Urban Affairs and Planning, 2001). Features a review of seven methods including citizens' juries, consensus conferences, deliberative polls, and search conferences. Downloadable from *duap.nsw.gov.au/ planfirst/pdf/principles_procedures_final.pdf*.

Carson, Lyn, and Brian Martin. *Random Selection in Politics* (Praeger, 1999). Explores random selection and citizen participation—yesterday, today and tomorrow. Includes notes about methods like citizens' juries.

Centre of Bhutan Studies. *Gross National Happiness* (1999). A major exploration of Bhutan's national success criteria in its early days. Available online at *bhutanstudies.com/pages/gnh/ contents.html*.

Chambers, Robert, and James Blackburn. "The Power of Participation: PRA and Policy," *IDS Policy Briefing*, Issue 7, August 1996. A concise description of Participatory Rural Appraisals. *ids.ac.uk/ ids/bookshop/briefs/Brief7.html*.

Chawla, Sarita, and John Renesch (eds). *Learning Organizations: Developing Cultures for Tomorrow's Workplace* (Productivity Press, 1995). Thirty-two essays about the theory and practice of creating organizational intelligence.

Childre, Doc, and Howard Martin. *The HeartMath Solution* (HarperSanFrancisco, 1999). Scientific evidence of the intuitive problem-solving capacity of the heart, and how to access it. See also *heartmath.org*.

Cooperrider, David, and Diana Whitney, *Appreciative Inquiry: The Handbook* (with CD) (Lakeshore, 2001). A surprising amount of improvement can be achieved by attending to what works instead of what doesn't. See also *appreciativeinquiry.cwru.edu*.

Coover, Virginia, et al. *Resource Manual for a Living Revolution* (New

Society Press, 1978). Vision, analysis and practices from the Movement for a New Society who brought consensus and affinity groups broadly into activist movements.

Craig, James H., and Marguerite Craig. *Synergic Power: Beyond Domination, Beyond Permissiveness* (Proactive Press, 1979), 2nd ed. Pioneers of power-with and win-win solutions explore their application from the personal realm to the world of social transformation.

Crosby, Ned. *Healthy Democracy* (Beaver's Pond Press, 2003). The creator of Citizens Juries describes their rationale and use, and their potential to help us collectively discover our best interests and to provide voters at election time with trustworthy general-interest advice about which initiatives and candidates are most likely to serve the common good.

Dass, Ram, and Paul Gorman. *How Can I Help? Stories and Reflections on Service* (Alfred A. Knopf, 1987). What does it mean to care? This challenging, compassionate book invites us into an inquiry most of us didn't know was there to explore, and leaves us changed. Some of its many stories were watersheds in my own thinking and feeling.

de Beauport, Elaine. *The Three Faces of Mind* (Quest, 1996). An integrated theory of multi-modal intelligence based on the functions of the three parts of the human brain – reptilian, mammalian and cerebral cortex.

de Bono, Edward. *Serious Creativity: Using the Power of Lateral Thinking to Create New Ideas* (HarperBusiness, 1992). Includes a popular non-political, non-typing, and very co-creative approach to human diversity: "the Six Thinking Hats."

de Sousa Santos, Boaventura, Gianpaolo Baiocchi, and Leonardo Avritzer. Papers on "The participatory budget experiment in Porto Alegre, Brazil" presented at the conference on Deepening Democracy: Institutional Innovations in Empowered Participatory Governance, January 2000, sponsored by the Real Utopias Project. See *ssc.wisc.edu/~wright/RealUtopias.htm*.

Dewey, John. "Democracy as a Way of Life" in *School and Society*, April 1937, quoted in Ammerman, Robert, and Marcus Singer (eds), *Introductory Readings in Philosophy* (Scribners, 1962). Sixty years ago, Dewey glimpsed the democratic implications of the "pooled intelligence constituted by the contributions of all."

Dominguez, Joe, and Vicki Robin. *Your Money Or Your Life: Transforming Your Relationship With Money and Achieving Financial Independence*, 2nd ed. (Penguin USA, 1999). So many people say "I don't have time" for citizenship or dialogue. Here is a proven approach for stepping from the consumerist treadmill into a quality life with quality time.

Doyle, Kevin, et al. (eds). "The People's Verdict: How Canadians

Can Agree on Their Future," a series of eleven articles in *Maclean's*, July 1, 1991, Vol. 104, No. 25, pp. 3-76.

Earley, Jay. *Transforming Human Culture* (State University of New York, 1997). The evolution of integral culture from prehistory into the twenty-first century, mapping the interplay of "ground qualities" (community, participatory consciousness, etc.) and "emergent qualities" (complex social systems, analytic consciousness, etc.), and suggesting that our next task is to create a culture that integrates them all. See *earley.org*.

Ecotrust. *Pattern Language for a Conservation Economy: What Does a Sustainable Society Look Like?* (c. 2000). A fascinating detailed map of design elements for sustainability at *conservationeconomy .net*.

Einstein, Albert. *The World As I See It* (Philosophical Library, 1949). Timeless insights from a great mind, heart and spirit at the center of the twentieth century.

Eisler, Riane. *The Chalice and the Blade* (Harper and Row, 1987). Traces the sources of domination-based culture and shows how partnership-based cultures preceded them, and that we can move once again towards partnership.

Eisler, Riane, and David Loye. *The Partnership Way: New Tools for Living and Learning, Healing Our Families, Our Communities and Our World* (HarperSanFrancisco, 1990). A practical companion for *The Chalice and the Blade*, filled with useful exercises and essays.

Elgin, Duane. *Awakening Earth: Exploring the Evolution of Human Culture and Consciousness* (William Morrow, 1993). Integrating science and ancient wisdom traditions into an inspiring vision of humanity's evolutionary journey. See also *awakeningearth.org*.
———. *Promise Ahead: A Vision of Hope and Action for Humanity's Future* (HarperCollins, 2000). As we stand at the crossroads of unprecedented problems and opportunities, we are poised to make an evolutionary leap.

Ellinor, Linda and Glenna Gerard. *Dialogue: Rediscovering the Transforming Power of Conversation* (J. Wiley & Sons, 1998). A major articulation of Bohmian dialogue. Begins with a transcript of a dialogue among leading dialogue advocates that exemplifies the method.

Etzioni, Amitai. *The Spirit of Community: The Reinvention of American Society* (Touchstone/Simon & Schuster, 1993). A foundational document of the communitarian movement which suggests that responsibilities are as important as rights in a democracy.

Ferguson, Marilyn. *The Aquarian Conspiracy: Personal and Social Transformation in the 1980s* (Tarcher, 1980). The book on the holistic "new paradigm" revolution which first laid the groundwork for co-intelligence. Decades old, it still inspires.

Fisher, Roger, and William Ury. *Getting to Yes: Negotiating Agreement Without Giving In* (Penguin, 1981). The classic introduction to principled negotiation. Fisher and Ury have many other excellent books. See also *colorado.edu/conflict/peace/treatment/pricneg.htm*.

Fishkin, James S. *The Voice of the People: Public Opinion and Democracy* (Yale University, 1995). The founder of deliberative polling describes its rationale, history and vision, educating us about real democracy in the process.

Follett, Mary Parker. *The New State: Group Organization, the Solution of Popular Government* (Pennsylvania State University, 1998). Originally published in 1918, this prescient book offers an advanced holistic vision of dialogue and democracy. Downloadable from *sunsite.utk.edu/FINS/Mary_Parker_Follett/Fins-MPF-01.html*.

Fricska, Szilard. "Popular Participation in Porto Alegre" (1996) based on Habitat II Conference document A/CONF.165/CRP.5 highlights of submissions to UNCHS (United Nations Human Settlements Programme), online at *unhabitat.org/HD/hd/latin.htm#popular*. A description of the Brazilian participatory budget process.

Friere, Paolo. *Pedagogy of the Oppressed* (Penguin, 1972). The classic articulation of education that uses the realities of people's lives to help them change their lives. See *infed.org/thinkers/et-freir.htm*.

Gardner, Howard. *Frames of Mind* (Basic Books, 1983). The first fully researched theory of multiple intelligences that opened the door to expanded views of intelligence.

———. *Multiple Intelligences: The Theory in Practice* (HarperCollins, 1993). Here Gardner applies his theory to education.

Gastil, John. *By Popular Demand: Revitalizing Representative Democracy through Deliberative Elections* (University of California, 2000). Describes five ways to use citizen deliberative councils to evaluate candidates and ballot initiatives and to oversee representative government.

Gerzon, Mark. *A House Divided: Six Belief Systems Struggling for America's Soul* (Tarcher/Putnam, 1996). Describes the divisions in America and a new brand of patriots who are trying to bridge those chasms.

Gibson, Tony. *The Power in Our Hands: Neighborhood-Based World Shaking* (Jon Carpenter, UK, 1996). How-tos and stories for those who want to make a creative difference in their communities.

Goleman, Daniel. *Emotional Intelligence* (Bantam, 1995). A direct and successful challenge to the "cult of IQ" which claims that how we deal with our (and others') emotions can be a greater indicator of success than more analytical types of intelligence.

Greenwood, Laura, et al. (eds). *PLA [Participatory Learning and Action] Notes 40: Deliberative Democracy and Citizen Empowerment* (International Institute for Environment and Development, UK, February 2001). Includes summaries of Tim Holmes and Ian Scoones work, among many other articles. Available through *iied.org/bookshop/sd_spla.html*.

Grundahl, Johs. "The Danish Consensus Conference Model," in Simon Joss and John Durant (eds), *Public Participation in Science: The Role of Consensus Conferences in Europe* (Science Museum, UK, 1995). A step-by-step description of consensus conferences.

Harary, Keith, and Eileen Donahue. *Who Do You Think You Are?* (HarperSanFrancisco, 1994). How to use the Berkeley Personality Profile to explore human differences without "typing" people.

Hawken, Paul. *The Ecology of Commerce* (HarperBusiness, 1993). How an economy that fully collaborated with nature would work.

Hawken, Paul, James Ogilvy and Peter Schwartz. *Seven Tomorrows: Seven Scenarios for the Eighties and Nineties* (Bantam, 1982). Here is the earliest reference I've found to "collective intelligence" at the societal level.

Hawken, Paul, L. Hunter Lovins, and Amory Lovins. *Natural Capitalism: Creating the Next Industrial Revolution* (Back Bay Books, 2000). More about a nature-based economy, including powerful technical developments. See also *naturalcapitalism.org*.

Henderson, Hazel. *Building a Win-Win World: Life Beyond Global Economic Warfare.* (Berrett-Koehler, 1996). Innovations that would allow ethical corporations and politicians - and human and natural communities - to win in a competitive world. Chapter 11, "Perfecting Democracy's Tools" features creative use of polling and telecommunications technology.

———. *Paradigms in Progress: Life Beyond Economics* (Knowledge Systems, 1991). Accessible futurist thinking which breaks some chains of traditional economic thinking.

Henderson, Hazel, Jon Lickerman, and Patrice Flynn (eds). *Calvert-Henderson Quality of Life Indicators* (Calvert Group, 2000). A sophisticated set of national quality-of-life statistics to guide public policy and public life.

Henton, Doug, et al. *Empowering Regions: Strategies and Tools for Community Decision Making* (Alliance for Regional Stewardship, 2001). A brief, useful guide with examples.

Hirsch, Sandra and Jean Kummerow. *LifeTypes: Understand Yourself and Make the Most of Who You Are* (Warner, 1989). A popularization of the widely-used Myers-Briggs system of personality typing based on the work of psychologist Carl Jung.

Hock, Dee. *Birth of the Chaordic Age* (Berrett-Koehler, 1999). A breakthrough vision of leaderful organizations that organize themselves benignly at the edge of order and chaos, articulated by the founder of Visa. See also *chaordic.org.*

Holman, Peggy, and Tom Devane (eds). *The Change Handbook: Group Methods for Shaping the Future* (Berrett-Koehler, 1999). Describes eighteen different approaches, including dialogue, future search, open space, appreciative inquiry and participative design, in doable detail – with thoughts on the future and a unique matrix chart comparing all the methods described.

Holmes, Tim, and Ian Scoones. *Participatory Environmental Policy Processes: Experiences from North and South* (Institute of Development Studies, UK, 2000). A very extensive analysis of dozens of "deliberative inclusionary processes" from around the world. Downloadable from the Web: Click on "IDS Working Paper 113" at the bottom of *ids.ac.uk/ids/env/citizenjury.html.*

Hopkins, Susan. *Thinking Together with Young Children: Weaving a Tapestry of Community* ($12.50 from 12959 Woolman Lane, Nevada City, CA 95959). Techniques and stories to facilitate collaboration with and among children and prepare them for responsible, active citizenship in the world.

Hubbard, Barbara Marx. *Conscious Evolution: Awakening the Power of Our Social Potential* (New World Library, 1998). We need to develop not only our individual human potential but our social human potential, and consciously evolve our cultures and our consciousness.

Janis, Irving. *Groupthink: Psychological Studies of Policy Decision* (Houghton Mifflin, 1982). Studies of the dynamics of co-stupidity in leadership situations, including the Bay of Pigs, Pearl Harbour, the Vietnam War, the Cuban Missile Crisis, and Watergate.

Johnson, Mark. *Moral Imagination: Implications of Cognitive Science for Ethics* (University of Chicago, 1993). Moving beyond illusions of objectivity and subjectivity into a co-created world.

Johnson-Lenz, Peter and Trudy. *Practicing Our Wisdom Together in Cyberspace* (Awakentech, 1998). An online collaborative exploration of wisdom and knowledgge at *awakentech.com/AT/ Wisdom.nsf/By+Title/FrameSet?OpenDocument.* The form is as fascinating as the content.

Johnston, Charles M. *Necessary Wisdom: Meeting the Challenge of a New Cultural Maturity* (ICD Press, 1991). Shows how opposites can dance together into creative co-evolution. Provides guidelines to help us build living bridges between us, where we come alive together.

Joss, Simon, and John Durant (eds). *Public Participation in Science: The Role of Consensus Conferences in Europe* (Science Museum, UK, 1995). A thorough discussion of Danish consensus conferences in English.

Joy, Bill. "Why the Future Doesn't Need Us" in *Wired,* April 2000. Explains how developments in biotechnology, nanotechnology and robotics will, with the expansion of computer power, almost surely result in human extinction, unless we monitor those developments much more carefully.

Kaner, Sam, et al. *Facilitator's Guide to Participatory Decision-Making* (New Society, 1996). A detailed guide to facilitated consensus process, organized so individual pages can be copied and used by the group.

Korten, David C. *The Post-Corporate World: Life After Capitalism* (Berrett-Koehler, 1999). A vision to move beyond corporatism to "eliminate the economic pathology that plagues us and create truly democratic, market-based, life-centered societies."

Krapfel, Paul. *Seeing Nature: Deliberate Encounters with the Visible World* (Chelsea Green, 1999). Engaging examples of nature as it dances entropy into life, and how we humans can join that dance. See also *krafel.net.*

Kremer, Jurgen. "Perspectives on Indigenous Healing," *Noetic Sciences Review,* No. 33, Spring 1995, p. 13. Clarifies the significant difference between the indigenous and Western approaches to science and healing.

Kretzmann, John P., and John L. McKnight. *Building Communities from the Inside Out: A Path Toward Finding and Mobilizing a Community's Assets* (Center for Urban Affairs and Policy Research, 1993). Set aside all those community problems for a moment, and forget about serving clients. Engage in some "asset based community development" in which *everyone* is a resource. See also *nwu.edu/IPR/abcd.html.*

Laddon, Judy, Larry Shook and Tom Atlee (eds). *Awakening: The Upside of Y2K* (Printed Word, 1998). Mostly articles selected from the Co-Intelligence Institute's 1998 Y2K website.

La Chapelle, David. *Navigating the Tides of Change: Stories from Science, the Sacred, and a Wise Planet* (New Society, 2001). A compassionate shaman of complexity theory – a storyteller of the underlying depths of time and space – speaks to us of our times.

Lao-tzu. *Tao Te Ching* (Harper & Row, 1988). Trans. Stephen Mitchell. My favorite translation of the Tao, short of the ones I do myself comparing this with others.

Lappé, Frances Moore, and Paul Du Bois. "Living Democracy" in *Thinkpeace,* July 24, 1992, Issue 37/38, Vol. VIII, Nos. 2 & 3, pp. 2-7. Online at *co-intelligence.org/CIPol_LivingDemoc.html.*

———. *The Quickening of America: Rebuilding Our Nation, Remaking Our Lives* (Jossey-Bass, 1994). Powerful examples and new theory about how Americans are "doing democracy." A foundational document on cooperative politics.

Lebensold, Ken. *A New Moral Vision* (1999). Insight into the evolving, ecosystemic nature of moral perspectives, inviting us to be partners in exploring morality and transforming the systems that influence life.

Lerner, Michael. *The Politics of Meaning: Restoring Hope and Possibility in an Age of Cynicism* (Addison-Wesley, 1996). There is political power available to those who can tap into people's deep yearning for meaning and values.

————. *Spirit Matters* (Walsch Books/Hampton Roads, 2000). A passionate, articulate statement of how active Emancipatory Spirituality can – with care, wonder and joy – heal and transform our lives, our society and our world. See *tikkun.org*.

le Roux, Pieter, et al., *The Mont Fleur Scenarios: What will South Africa be like in the Year 2002?* (Global Business Network, 1992). Details about a highly influential scenario project, available at *gbn.org/public/gbnstory/articles/ex_mont_fleur.htm*.

Leuf, Bo, and Ward Cunningham. *The Wiki Way* (Addison-Wesley Longman, 2001). Details how to collaborate online to create and modify documents and hot-linked dialogues.

Loden, Marilyn. *Feminine Leadership: How to Succeed in Business Without Being One of the Boys* (Times Books, 1985). Women's collaborative style has a demonstrable power all its own.

Macy, Joanna, and Molly Young Brown. *Coming Back to Life: Practices to Reconnect Our Lives, Our World* (New Society, 1998). Exercises to do together to find our place in the whole once again.

Manitonquat. *Ending Violent Crime: A Vision of a Society Free of Violence* (Story Stone, 1996). A visionary but simple co-intelligent prison program, downloadable at *futureworld.dk/society/books/nonviolence/nonviolence.htm*.

Mansbridge, Jane J. *Beyond Adversary Democracy* (Basic Books, 1980). Describes adversarial and consensus ("unitary") approaches to democracy and when it makes sense to use each approach.

McLaughlin, Corinne, and Gordon Davidson. *Spiritual Politics: Changing the World from the Inside Out* (Ballantine Books, 1994). A spiritual view of political dynamics, and a compendium of great things being done.

McMaster, Michael D. *The Intelligence Advantage: Organizing for Complexity* (Butterworth-Heinemann, 1996). A source of some remarkably clear thinking about collective intelligence and organizational learning.

Meadows, Donella H. *The Global Citizen* (Island Press, 1991). Dana Meadows was one of the most down-to-earth, accessible systems thinkers and writers. You can read more of her essays about our role in the whole at *iisd1.iisd.ca/pcdf/meadows/default.htm*.

Mindell, Arnold. *The Deep Democracy of Open Forums: Practical Steps to Conflict Prevention and Resolution for the Family, Work-*

place and World (Hampton Roads, 2002). Practical tools for "psycho-social activism" – for creating space in which awareness can grow and deep personal and social transformation can take place safely.

———. *Sitting in the Fire: Large Group Transformation through Diversity and Conflict* (Lao Tse Press, 1997). How to work in community with abuse, rage, revenge, revolution, racism and more, with examples.

———. *The Leader as Martial Artist* (HarperSanFrancisco, 1992). The Aikido of conflict resolution, relationship and change.

Mitchell, Natasha, and Alexandra de Blas (reporters). "Citizens Speak Out About Stormwater in Democratic Experiment." ABC Australia radio broadcast, 22/09/01. Transcript at *abc.net.au/rn/science/earth/stories/s376084.htm.*

Mollison, Bill. *Permaculture: A Practical Guide for a Sustainable Future* (Island Press, 1990). Collaborative design principles for creating self-sustaining systems that include both nature and humans. (I find it significant that permaculture advocates were early adopters of co-intelligence ideas.) See also *permaculture activist.net.*

Morris, David. *Self-Reliant Cities* (Sierra Club Books, 1982). The classic visionary text on the relationship of American cities to energy. See also *ilsr.org.*

Nader, Ralph. "The Concord Principles" (1992). Guidelines for The People taking control of what they own, such as their public lands, pension funds, savings accounts and public airwaves. *co-intelligence.org/CIPol_ConcordPrinciples.html.*

Nash, Terre. *Who's Counting: Marilyn Waring on Sex, Lies, and Global Economics* (National Film Board of Canada, 1995). A powerful film about the measurables and immeasurables in our lives, and how economic measurements and policies affect them. Who counts the work of women and nature? Get the 94-minute version if you can. See also *home.earthlink.net/~mediatorken.*

Nhat Hanh, Thich. *Peace is Every Step: The Path of Mindfulness in Everyday Life* (Bantam, 1991). Perhaps we should call him a mindfulist instead of an activist: He practices his mindfulness on the world stage as well as in the kitchen. "If we make it possible for [our government] to change policies, they will do it."

Oliver, Leonard P. *Study Circles: Coming Together for Personal Growth and Social Change* (Seven Locks, 1987). The history and practice of small-group, democratic, adult education and social learning. See also *studycircles.org.*

Ornstein, Robert, and Paul Ehrlich. *New World, New Mind* (Touchstone, 1989). One of the biggest obstacles to social change is that our 10,000 year old human nervous systems, wired for a life in nature, leave us unable to directly perceive and respond to the many "invisible" threats generated by civilization.

O'Shah, Nasrudin. *The Zen of Global Transformation* (Quay Largo, 2002). Careful study of our global predicament – including elite power – reveals the best way to create a decent, sustainable world is by drawing all sides into creative dialogue. Available online at *QuayLargo.com/Transformation*.

Owen, Harrison. *Open Space Technology: A User's Manual* (Berrett-Koehler, 1997). The how-to manual for one of the simplest, most powerful self-organized collective processes we have: conferences of, by and for the participants. See also *openspaceworld.org*.

Peavey, Fran. *By Life's Grace: Musings on the Essence of Social Change* (New Society, 1994). Heartful, insightful essays – including a detailed description of strategic questioning.

Peavey, Fran, with Myra Levy and Charles Varon. *Heart Politics* (New Society, 1986). A moving, creative inquiry into what it means to live a life trying to change things for the better, sensitive to the interconnectedness, mystery, beauty and quirkiness of life.

Peck, M. Scott. *A Different Drum: Community Making and Peace* (Simon & Schuster, 1987). Peck tells us what needs to happen for us to feel like we're in genuine community. Interestingly enough, it involves a passage through chaos and emptiness.

Pimbert, Michel, and Tom Wakeford. "Prajateerpu: A Citizens' Jury/Scenario Workshop on Food Futures for Andhra Pradesh, India" (International Institute for Environment and Development, 2001). Downloadable from *iied.org/agri/IIEDcitizenjuryAP1.html*.

Potter, Dave, et al (eds). *Centered on the Edge: Mapping a Field of Collective Intelligence and Spiritual Wisdom* (Fetzer Institute, 2001). Explores the underlying dynamics of spiritually powerful group process. Available through *fetzer.org/resources/Centered OnTheEdge*.

Ray, Paul H., and Sherry Ruth Anderson. *The Cultural Creatives: How 50 Million People are Changing the World* (Harmony, 2000). Marketing research shows the U.S. population (and many other societies) can be divided into three values-based cohorts: "Traditionals," "Moderns," and "Cultural Creatives." Cultural Creatives constitute a quarter of the population and are growing fast, with profound implications. See also *culturalcreatives.org*.

Redburn, Ray, et al. *Confessions of Empowering Organizations* (Association for Quality and Participation, 1991). Ninety-two case studies of partnership and empowerment, self-managed work crews, self-directed reorganizations—with names and phone numbers.

Renn, Ortwin, Thomas Webler, and Peter Wiedemann. *Fairness and Competence in Citizen Participation: Evaluating Models for Environmental Discourse* (Kluwer Academic, 1995). Volume 10 of *Technology, Risk and Society: An International Series in Risk Analy-*

sis, Jeryl Mumpower and Ortwin Renn (eds). Describes and evaluates eight models, including citizens' juries and planning cells.

Riso, Don Richard. *Personality Types: Using the Enneagram for Self-Discovery* (Houghton Mifflin, 1987). An introduction to one of the most popular personality typing systems, originally designed for serious students of personal growth.

Rosenberg, Marshall B. *Nonviolent Communication: A Language of Compassion* (PuddleDancer Press, 1999). Excellent process for creatively handling difficult interpersonal situations – including intense conflict – and understanding human needs. See *cnvc.org.*

Rough, Jim. *Society's Breakthrough! Releasing Essential Wisdom and Virtue in All the People* (1stBooks, 2002). Describes Dynamic Facilitation and its use in Wisdom Councils – and a "Citizens Amendment" to establish a national Wisdom Council in the U.S. See *SocietysBreakthrough.com.*

Sandra, Jaida N'ha. *The Joy of Conversation* (Utne, 1997). *Utne Reader*'s guide to co-creative salons of all types. Excellent write-ups on study circles, listening circles, etc.

Savory, Allan, with Jody Butterfield. *Holistic Management: A New Framework for Decision-Making* (Island Press, 1999). Get the whole system's stakeholders to think together about the whole system's long-term needs. See also *holisticman agement.org.*

Schutt, Randy. "Notes on Consensus Decision Making" and other papers downloadable from *vernalproject.org/RPapers.shtml#Coop DecMaking.* Concise guidelines for facilitators and groups wanting to use consensus.

———. *Inciting Democracy: A Practical Proposal for Creating a Good Society* (SpringForward, 2001). A detailed vision for a path of nonviolent social change. See also *vernalproject.org.*

Sclove, Richard. *Democracy and Technology* (Guilford, 1995). Shows how technologies support – and undermine – democracy, and asks: "What role should democracy have in the development of technology?" See also *loka.org.*

Semler, Ricardo. *Maverick: The Success Story Behind the World's Most Unusual Workplace* (Warner Books, 1993). Not only the most unusual workplace, but one of the most co-intelligent. A great study of leadership that nurtures the capacity of the system to increasingly care for itself.

Senge, Peter. *The Fifth Discipline: The Art and Practice of the Learning Organization* (Doubleday Currency, 1990). This book introduced the world to the idea of an organization that can learn. One of the first to explicitly explore collective intelligence.

Senge, Peter, et al. *The Fifth Discipline Fieldbook* (Doubleday Currency, 1994). Packed with strategies, tools and exercises to help us build learning organizations.

Shaffer, Carolyn, and Kristin Anundsen. *Creating Community Anywhere: Finding Support and Connection in a Fragmented World* (Tarcher/Perigree, 1993). M. Scott Peck called this "the most comprehensive book I know of about the community movement." It covers all forms of community, providing guidance on conflict, decision-making, celebrations, communication, and dealing with community evolution and the "shadow side" of community.

Shuman, Michael H. *Going Local: Creating Self-Reliant Communities in a Global Age* (Free Press, 1998). The title says it all.

Smith, Anna Deavere. *Twilight: Los Angeles, 1992.* A one-woman performance about the violence that broke out after the Rodney King beating verdicts. Available through *shop.pbs.org.*

Spangler, David. *Everyday Miracles: The Inner Art of Manifestation* (Bantam, 1996). A rare vision of a truly co-creative spiritual metaphysics. Spangler suggests we live in a co-incarnational universe, and shows how we can use that fact to serve the well-being of the whole through our own intention and evolution.

Starhawk. *Truth or Dare: Encounters with Power, Authority and Mystery* (Harper and Row, 1987). *Power-with* and *power-from-within* are the magical powers needed to dissolve *power-over* in the mystery of Life. It turns out that this is all very practical.

———. *The Fifth Sacred Thing* (Bantam, 1993). An intense novel grounded in the ultimate mystery and power of wholeness, in partnership with *everything.*

Tannen, Deborah. *The Argument Culture: Moving from Debate to Dialogue (Random House,* 1998). Tannen questions the assumption that a war of ideas produces the greatest truth.

Teledemocracy Action News+Network, "Scientific Deliberative Polling and Deliberative Democracy," *auburn.edu/academic/ liberal_arts/poli_sci/tann/tann2/project2.html.* Describes and links ten leading citizen deliberative methods and projects, including citizens' juries, deliberative polling, planning cells, and consensus conferences.

Theobald, Robert A. *Turning the Century: Personal and Organizational Strategies for Your Changed World* (Participation, 1992). Specific recommendations for radical change towards a caring, sustainable society.

———. *Reworking Success* (New Society, 1997). An accessible re-examination of how to help communities and societies work better in the twenty-first century. Downloadable from *transform .org/ transform/tlc/rsuccess.html.* See also *resilientcommunities .org.*

Toms, Michael. *A Time for Choices: Deep Dialogues for Deep Democracy* (New Society, 2002). A collection of post–9-11 wisdom from more than one hundred leading thinkers, educators, political analysts, activists, social innovators, clergy, journalists, philosophers and spiritual teachers.

Verhulst, Jos. "Orcamento Participativo: The remarkable experience of direct democracy in a Brazilian town," (c. 1998) at *ping.be/ jvwit/directdemorcamento.html*.

Waldrop, M. *Complexity* (Simon & Schuster, 1992). This book opened my eyes to the way nature generates totally new phenomena through the co-evolution of complex synergies.

Watterson, Kathryn. *Not by the Sword: How the Love of a Cantor and His Family Transformed a Klansman* (Simon & Schuster, 1996). A compelling true story showing the power of caring and empathy as forms of strength, not weakness.

Weatherford, Jack. *Indian Givers: How the Indians of the Americas Transformed the World* (Crown Publishers, 1988). Native Americans innovations—the federal system, caucuses, taking turns, peacefully removing leaders, an egalitarian culture of personal liberty—inspired Rousseau, Franklin, Paine and other "founders."

Weisbord, Marvin, and Sandra Janoff. *Future Search: An Action Guide to Finding Common Ground in Organizations and Communities* (Berrett-Koehler, 1995). A how-to book to help communities and stakeholders explore and co-create their shared past, present and future. See also *futuresearch.net*.

Weisman, Alan. *Gaviotas: A Village to Reinvent the World* (Chelsea Green, 1998). A breathtaking true story of sustainability co-created in a very challenging environment, on behalf of us all.

Wenk, E. *The Double Helix: Technology and Democracy in the American Future* (Ablex, 1999). Describes the threats to democracy from technological innovation, focusing on those that require a political rather than a technological solution.

Wheatley, Margaret. *Leadership and the New Science: Discovering Order in a Chaotic World* (Berrett-Koehler, 1999). How to relate to organizations as natural systems. See also *berkana.org*.

———. *Turning to One Another: Simple Conversations to Restore Hope to the Future* (Berrett-Koehler, 2002). Guidelines, inspiration and questions to help us turn to each other instead of against each other, by realizing newly the innate power of talking and listening. See *turningtooneanother.net*.

Wilber, Ken. *A Brief History of Everything* (Shambhala, 1996). Useful insights for expanding our thinking in more holistic directions, including his widely-used "four quadrants model."

Zimmerman, Jack, and Virginia Coyle, *The Way of Council* (Bramble Books, 1996). Council process practiced by the Ojai Foundation.

Zubizarreta, Rosa, and Jim Rough. *A Dynamic Facilitation Manual and Reader: Evoking Practical Group Creativity through Generative Dialogue* (Center for Wise Democratic Processes, 2002). To order, email *seminars@tobe.net*.

INDEX

About the Author

Tom Atlee, founder of the non-profit Co-Intelligence Institute, has written and spoken for twenty years on politics, democracy and cultural transformation. His two resource-packed websites – *co-intelligence.org* and *democracy innovations.org* – are used by thousands of people every month, and a thousand of them subscribe to his email newsletter.

Tom's articles on social issues and co-intelligence have appeared in *National Civic Review, Communities, Co-Op America Quarterly, IONS Noetic Sciences Review, In Context, Yes!, Permaculture Activist, Earthlight, Thinkpeace* and numerous other journals.

Raised in a Quaker activist family, Tom has been exploring social issues and personal and social transformation since an early age. His participation in the nine-month cross-country Great Peace March of 1986 marked a watershed in his life. He has served on the boards of the Berkeley Ecology Center and the Center for Group Learning. In 1991 he was invited to Belize and to Czechoslovakia (with his life partner, Karen Mercer) to consult on green social change and community-building.

Tom lives in Eugene, Oregon, with Karen and several of their friends. In his rare departures from his desk, he takes aerobic walks, bikes to the post office, plays twelve-string guitar and writes an occasional poem or song. His daughter Jennifer Atlee, a green product design engineer, lives and works around New England.

NOTES

NOTES

NOTES

NOTES

NOTES

NOTES

For permissions contact

Tom Atlee
c/o The Co-Intelligence Institute
PO Box 493
Eugene, OR 97440
Email: cii@igc.org

Published by

The Writers' Collective,
780 Reservoir Ave., Ste 243
Cranston, RI 02910
Phone/Fax: 401-537-9175
writerscollective.org

To share this book

Send your friends and associates to

taoofdemocracy.com

This book was set in Bookman,
    Bookman Old Style and Arial.
Book design by Tom Atlee.
Cover design by Grá Darjeeling and Tom Atlee.

Get Involved

If you would like to get involved in the co-intelligence work, see pages 276-281 and read
"How you can be involved with the co-intelligence work"
co-intelligence.org/CIInvolved.html
and contact us though that web page.

FREE e-mail bulletins

You can subscribe to Tom Atlee's free email bulletins on co-intelligence, social issues and cultural transformation. Just send an email to cii@igc.org with "SUBSCRIBE CII LIST" in the "Subject" line.

FREE recent articles by Tom Atlee

Tom Atlee writes many articles each year, some of which update material in this book. Many of them are not otherwise available. We are happy to mail you two of his most recent articles FREE. Just send an email to cii@igc.org with "TOM ATLEE ARTICLES" in the "Subject" line, or send a letter or postcard to

> Tom Atlee Articles
> Co-Intelligence Institute
> P.O. Box 493
> Eugene, OR 97440

Please include your name and address (which we won't sell or share with anyone else.)